The Dream Story

Marie-Louise von Franz, Honorary Patron

**Studies in Jungian Psychology
by Jungian Analysts**

Daryl Sharp, General Editor

The
Dream Story

DONALD BROADRIBB

The Dream Story was orginally published in 1987 by Cygnet Books, distributed by University of Western Australia Press.

Canadian Cataloguing in Publication Data

Broadribb, Donald, 1933-
  The dream story

(Studies in Jungian psychology by Jungian analysts; 44)

ISBN 0-919123-45-7

1. Dreams.
2. Dreams—Psychological aspects.
3. Jung, C.G. (Carl Gustav), 1875-1961.
I. Title.   II. Series.

BF1091.B76   1990   154.6'34   C90-093301-1

INNER CITY BOOKS
Box 1271, Station Q, Toronto, Canada M4T 2P4
Telephone (416) 927-0355

Honorary Patron: Marie-Louise von Franz.
Publisher and General Editor: Daryl Sharp.
Senior Editor: Victoria Cowan.

INNER CITY BOOKS was founded in 1980 to promote the understanding and practical application of the work of C.G. Jung.

Cover: "Second Opening," oil on linen, by Nancy Witt.

Index by the author

Printed and bound in Canada by John Deyell Company

CONTENTS

INTRODUCTION

Dreams have fascinated mankind for all of known history. There never seems to have been a time or a people that believed that dreams are meaningless. Instead, history is filled with works on dream interpretation, and every known people has had its dream interpreters. This interest is fully as alive among us today as ever. Bookstands are filled with books on dreams, universities conduct dream laboratories and include classes on the meaning of dreams. The author of a new book on the subject is asked, not why a book on dreams, but why yet another book on dreams? Is there anything new left to be said amid the spate of new dream books that seems to be a never-ending flood?

The answer is yes, there is. In particular, there is a need for a new way of looking at dreams. The body of dream books that are flooding the market is based on a small amount of theorising and a minimal examination of dreams. Three main streams have fed into this flood. There is a traditional view that images in dreams are symbolic, and that the symbols can be deciphered in some standard way, a viewpoint that goes as far back as written literature itself. But in the modern day, Freud's discovery of the unconscious origin of dreams, and his predominantly sexual interpretation of dreams, has had tremendous impact. His interpretations are primarily based on the view that dream images are symbolic. Jung's discovery of complexes and archetypes, with stress that imagery in dreams can be understood better when we take myths, legends and figures of speech into account, has in recent years had an equal influence with Freud's views. Jung also places great emphasis on the viewpoint that dream images are symbolic. The third stream has been derived from observations based on laboratory dream research, with special attention to types of dreams, and typical features and figures appearing in dreams. Most of the dream books today are based on one or more of these three streams, although there is still great popularity for the classical 'dream dictionaries' and modern imitators.

This book attempts to look at dreams from a different angle, making use of, but not limiting itself to, the contributions of those who have gone before.

Why should we look at dreams at all? Apart from natural curiosity about the fact that dreaming takes up a very large slab of our sleep time each night, with the intriguing suggestion that the dreaming process may be continuous both day and night, the recording and examination of our dreams has a very profound effect on our moods, our attitudes, even our thoughts. Dreams help reveal to ourselves the hidden parts of our personalities of which we are usually unaware. This revelation — for that is how it usually feels — has, in turn, a profound effect on our characters, so much so that it could almost be said that we know only half the truth about ourselves, and our dreams help us to meet the other half. Many of the problems that vex us during the day can be seen in a different light when we look closely at our dreams.

At first, just a simple recording of our dreams on paper is enough to astonish us with the rich variety of thought and adventure that goes on within our minds during sleep. But viewing our own dreams by ourselves rarely gets us very far. That is why it has been the practice since time began to tell dreams to others, for their help in understanding what the dreams have to say to us. This help need not necessarily come from a professional analyst. As I discuss in Chapter 8, dream discussion groups, consisting of people interested in mutually examining their dreams and helping each other see the messages the dreams are conveying, can be a very real help. While dream analysis may be valuable to the professional analyst in dealing with a patient's emotional problems, it can also be of great value to the ordinary individual who wants or needs to enlarge her/his self-understanding. At one time or another, most of us feel that life has become stagnant, and is in need of some kind of revitalisation. Often, too, we face major problems where we really do not know what to think or do. This is when looking at our dreams can be most helpful.

Dreams, however, are not oracles. They cannot tell us what to do. Their expression of life's problems is as one-sided a view as our conscious view, no more, no less. It would be a very serious mistake to suppose that by examining dreams, you are going to find the answers to all your problems. You are not. But what you will find is the other side of the coin, the attitudes and viewpoints that you have not been looking at, and that may help to pull you out of the mire.

From time to time in history, and now enjoying a widespread renaissance, has been the hope that a person can influence her/his dreams, manipulate their contents, change their direction — in other words, take control of the dreaming process. There have been various reasons proposed for this endeavour. Practically everyone has, at one time or another, wished, even hoped, to be able to control nightmares. One woman, for example, of a very puritan background, regularly had the very common dream of appearing naked in public. Typically, in this dream, the dreamer is very embarrassed at being naked, but no one else in the dream seems to notice or be concerned. Probably everyone has had a variation on this dream motif at some time. Now this dream, as we will discover as we work through anxiety dreams, has an important message. The woman finally determined that her puritan sensitivities were just too much offended for her to allow this to continue, so she resolved that she would never allow herself to have such a dream again. This very firm resolve, which was strengthened by a strong determination to wake herself up if such a dream began, was successful. She has not had that dream motif again. Not being acquainted with dream analysis or the value of working with dreams, the woman felt pleased by her achievement. But from my viewpoint, as expressed in this book, the woman actually became impoverished by this process.

The dream itself, as said, is a very widespread motif found almost universally among people. It has a meaning — basically, that the dreamer feels exposed to the public gaze, feels her/his defences are down, that her/his innermost self is open to all and sundry; but, through the fact that no one else in the dream notices or cares about the dreamer's nudity, the dream expresses the point that the feeling is purely subjective, and not in fact the way others perceive her/him at all. The dreamer's sense of inadequacy for the situation s/he is in is unjustified. This is an important message. By blocking out the dream, the woman was simultaneously blocking out an important fact vital to her self-esteem and ultimately to her career, for her feeling of inadequacy greatly affected how she approached authorities and peers.

How this interpretation of the dream is arrived at is something I hope you will discover as you read through this book. But I want to stress the point that dreams *mean* something, and that to block them out or denature them is to deprive ourselves of a valuable piece of self-knowledge and, ultimately, of discovering new ways to confront the world and life in general.

Systematic attempts to control the content of dreams can be traced far back in history, where, in the ancient world, religious rituals and indoctrination were used at sacred sanitariums to cause the sick person to dream of being visited by the healing god, such as Asklepios, who would explain what was to be done to heal the illness. Countless votive inscriptions indicate that this practice enjoyed great success. In present-day groups, such as Australian tribal Aborigines, the medicine-man, or shaman, is trained to enter trances in which, during a pre-programmed dream, she/he undertakes supernatural activities, for better or for worse. Carlos Castaneda, in his Don Juan series of books, describes training and practice in similar dream control in order to conduct acts of sorcery as American Indians have developed the shamanistic traditions.

In line with these is the viewpoint that to learn to control our dreams, through special exercises and practice, will give us control over our unconscious minds. This is sometimes based on the assumption that the unconscious mind is a secondary, inferior and intrusive part of the personality; but much more often, the opposite idea is held before us: that our unconscious minds are a conglomeration of very great powers and abilities whose

resources we would like to tap. Without going into the psychological discussion of why these two assumptions are seriously incorrect, I wish to point
out that to control your unconscious mind leads to an impoverishment of
your personality rather than an enrichment. As will be discussed rather
frequently in this book, the unconscious mind is pure nature, and represents the adaptation of each individual with her/his natural environment.
In our conscious world, we have become so alienated from nature that we
often no longer recognise that we are children of nature. As a consequence, we live only half-lives.

To learn to understand the language of dreams — that is the goal of this
book, to enable us to encounter and comprehend this other half of ourselves.

*   *   *

In this book, dreams have been given verbatim, as related to me by the
dreamers. No attempt has been made to smooth out incongruities, to summarise repetitious bits, or to add in explanatory material. The only exception is that all proper names and references that might identify the
dreamers have been replaced by fictitious names bearing no resemblance
to the originals. Descriptions of the dreamers have been limited to information necessary for working with the dreams. Dates, places, occupations
have been altered. Care has been taken to ensure that this one change does
not affect the interpretation of the dream.

Dreams are meaningful only within the context of the dreamer's life.
That is why, in discussion of dreams, the dreamer needs to be as open as
possible, and the message of each dream must be related to specific events
taking place in the dreamer's life. I have attempted to show this in regard
to each dream discussed, so as to enable a full understanding.

In this book, I work with the assumption that dreams do not lie, that a
dream means what it says; this means sometimes taking at face value much
that is difficult to accept or acknowledge. But if we are to find value in our
dreams, we must be prepared for the unexpected.

What are my qualifications for writing about dreams? I have been
fascinated by them since a child and Freud's *The Interpretation of Dreams*
stayed with me for many years. It was, though, only when I began to study
the content of biblical writings, at Union Theological Seminary in New
York City, that the role of dreams began to fascinate me. It was then, too,
that I had my first experience of psychoanalysis. In this, dreams were a
regular topic of discussion. While I did not feel that I understood dreams,
it seemed clear that they had some meaning and message. I could not
accept the claim that dreams in the Bible came from some supernatural
force, let alone dreams in our own daily lives. But it became clear that

there is some natural centre in our personalities where dreams originate, and which is reacting to events of life.

I found it easier to understand the language of dreams when I became familiar with the poetic language of the prophets of the Old Testament and the parables in the New Testament, and I was struck by the seriousness with which biblical writers took what they found in dreams (they usually called them visions). It came as no great surprise to me to discover how riveted Jung was to dreams for understanding our inner depths. I taught biblical studies for about ten years after leaving Union Seminary, ever increasingly fascinated by the poetic speech which seemed able to communicate far more meaningfully than philosophical treatises. Even my beloved Plato turns to parables and poetic myths of his own creation when he attempts to express his deepest convictions.

It is fascinating how similar ancient dreams are to those of today, and I am speaking now not only of the material that formed the Bible. When I began to embark on the teaching of the general mythological and cultural heritage of the very ancient world, I came upon Jung's book, *Symbols of Transformation*. There I found, as have many others, a completely fresh and inspiring approach to looking at the spontaneous productions of the modern mind and of the poetic and mythological traditions of those parts of the world with which our culture has only recently become acquainted, beyond the confines of the Jewish, Christian, Greek and Roman cultures. For about ten years, I was engaged in the study and teaching of comparative religion, and the 'non-western' sector of humanity. The public upsurge of interest in fairy-tales and folklore contributed a large share. And modern experimental drama insists on being taken into account. What can it be that all these 'remote' things share with dreams? The answer is that they all speak the language that dreams are made of, all well up from the same unconscious depths within us.

All this was not left to theory, though. In the 1970s, I trained as an analyst at the C. G. Jung Institute in Zürich, and received my diploma from there in 1975. By this point, I had come across and studied Jung's extraordinarily practical seminars published under the title *Dream Analysis*. Since then, I have had ample opportunity to test out my own grasp of dream language, not only in working over my own dreams, but in working over many thousands of dreams of other persons, discussing the dreams with them and being corrected and guided by what I found. For the most part, this experience has come in the context of psychotherapy with persons who have come to consult me professionally.

It was a challenge and, as it proved, a great boon to be invited to conduct dream discussion groups in which, usually, eight to ten people would meet on a regular basis to discuss their dreams among themselves, using me as a reference person and general convenor. Many of these groups were conducted at a psychiatric hospital, where troubled people were undergoing psychotherapy. But many other groups have consisted of 'ordinary' people who would meet of an evening with me, simply interested in furthering their own self-development by examining dreams. I have become impressed by the wisdom of the shared knowledge of dreams which lies latent within us, even in those who heartily insist that they 'never' dream, or that they can never understand what it is that they dreamed. I have supplemented these dream groups with formal seminar series, in which we have looked at the mechanics of dreams, the many theories that have been put forward, and the inspirations of individuals as they have applied their talents to the investigation of what makes dreams tick.

What emerged from all this was a distinctive approach, different from the others, which is worthy of presentation in a new book. Like all studies, nothing is completely new, and nothing is completely the way it was. But all the material originates in firsthand experience and examination of dreams with their dreamers.

This book has been written systematically. No chapter stands on its own — it must be read in order — and there are many cross-references between chapters. What is presented here is not quite a handbook but rather a description of how dreams may be approached. Every discussion presupposes the chapters that have gone before it. Thus, for example, the chapter entitled 'Sex in Dreams' requires, for much of its meaning, what is said in Chapter 2, 'The People in Our Dreams'. To attempt to read the later chapter before the earlier one is to invite serious misunderstanding.

I have tried to avoid the pitfall of assuming that all dreams fit into the same categories. To say that all dreams are symbolic, or sexual, or relate to the dreamer, or to the dreamer's relationships, for example, simply would not be true. Dreams span all that the human being encompasses mentally, emotionally, and physically, which is a lot.

One chapter is sadly missing from this book. Originally, I had hoped to include a chapter on 'Dreams and ESP', but limited amounts of verifiable material and necessary discretion in presenting authenticated facts about the dreamers have made this chapter impossible to include at this time. I would greatly appreciate readers sending me verified accounts of ESP material, with authenticating evidence, for a future edition of this book. Verified and authenticated means, among other things, that the dream was written down before the ESP event was discovered, and that the account does not rely on memory alone.

The structure of this book is important. As explained, each chapter depends on what has been said previously. To ease study of this book, apart from cross-references in the chapters, an index of dreams has been given at the end of the book, and every dream has been given a code to enable it to be identified quickly and easily.

We begin, in Chapter 1, by looking at the story that each dream tells. We look at each dream as a separate little drama that can and should be looked at in its own right before any attempt at interpretation is made. I owe this particular insight to Dr James Hillman, and would like to thank him for his (unknowing) help in formulating the basic premise of this book.

In Chapter 2, we move on to examine the people in our dreams. We look at the role individuals play in our dreams, and pay special attention to a question that many people find vexing: do the people in our dreams have anything to do with the real people outside our dreams? Also, what are we to make of the people 'invented' by our dreams?

Chapter 3 takes up the subject that dominates most books on dreams, the nature and use of symbolism. I hold that symbolism plays a far lesser role in dreams than has commonly been claimed. I also hold that no image has a fixed 'symbolic meaning', and that a 'dictionary of dream symbols' cannot be compiled. But for an individual dreamer, various dream images may have a true symbolic meaning, as determined by her/his experiences and culture. In this chapter, we examine how to identify symbols and understand them.

With Chapter 4, we turn from observing the content of dreams to considering what the purpose of dreams is. We discover that dreams have a definite purpose in each instance, and are not just incidental imaginations. Their purpose may vary, from person to person and dream to dream. Here, we learn to look for the purpose underlying each dream.

Chapter 5 takes up the bugbear of nightmares, which prove to be some of the most important dreams we have. They help us identify what it is that is going wrong in our lives, and to understand how to attack these problems. Even the most gruesome nightmare includes a ray of hope, in that it indicates the point at which things are going wrong, thus indicating where we may begin to set things right.

Sex is the subject of Chapter 6, both sexual symbolism and outright sexual references and activities. Of course, sexual dreams are found throughout the book, but in this chapter, I attempt to look at the matter systematically. Although it is a wild exaggeration to say that most dreams have sexual content or sexual symbolism, it is equally absurd to deny that sex plays a major role in our dream lives.

In Chapter 7, I present a series of dreams of one person, showing the cumulative effect of discussion of dreams. Every time we discuss a dream, the dreams that follow are influenced by the discussion and it is even possible to set up a sort of 'dialogue' with dreams in this way. In this chapter, I am also concerned with pointing out that a dream series indicates a direction and wider meaning than an individual dream can do, and that one dream may be helpful in throwing light on another dream of the same person.

The subject of dream discussion groups is the topic for Chapter 8, along with a general conclusion about approaching dreams and a specimen account of a discussion between dreamer and analyst in working over a dream. The chapter concludes with a summary of the role dreams play in our lives.

Finally there is an Appendix, which contains eleven selected dreams ranging from relatively simple to fairly complicated, each with the necessary explanatory material, for you to try your hand at interpreting. In the second half of the Appendix, I give my own suggested interpretations to compare with yours. There are also cross-references to material in the book that is relevant to the interpretations.

I would like to acknowledge my indebtedness, not only to the dreamers who contributed the material for this book, but also to: Dr Mario Jacoby, who in his work with my own dreams helped guide me to find the kernal structure of a dream; Mrs M. Pope-Heumann, who taught me rigour in examining the details of a dream and its symbolism; Dr John Melville Jones, who suggested the Appendix; Dr Marilyn Holly, who served as a most helpful philosophical consultant, scrutinising each chapter for its soundness and eliminating many *non sequiturs*; and Norma Broadribb, who read and criticised the manuscript for me, which was of great help. Finally, I thank a number of 'guinea pigs' who kindly read the manuscript and guided me in what needed further clarification. I have also had opportunity to check over earlier drafts of the manuscript with the original dreamers, who have helped sharpen and redirect many of the discussions of their dreams.

Chapter One

A DREAM TELLS A STORY

People who have not watched their dreams very closely often have the impression that their dreams are very fragmentary, incoherent and, frankly, bewildering. It often comes as a surprise to them, when they do examine each dream closely, to discover that each dream is a little story in itself, sometimes like an anecdote, sometimes like a scene from a drama, sometimes more like an adventure. The comparison with drama is often good: the dream seems sometimes like a small skit, sometimes like a three-act play complete with a long cast of characters. Whichever analogy we use, the important point remains the same. On inspection, a dream proves to be a very meaningful, well-constructed product of the imagination. No matter how bewildering the theme turns out to be, so that we exclaim 'Why on earth did I dream that?!', the dream taken in its own right usually seems coherent and to be a complete snippet. Since we all dream every night, the number of these productions boggles the imagination. In seventy years of dreaming life, there seem to be well over 150,000 separate dreams; and most extraordinary of all, it appears that, like fingerprints, no two of them are completely identical. There are, of course, 'recurring dreams', dreams which seem to repeat themselves and often, if not usually, make their first appearance in childhood. There are also 'typical dreams', dream themes that virtually everyone has in her/his dream repertoire. But when examined in detail, these recurring and typical dreams also show important differences between them.

Sometimes, it is most helpful to disentangle the basic pattern in dreams and to deal with that as a recurrent or typical way of responding to the situations of life. Other times, it is more helpful to look at the detailed differences between dreams, to discover how the response to life's situations is altering.

Every person has her/his own style of dreaming, and often, these styles differ enormously. We begin to wonder which is more extraordinary: that one person's mind can be so fertile as to produce hundreds of thousands of meaningful dramatic stories without ever quite repeating itself, or that there can be a faculty within us to produce such meaningful material while we are asleep.

Since Freud, it has become traditional to say that dreams are the works of the unconscious. This means that we do not lie down and consciously strive to produce a dream, but that, nevertheless, there is good reason to say that dreams are communications of a part of us which has virtually all of our mental faculties at its disposal.

It has also become traditional, in professional circles, to say that dreams are expressions of the 'psyche' rather than of the 'mind' or 'personality'. When we look at dreams closely, we often find reflections of our bodily condition in them. The word 'psyche' is meant to encompass both mind and body, and to point out that the division between them is very tenuous, and probably does not exist at all. I would like to emphasise that our familiar distinction between mind and body has very little to commend it. Each of us is a psychosomatic whole, in which it is impossible to say where 'mind' begins or 'body' ends. Frequently, it is useful to speak about the 'mental' aspect of an experience, or of the 'somatic' (bodily) aspect, but this is purely for convenience and begs a good many questions. Dreams, as a whole, are spontaneous expressions of our entire psychosomatic being, and show every indication of being the product of the central core of our being.

But how reliable is our memory of our dreams? How confident can we be that our memory of our dreams is an accurate portrayal of what we experienced while we were asleep? Although experimental research in dream laboratories shows promise of someday being able to address that question, as yet it is unanswerable. Experience indicates that we do distort the dream content a lot. When a dream is recited or written down right after the dreaming, and matched with the memory of it the following morning, much of the detail is usually found to be missing or altered, and, often, whole major segments are forgotten. Similarly, when we write dreams down as soon as possible on awakening in the morning, and compare the written record with our memory for the same dreams later in the day, there are usually major discrepancies. Usually, these are not so much a change in story-line of the dream as the deletion of scenes and characters.

Some people are, however, much more adept at remembering their dreams accurately than others. Occasionally, it is possible to find a person who does remember the dream content quite accurately and fully without consulting the earlier written text or the person to whom the dream was told, not only later in the day but even days later. Thus, memory varies considerably. Nevertheless, it is safe to assume that, generally, our memory for the content of dreams is not so good. At first thought, this seems to vitiate any kind of dream analysis at all. But experience shows otherwise. Careful investigation, through detailed discussion with the dreamer, indicates that, while details or segments of the dream are forgotten or altered, the essential content of the dream appears unaffected. This is surprising only until we consider that our conscious imagination is as much an activity of our whole psyche as is our dreaming. What we write or say when just waking and still strongly under the influence of the dreaming state follows directly on the same theme as the dream expression. And our spontaneous thoughts and memories later on, when we discuss the dream, also link up directly with the earlier recorded dream content; they lead us directly into the communication, the story that the dream tells.

Readers of Freud's *The Interpretation of Dreams* will see that I take a very different viewpoint on many issues, especially including this one. This is, in part, due to the research on dreams that has been undertaken in the eighty-five years since the publication of Freud's book; and, in part, to a different perspective, which has come out of my experience in examining dreams.

Let us begin our study of dreams by taking a short, sample dream and looking at it as a dramatic story:

> *I walk down the street and after a ways I stop to do up my shoe-laces. Some hoodlums see me and come over and it looks like they will attack me. I try to appear calm. After a while they go on their way, leaving me untouched. I tie my two shoes together by the laces, which seem to be made of rubber bands, while the shoes are still on me. Then I realise that I cannot walk that way, and I try to break them apart, which is a very difficult task.*
>
> JOHN W., #1

For convenience in cross-referencing, I have given each dreamer a pseudonym and numbered that person's dreams consecutively. All the dreams are listed at the end of this book in the Index of Dreams, arranged alphabetically by author's pseudonym.

We may become quite bewildered if we ask right off 'What does this dream mean?', with the assumption that the dream must be translated in some way, that it means something different from what it says. Let us approach it from a different angle, looking at it as a story.

In this story, John is out walking, but his shoe-laces have come undone. Before he can do them up again properly, hoodlums appear and he is afraid that they will attack him. But they do not attack him; the threat is imaginary. Then John returns to the task of doing up his shoe-laces, and makes quite a mess of it. They are not proper laces but seem like rubber bands. John ties the laces together, so that he cannot walk. Rather than undo the knot, he tries to break the laces which, since they are made of rubber, he finds difficult. The story ends at this point. We do not learn whether or not he eventually manages to get his laces in order and to proceed on his walk.

Some interesting observations arise from reading this story. John fears being attacked, but that fear is unfounded. He himself, rather than other people, is responsible for making it impossible for him to walk. There may be a hint of panic in the last sentence of the dream. John awakens, apparently, before he has succeeded in getting his shoes in walkable condition. It is an anxiety dream.

There is an interesting question to be raised in thinking about this story: are the hoodlums that he fears other people who he thinks will attack him, or are the hoodlums his own subjective fears within himself? Are we to take the dream as an objective description of John vs the world, or is it a subjective image of his inner condition, his own emotional state?

Posed that way, the question rather tends to answer itself. The dream says that he views the world as threatening, but that in fact there is no threat. The fear that he feels has no basis in objective fact. If he is afraid that others will attack him, he presumably feels very insecure in himself about his own ability to withstand confrontation from any direction. Attacks might be feared from other people, or from complexes within himself, or from physical conditions. Anxiety-ridden people often fear that they are threatened by horrendous illnesses, heart attacks, cancer, brain strokes, or the like. Wherever John's fears come from, and the dream portrays it as from violence-prone hoodlums, the dream says the fear is unfounded. John is himself hampering his own movement, but does not seem to be aware of how he is doing it or how to undo the situation. This would appear to be the theme of the story. Something we are not told is whether the dream deals with his outlook on life generally, or to some one particular incident or experience he has had.

Is there any further 'interpretation' needed for this dream? It looks as though simple contemplation of the story of the dream gives all that we need to understand it. Are there depths that we might be missing if we left it at that?

Here, we must be careful. The 'depths' we might miss really are: 'To what in the dreamer's life does this dream apply?' The message may be clear, but the dreamer must answer the question: 'In what ways in your life are you hampering your own progress, and what are the apparent but unjustified fears that you have?'.

In working with dreams, it is frequently not the message of the dream that is perplexing, but the application of that message to the dreamer's life. When you examine your own dreams, you may often be able to understand what they are 'saying', but not their relevance to your everyday life. This is where the help of another person, or of discussion in a dream group, is usually most needed. It is the persons who know us who are usually most able to say; you fear such and so, but the real fact is that you have made it impossible for yourself to move ahead, by stopping yourself'. They then can often point out just what it is that the person is doing that makes this ludicrous scene. There will usually be resistance to the suggestions made. Generally, dreams state rather unpalatable facts about ourselves or our situation. Something within us does not want to take responsibility for the situation. We may speculate that the purpose of a dream is to point these things out. In Chapters 4 and 8, I attempt to support this speculation with hard evidence. But, at the same time, I must mention that some dreams seem, instead, to bring our attention to comforting or supportive considerations, when we mistrust what we are doing or lack confidence in our way of handling life.

We will not proceed further with John's dream, because I wished merely to indicate how a dream can portray a dramatic story which has meaning in itself. Interested readers may wish to follow up what John's dreams reveal about his character by examining the other dreams he has contributed to this book. Six of his dreams are discussed, as listed at the end of the book in the Index of Dreams.

The second dream that we will examine looks very complicated in comparison with the first, but we will find that it, too, yields to treatment as a dramatised story about the dreamer's life-style and attitudes towards life's situations. The dreamer, Jim K., is a young man whom we will meet twelve times in this book. In age and nationality, he is quite different from John.

I was sitting in the train on the way to a business conference (I was a business man). I did not want to waste time on this trip, so I took out my typewriter to do a bit of work. The train compartment had, in the meantime, turned into an office, though I was sure I was still on the train. I tried to type, but it was hopeless. A perfectly unintelligible series of letters appeared on the paper in the machine. A dark-haired girl was standing by the right wall of the room; she was staring at me so intensely that it felt like she was criticising my clumsy attempts to type. Apparently, she wanted to use the typewriter herself. But then I immersed myself in my work altogether, and paid no further attention to my surroundings. Suddenly, there was an old man (about sixty) standing beside me. He told me, in a friendly fashion, that we would soon be in W.... I was alarmed, because that meant that I had neglected to get out at the right station, and would not be able to keep my appointment.

I also remember standing at the stop in W.... I was quite convinced that it really was W.... (although the real city looks totally different). What I saw was a very idyllic little village with beautiful houses and trees surrounding a large, well cared for, rectangular green. I wondered how I could get to a telephone. I could not see any public building or restaurant among the houses on the edge of the green. But as I looked about, I saw that I had passed two telephone booths beside the path that I was following; somehow I had missed seeing them. Both were occupied, and a couple of people were waiting beside each one. I could not decide which booth to stand in line for, and went back and forth from one to the other a couple of times. When it looked like the booth to the right was about to be free, an Italian-looking young man ran in front of me. I told him I was there first, but he insisted, in a sort of bashful way, that he was first. Then I

asked him whether his call would take very long. He said that it would
only take a few minutes, so I let him go first.

JIM K., #1

(The W . . . . in the dream text indicates that I have replaced the real place
name with a different initial, to help ensure the anonymity of the
dreamer.)

This dream has portrayed for us the troubles of a business man on the
way to a conference. This business man does not like to waste time, so his
train compartment turns into an office where he can type, but his typewriter will not type anything sensible.

In reality, Jim is not a business man at all, but a student. Why, then, has
the dream turned him into a business man? This problem would be solved
by the insertion of one tiny word, 'like': 'I was like a business man'. It is an
'as if' story, a point that could also be made about the first dream we
examined. Dream language is often made comprehensible when we fill in
this 'as if' or 'like' — in this instance, 'My life is as if . . . I were not a student
but a business man'.

What is the difference between a student and a business man? A student
may take time off, goof about, do tomorrow what has not been done today.
A business man must be industrious, devoted to his job, utilising every
moment of his time for his all-important work. A business man may have
wistful longings for a dark-haired girl or an idyllic country village with no
commercial establishments or even apparent telephones, but he must
brush these aside in favour of his work. Jim tells us a lot about how he views
his life in the very first sentence of his dream.

So as not to waste time, the train compartment doubles as an office
where the business man can type. But the typewriter will only print gibber-
ish for him. The frantic business activity results in nothing. In fact, the
whole dream is a long frustration of the business man's intended activities,
right to the final episode of the phone booths.

In the series of irritations that plague this business man is a dark-haired
girl over by the wall, who seems to be impatient to use the typewriter herself. Then another major irritation: an 'old' man comes to announce the
next station. Presumably, it is the train conductor, though the dream does
not say so. Jim is alarmed, for he has missed his stop.

Jim gets off the train at a village that is very different from the bustling
city of today. It is a quaint, old-fashioned village surrounding a central
green. Something in Jim is attracted by this village, for he describes it as
idyllic. It is idyllic enough to distract him from seeing at first the two telephone booths that he passes while searching for a phone! He has to wait to
use either booth, but cannot make up his mind which to wait for. When
one booth is finally free, a newly appeared Italian-looking youth claims
priority in using it, and Jim submits after a brief argument.

If this dream is, so to speak, the story of Jim's life at the time, we get a pretty good description of what that life feels like — busy, the feeling of never a moment to lose; a nostalgic longing for a quiet, rather isolated village life; difficulty in expressing just what he feels to be important, imaged by the typewriter that won't type what he intends; a dark-haired girl trying to intervene, to use the typewriter, but he does not want to disrupt his busy attitude of getting down to work at every opportunity.

Is this dark-haired girl a real person in his life? Or does she represent women in general, for him? As with the hoodlums in the first dream, on reflection, this question does not seem very important. Whether she is an objective person in the real world, whom for some reason the dream does not name, and who wants to draw his attention, or whether the incident represents his way of relating to people, especially women, amounts to much the same thing: he ignores her and devotes himself scrupulously to his work, allowing no other interest to distract him.

There is, however, another aspect to this story, which I have already alluded to. The dream contrasts the intense life of a business man, which, since in reality he is not a business man, we should perhaps take as 'busy-ness-man', who has no time or interest for the dark-haired girl, with a sort of nostalgic, wistful image of the idyllic country village with its central green. Actually, this represents one aspect of Jim's life, for he takes vacations out in the countryside, and enjoys the restful life of camping and touring, a stark contrast to his very busy, 'never-a-moment-to-be-lost' regular life as a student.

That Jim is caught by conflicting feelings, both in real life and in dream fantasy, stands out when we look at the marked contrast in the two parts of his dream. On the one hand, a busy office-even-on-the-train life-style; on the other hand, a nostalgic picture of getting off that train and entering a little country village where communication with the rest of the world seems to be limited to two telephone booths. Jim's isolation continues in this second part of the dream. Only one interaction takes place, and that is the brief argument with the Italian-looking chap who claims priority in using the phone.

With this dream more than the first, we have the feeling that we would like explanations. Why a sixty-year-old man? Why an Italian-looking young man? Why the city/village of W . . . .? Surely these descriptions mean something in the dream that would enlarge our understanding. Brief comments about them are available, after talking with Jim about his dream. Here again, the help of a second person, or of discussion in a dream group, proves desirable to pick out points that the dreamer might tend to pass by. And for us, discussion with the dreamer is imperative if we are to understand the dream fully.

Jim says that a sixty-year-old man reminds him of his father, and also a psychoanalyst whom he consulted and who took him 'part of the way' in working over his problems. But the man in the dream does not resemble either of these persons, except vaguely in age. There is some more resemblance to the psychoanalyst, though. It feels pretty clear, from talking with Jim, that the psychoanalyst took him rather further than he had intended, and, so to speak, landed him in unfamiliar territory, leaving him at rather a loss as to what he wanted to do with his life.

The Italian-looking youth reminds him of various friends from his earlier years, though of no person in particular. Like the girl on the train, it is no one special. Rather, he says, he has a feeling about Italians, that they are more easygoing, have a zest for life, an enjoyment of nature and natural beauty, and a facility in relationships.

So the dream has picked figures that bear some similarities to real persons, but are not imaged as those particular persons. In other words, real persons have served to conjure up dream images that represent types: female relationships that might impinge upon Jim's busy life if he were to allow it; guidance from an older man which takes him beyond where he intended; a hesitating willingness to permit a free and easy life-style, providing it does not take up too much of his time.

This tendency of a dream to portray persons who do not exist but are modelled on people known to the dreamer is very frequent and has a very important role to play. We will examine it in more detail in Chapter 2. In regard to Jim's dream, we can say that the dream portrays Jim's life situation and character as seen from the inside. A dream may deal with specific problems encountered in life, often by directly mentioning the problems and persons involved. But when it portrays 'invented' persons, it does so for a purpose. They portray parts of the dreamer's own character, modelled on real persons. Thus, Jim's character has been enriched by incorporating features of real persons, but this enrichment has taken place at an unconscious level. In his waking state, Jim is not usually aware that they are there inside him. They are lying latent, under the surface, awaiting the chance to come into his waking awareness from time to time.

Jim's dream can be seen as an attempt to enlarge his conscious personality by portraying these figures: the possibility of a female relationship, which he tends to brush aside; goals evoked within him by sessions with his psychoanalyst; and the desire for and possibility of a much more free, relaxed life with a touch of *joie de vivre*. At the same time, the dream portrays Jim's reluctance to accept these potentialities of enrichment of life. There is some progress in this regard, however, in the dream story. Jim knows the dark-haired girl wants to communicate but he is determined not to let her interfere with his busy life; the train conductor informs him of a *fait accompli*, that he has already passed his original 'business' destination and moved onwards to a new kind of situation; and he does let the Italian youth use the telephone to contact the outside world, even if only under the stipulation that it be brief. But the dream also indicates his determination to keep these potentialities for enrichment from being given their due.

One person in the dream whom we must be very careful not to overlook is Jim himself. Jim, in relating his dream, naturally says 'I' did such-and-such: 'I was sitting in the train', 'I did not want to waste time', 'I took out my typewriter', etc. He interacts with the other persons portrayed in his dream, to a greater or lesser degree: with the dark-haired girl, the train man, the Italian-looking youth. The type of interaction portrayed in the dream gives us a very good entry into an understanding of what has prevented the potential for enrichment from being fulfilled. Let us look at what Jim says about himself in his dream:

1. I was sitting in the train
2. I was a business man
3. I did not want to waste time
4. I took out my typewriter
5. I was sure I was still on the train
6. I tried to type
7. I immersed myself in my work altogether
8-9. I was alarmed, because ... I had neglected to get off at the right station
10. I also remember standing at the stop
11. I was quite convinced that it really was W . . . .
12. What I saw was a very idyllic little village
13-14. I wondered how I could get to a telephone
15. I could not see any public building or restaurant
16-18. As I looked about, I saw I had passed two telephone booths
19. Beside the path I was following
20. Somehow I had missed seeing them
21. I could not decide which booth
22-23. I told him I was there first
24. I asked him whether his call would take very long
25. I let him go first

What has happened in this dream is that a dramatic story has been composed, and the dreamer takes part in it as if it were a real event, reacting to the persons and situations he encounters as the story proceeds. From this characterisation we get a good picture of what Jim's attitudes and feelings are.

Thus, the dream story has presented to us two major features of Jim's personality: features that come from his experiences with other people, but that are still dormant within his character; and also his own natural response to these dormant inclinations. His primary concern and reaction to female relationships are represented in items 1-7; his response to the elderly figure in items 8-9; his response to the village features in items 10-21; his response to the Italian-looking young man in items 22-25.

This is a general feature of dreams, although there are exceptions, that a dramatic scene is presented, in which the dreamer encounters various people or situations and reacts to and interacts with them. Most dreams, though not all, do feature an 'I' = the dreamer, and portray how she/he acts in the face of various situations. The situations or people encountered are usually aspects of life that, for some reason, are foreign to the dreamer's waking life pattern, aspects of life that she/he cannot handle, or has not recognised, or has not acknowledged the strength and importance of. There are many exceptions, but as a general principle for helping us on our way, it works well. We can, initially at least, ask of each dream: 'What sorts of situations, what aspects of life, are portrayed as being encountered by the dreamer, and how does she/he handle them?'

In the case of Jim's dream, there is a marked progression in the dream story as it proceeds, which gives the story a feeling of hopefulness: whereas, initially, Jim is unwilling to be concerned with the girl by the wall, he later interacts a little bit with the elderly man, and he is finally willing to let the Italian-looking youth take precedence, even though only briefly. The dream is, so to speak, saying 'You start by being unwilling to let anything interfere with your busy-ness; but gradually, you give in and allow a bit of time, even though brief, to the spirit of the zest for living'.

As with our first example, we have not really 'interpreted' the dream here. We have merely looked at the story it tells, taking it at face value, and characterised what it says basically in its own terms. To make full use of this dream, discussion with Jim would be required: 'To what do you devote your life so exclusively? What potential relationships with women are you disregarding? How could you find a restful, peaceful oasis in your busy life where you could relax, and what would you have to give up in order to make room for it? And finally, how could the Italian approach to life be given an opportunity to express itself in your own attitudes towards life?'

The approach to dreams that I have been illustrating is not universally applicable to all dreams, but it is particularly helpful for many, and makes a valuable beginning for the examination of others. In later chapters, I examine further aspects of dreams and the technique of 'interpreting' them — by which I mean coming to understand them. For the remainder of this chapter, I wish to give further examples of how to examine the story of a dream, and to pick out its kernel structure.

In the first two dreams we examined, the people and events portrayed have been imaginary. But often, they are specific people or events taken from waking life. In the following dream, one of my patients examines his interactions with me:

I am talking to Donald Broadribb—an American psychology student is present. Some old lady, who I think is related to Donald Broadribb, asks what is happening tonight. Donald Broadribb explains that I am having my lectures with him tonight. He also says that I had made an offer to bring my parents over to Perth so that they could understand what psychoanalysis is all about. He says this usually works out to be a total failure or a complete success, depending on the relationship of the parents and the analyst. The American student says his parents accepted the fact that he was studying psychology with no difficulty. Donald Broadribb explains that psychology is far more acceptable in USA than in Australia.

GERALD D., #1

This dream came fairly early in the dreamer's analysis. Two very striking points in the dream stand out: the dream talks about the 'study' of psychology, which is identified with psychoanalysis, and there is the strange statement about Gerald's parents. Now, in the dream, I state that I am giving Gerald lectures tonight, and Gerald explains that I also proposed that his parents come to Perth, which is where my practice is, to learn what psychoanalysis is all about, and it is said that usually this works out to be a total failure or complete success. Another person, an American student, says that his parents had no difficulty in accepting that he was studying psychology. Then I seem to point out that things may be different with Gerald's parents, because psychology is more acceptable to Americans than to Australians.

We need to clarify, right at the start of examining Gerald's dream, to what extent the dream is concerned with real facts, and how much is imaginary. Gerald had, in reality, heard a great many of my lectures and seminars, but at the time of the dream, no lectures were in progress, Gerald's relationship with me was that of a patient with his analyst, rather than that of a student attending my lectures. But in the dream, there is no suggestion of analytic therapy, only of study. This implies that Gerald sees, or would like to see, his relationship with me as that of a student rather than of a patient.

This is not at all unusual when people consult an analyst. They frequently imagine that it will be a course of study of some kind; or, very frequently, they tell other people that they are undertaking a course of study, in order to avoid the social stigma attached to consulting an analyst. But in this particular instance of Gerald, the matter is a bit more complicated: he had already undergone some analysis sessions with me, and from my lectures and seminars, he should have derived the impression that analysis is not a course of study. In his dream, Gerald says I will be giving a lecture tonight, which he will attend. But his sessions were during the day, not the evening. So it is not just that he may regard his sessions as study classes, in which, heaven help me!, I lecture him. There is a reticence to acknowledge the therapy aspect altogether.

Gerald's parents play a strange role in this dream. In the dream, it is said that I suggested bringing his parents to Perth to find what psychoanalysis is all about. I am also made to say that it is a black and white situation: total failure or complete success. There is some background to this part of the dream: quite some time before, I suggested that a particular problem of Gerald's is understandable in the light of his childhood experiences. He could not, at the time, see the connection. It did, in fact, take a considerable while before he came to understand that his childhood experiences had a great deal to do with the way he relates to people, and to life in general, now. At that earlier time, I suggested that he write up an autobiographical sketch with emphasis on his childhood and family. I hoped that, by doing this, he would see the relevance of his earlier experiences to his way of experiencing the world now. He did write the sketch, to oblige me, but I had the feeling that he did it because I had asked for it, rather than from the realisation that he could discover some important facts about himself in the process.

In my way, I was saying 'To understand you, we need to understand your parents, and especially your relationship with them, for they are the ones who moulded your emotions and gave you your outlook on life'. I had him write out the account instead of giving it verbally, because I thought the writing would force him to look at his childhood systematically, and to notice, perhaps with my help, regular themes that ran throughout his years of life as a child at home. The dream suggests that he felt that it would be even better to bring the parents in person, so I could analyse them. What he had failed to realise was that my own direct impression of his parents would bear little resemblance to the parents he had experienced, for he had known them in a parent-child relationship, and with a child's own understanding, and there would be much that an adult outsider would never discover. So his memories of them were quite vital.

That this would be 'a total failure or a complete success, depending on the relationship between the parents and the analyst', via his memories, would really mean that success or failure depended on the way I related to his life material. While this is true to an extent, it leaves out one vital ingredient, namely, himself: his personal relationship with me would be the decisive element in the success or failure of the undertaking. In the dream, at least, he fails to see this point yet; he understands it as a lecturer-student situation, in which it is information that I give out that will furnish him with the foundation on which to succeed or fail.

Now let us look at the dramatis personae in the dream. These include me, himself, and his parents, all of whom are real people; and an American psychology student, an old lady, and the American student's parents, all of whom are dream inventions. The parallel is made quite explicit in the dream: Gerald is compared with the American student, and his parents are compared with the American student's parents. The relevance of the old lady is not immediately apparent. But the core theme of the dream seems to be 'You, Dr Broadribb, as an American student of psychology, had your parents' support, and I then agree: yes, in America, psychology (= psychoanalysis, in Gerald's language) is much more readily accepted than in Australia.'

This leaves us, of course, wondering why the parents' attitudes should come into the picture at all. In the dream, it is as if they hold a veto power over their son's 'studies'.

This dream is a 'transference dream'. Psychologists are very familiar with this phenomenon, but the lay reader may not be. In analytic usage, a transference dream is a dream in which the patient's fantasies about the analyst are expressed. A patient usually knows little or nothing about the analyst personally, but she/he generally makes a lot of conjectures about the analyst, which very often, for one reason or another, are not voiced directly, but have to be surmised by the analyst via the patient's dreams and general attitude toward the analyst in the sessions. Often, the conjectures are based on deductions made from the analyst's age, appearance, voice, taste in pictures and other room decorations, car, mannerisms, books and journals visible, and much more. For example, one patient spoke, in his dream, about my son who is studying in Cambridge. There is, in fact, no such son, but the patient had constructed him for me in his imagination, based on conclusions drawn from my age, marital status, obvious educational background, and imagined wealth. He was both surprised and disappointed when I had to tell him this son was imaginary.

Usually, there is more to transference than simply these conjectures. The patient customarily 'transfers' her/his experience of someone else, most often a parent, to the analyst, and acts emotionally as if the analyst were in fact that parent. In general, there is no good reason to restrict the concept of transference to the fantasies and feelings of a patient towards the analyst. Transference can occur in any human encounter. We will see this phenomenon many more times before the close of this book. But for the time being, let us restrict our discussion to Gerald and his dream about me.

In point of view of historical fact, Gerald's dream had very little substance behind it. I was neither an American psychology student, nor did I have parents who encouraged me in this line. From my experience, it does not appear to me that psychoanalysis, of whatever school, is any more socially accepted in America than in Australia. This is despite the usual Australian's conclusion from watching Hollywood movies that every American sees a psychoanalyst every day. But Gerald's dream is not about historical fact, it concerns his inner feelings about me and his relationship with me.

The old lady in the dream is a bit of a puzzle. She is said to be possibly related to me. The immediate answer is that she is probably the dreamer's idea of my mother, though Gerald was unable to confirm this. Another, less-pleasant conclusion is that Gerald sometimes sees me as an 'old lady'. We cannot rule out the possibility that that is how he felt about me at times. Actually, there is another candidate for the role of 'old lady'. The first qualified analyst in Perth was Rix Weaver, an old lady at the time of this dream, whose book *The Old Wise Woman* Gerald was familiar with. The 'old lady' designation may in fact be a compliment to me, as being an 'old wise woman'. It is by no means unusual for a patient's dream or fantasy to picture the analyst as a mother, even though the analyst is male. Dreams concern the dreamer's feelings and emotional experiences; I may be pictured 'as if' I were a mother, in the way the patient experiences me. Or as if I embodied the ages-old wisdom incarnated in the 'Old Wise Woman' of Ms Weaver's book.

I have already spoken of the point that Gerald, in his dream, claims to be my student hearing lectures from me, rather than a patient undergoing therapy from me. This could be a façade that he maintains in order to make his analysis acceptable to himself, or to outsiders. But there is another, complicating factor, which is also found very frequently. Gerald had his doubts about some of what was going on in his analysis. As an experience and a form of therapy, analysis aims at effecting changes in the patient's personality and life. These changes are very often strongly resisted. The simplest form of resistance is to say that the analyst is wrong. The next simplest form of resistance is to take it all in intellectually, but shield off any emotional involvement. It is a widespread idea, among the public, that to know the origins or cause of a problem automatically dissolves the problem. It is, thus, possible for a patient to attend many analytical sessions with no particular change taking place in the problems for which she/he came. This is especially a danger when dream analysis is used, because it is all too easy to say 'That's an interesting interpretation', without going into the emotions involved at all. For dream analysis to have any value, it has to be linked up intimately with current events in the dreamer's life. Dreams frequently speak of the past, but the danger of stopping there is that the dreamer will say, 'Well that's all over with'.

In one, very real sense, working with dreams is truly subjective. It requires not only emotional confirmation by the patient, but linking up with the realities of the dreamer's daily life. Gerald had studied a number of books on dream interpretation, and participated in seminars on the practice of dream interpretation, but he found it difficult to apply his dreams to his own life. This is the rule, rather than the exception. Gerald hoped for some easier, objective method to turn to than the intangible area of emotions. So, in his dream, he turned to a side of me that he knew, even though it was not relevant at the time of his dream — my role as a teacher.

He still had the hope that my lectures would provide the 'solid' content that would smooth his way to understanding his dreams. It had not yet really become clear to him that the meaning of a dream is something that can only come out through discussion, and that is emotional rather than intellectual. The meaning cannot be arrived at by some specific methodology applied to the dream in isolation.

By examining Gerald's dream story, viewing it as giving an insight into his relationship with me, it has been possible to seek out the main points of his dream. The dream gives emphasis to two main points: the necessity of examining in detail his relationship with his parents as a major factor in his personality structure; and the vexing conflict between the therapeutic experience of undergoing analysis and the academic experience of studying and going to lectures, which does not affect the nature of the conduct of his life.

Thus far, we have been examining dreams dealing primarily with emotional relationships and the dreamer's relationship with life. This will prove to be a typical set of themes. Sometimes, they are easy to discover in the dream text, sometimes not. Let us try our hand at a short dream that looks, at first glance, rather formidable to understand:

> *I am with a girl in some place. We look through the pages of what seems to be an old* National Geographic. *In it is a photograph of the rock group Led Zeppelin, an FJ Holden and the Queen [i.e. Queen Elizabeth]. The girl and I are close, with our hands on one another's legs, though I seem hesitant because it seems she is involved with another guy. We leave the place and later she asks if I have the magazine, she had wanted to keep it as it had represented the two of us. I said no, but I had set it aside, knowing its importance. The girl says we must buy it now, after looking through it.*

> ALFRED M., #1

This is the first of three dreams of Alfred's that we will be examining in the course of this book. We need a few explanations, before we proceed:

Led Zeppelin is the name of a rock group that sprang to prominence in the late 1960s. As Alfred described the group, they were into 'hard' rock and roll, a type of music of which he is particularly fond. Alfred described his love for them as, basically, because of their spontaneity, their production of music that allows for a great deal of improvisation, the way they throw themselves into the music, all of which, he feels, epitomise the soul of rock music.

The FJ Holden is an Australian phenomenon, an attempt to design a purely Australian car. The FJ was an early model, produced shortly after the Second World War. It is something of a collector's item now. As an attempt at local car design and manufacture, it was a failure. The Holden company was bought by General Motors, which continues to use the name Holden for its cars marketed in Australia. We will see the FJ Holden turn up in another person's dream later in the book. It holds an especially warm place in Australian hearts, including this dreamer's.

Queen Elizabeth II is nominally Queen of Australia, though she holds no authority there. She came to the throne in 1952, so that her reign spans the periods of both the FJ Holden and the Led Zeppelin group, as well as the intervening years up to the time of Alfred's dream.

The girl in Alfred's dream, as well as her other male friend, is a dream invention. The girl's relationship with Alfred is ambivalent: she was once emotionally close to Alfred, and still keeps fond memories of that, although she is now involved with another man. There is a slight degree of similarity with Jim's dream of the business man on the train, in that both dreams portray a missing relationship with the dreamer. In Jim's dream, the girl, who, like the girl in Alfred's dream, was a dream invention, wanted to communicate, but Jim was unwilling to give her any time. In Alfred's dream, the girl wants to remember the fact that they once had a relationship, but no longer.

Both dreams, Jim's and Alfred's, portray the problem of relating to a woman. However, unlike Jim and the dark-haired girl, Alfred and his friend share a common interest: something to do with Led Zeppelin, the FJ Holden, and Queen Elizabeth. The dream actually puts it a bit more strongly: the photograph in the *National Geographic* is more than a common interest, the girl says that it actually represents herself and Alfred. The girl seems more aware of this than Alfred. He says that he knew its importance and put the magazine aside. She wants to keep the magazine by buying it, now that they have looked through it. The dream story lays great emphasis on this issue of the *National Geographic*, and it would seem that the point is to make Alfred aware of its emotional value in representing them both.

I have already mentioned Alfred's enthusiasm for Led Zeppelin's music, which for him epitomises the theme of emotional spontaneity and freedom. The FJ Holden holds something of the image of being 'the people's car' and, incidentally, appeared in the mid-1950s, at the time rock-and-roll emerged as a musical form. Queen Elizabeth was in her late twenties then, and her youthful figure on a horse was a much beloved image.

There is, then, an air of nostalgia in this dream. The girl is now involved with someone else, but there was a time when she and Alfred shared a common love for spontaneous expression (Led Zeppelin) and innovation (the FJ

Holden, new and valued then), and the youthful zest for life that Queen Elizabeth personified. Now, years later, all this seems to him to be in the past, his heart has turned elsewhere, but he is reminded that these past feelings must not be lost, but be kept and treasured. The presence of the girl indicates his desire for a close relationship with a woman who shares his interests — a soul-mate, in short — but she also represents his fear that any such woman would already be spoken for. In some way, his heart lies in the memory of the past, commemorated by a picture survey, for that is what the *National Geographic* is. This dream makes us aware that the inner dialogue of a man with his heart is not a mere metaphor but a living reality, even if it may not be carried out during waking time. As we continue examining dreams, we will find this a consistent pattern, that the dream examines and, so to speak, contains a dialogue between the emotions and the waking day mind.

The *National Geographic* is a magazine that examines little-known areas and breathes life into them for the reader by means of pictures. It also looks at natural phenomena and better-known cities, to keep its readers up to date with the world around them. But most of all, the *National Geographic* is renowned for its maps. These features make it an eminently suitable image for the function of dreams, which is to explore little-known areas of the psyche, give a new look into well-known bits, and chart the dreamer's progress among the mountains and valleys of life.

Alfred is troubled by the problem of keeping hold of what was precious to him of the old and progressing into the new. His tendency to think of 'real life' as being in the past is emphasised for him by the dream girl who values this issue of the *National Geographic* for its images of life in past decades, but the images also point the way into the present and future by including Queen Elizabeth, who serves as a link between the past, present and future for Alfred's life, the overriding theme of continuity.

There are two women in Alfred's dream: one imaginary and one known to him only via the media. Queen Elizabeth is much idealised, at least by Australians, and is a fairly frequent figure in their dreams, along with other members of the Royal Family (Prince Charles tends to take the leading role in Australian women's dreams). The first woman, the 'girl' in Alfred's dream, is a purely fantasy figure, but Queen Elizabeth hardly less so for him, with one important difference. Led Zeppelin, the FJ Holden and Queen Elizabeth are all features of external life, while the girl in the dream represents no one in Alfred's life, but is purely an inner, imaginary figure. This contrast between the appearance of 'real' figures and 'imaginary' ones is a point that is going to occupy our attention quite frequently in this book. For now, knowing Alfred's life and consistent inability to form a lasting relationship with a woman, I would like to leave the matter as the girl representing Alfred's feeling of relationships being in the past with little hope for the future. Some of Alfred's later dreams fill in this aspect of his life for us in rather more detail. Queen Elizabeth, I would be more inclined to take literally, as an image of the highly respected woman who symbolises the special relationship felt by the members of the British Commonwealth of Nations and its continuity.

Alfred's use of the term 'girl' is more probably an influence of popular speech than an attempt to indicate age. To members of the present generation of Australian youth and young adults, the world is divided into 'guys' and 'girls'; to the older generations, it is divided into 'guys' and 'ladies', with 'sheilas' an alternative term for the latter, and 'women' used but rarely. Since many of the dreamers who have made their dreams available to me are Australian, it has been impossible to keep Australian usage and, occasionally, slang out of the dream texts, but I have tried to give translations into standard English in my comments, when necessary.

At this point, the reader may well be rather discontent, feeling that working over a dream requires a lot of information about the dreamer, and that, in my discussions, I am bringing in a great deal of material unavailable to the readers. This is quite correct. It is *not* possible to understand a dream without detailed acquaintance with consultation with the dreamer. For this reason, I must bring in information apart from what is given in the dream text. For example, Alfred's dream might be taken in quite a different way if he were an elderly man troubled by a break-up in his love life thirty years ago; or if he were a teenager with a crush on a geography teacher.

In looking at the dream's story, it is important to see it as talking about the dreamer's situation now. Events and persons and places of the past do turn up in dreams, particularly when the situation at present is one that causes the dreamer to look over her/his past. But as a generalisation, the principle holds well that the dream's story is concerned with now, although the images and events it uses may well come from the past. When, in Chapter 2, we come to discussing the roles of the people in our dreams, it will become clearer how persons of the past can represent influences upon us in past times that continue to live as parts of our personality make-up at the present.

The question often arises whether children's dreams are very different from adults'. One factor that has struck me particularly is that, on the whole, young children's dreams tend to use more symbolism than do adults'. This may be because their range of experience is much more limited than the adults', so that their dreams must rely on symbols more as a means of expression, while adults have a far greater stock of persons, places and events in their memory to call upon when dreams are being composed. I would mention that, like all generalisations, this does not hold true for all child dreamers, or all the dreams of one child.

With a child's dream, too, the dream's story is all-important to look at when beginning to try to understand it. Carl N., whose first dream follows, has kindly made available to me a number of his dreams for discussion, and has taken interest in their interpretation. Four of his dreams are used in this book. After reading through the book and trying your hand at the sample dreams exercise in the Appendix, you may find it helpful to locate all the dreams of Carl N., or another dreamer, using the Index of Dreams, to compare the light shone on an individual's personality through examining a variety of that person's dreams.

I was with my sister. Daddy was driving the car. We came to the supermarket and we decided to go to the underground parking. After we had done our shopping, we went across the road and I found some marbles growing on little trees. My sister got more marbles than me.

CARL N., #1

This dream is pretty straightforward. It picks up imagery from everyday life. The child is in a car with his (older) sister, and his father is driving. They come to a supermarket, park in an underground parking lot, do their shopping. But across the road are tiny trees with marbles growing on them. The two children pick the marbles, but the sister gets more than Carl.

Carl's jealousy of his sister appears in the comment on how many marbles each manages to pick. There is a fairy-tale-like quality with the marbles growing on trees and not needing to be purchased. Apart from the obvious sibling rivalry, there is also a failure to completely understand the workings of the world, as we might expect in a young schoolchild. Essentials must be purchased, and in waking life, the child is quite aware that toys, like marbles, also must be purchased. But his dream reveals the emotional difference: marbles are normally gifts, and the child is not in the habit of having his father include them in the grocery shopping. Necessities of life require payment, but the pleasures of life are a gift, they are there for the picking.

Since the marbles grow on trees, we might expect the two children to have equal opportunity in the picking. But the sister, who is several years older, gets more — the feeling of a young child that the older you are, the more you get. At the same time, the dream seems to be saying, by implication, 'You have equal opportunity with your sister, but you are not as able as she to seize opportunities'. We can legitimately point out that, being considerably bigger, her hands are larger and can hold more marbles.

Again, questions arise: have we missed out something in this examination of the dream? Why should it be marbles? Do they feature because the child was jealous earlier in the day that his sister really does have more marbles? Or do marbles represent something? Is the child familiar with such expressions as 'to lose your marbles', meaning 'to go crazy'?

In an instance such as this, it is rarely possible to ask the young child for details. Carl was able to tell me that his sister did not have more marbles in reality, though there was considerable rivalry between them on this issue. Both children managed to lose marbles frequently, so that it was necessary to replenish the supply often. Usually, they asked their Daddy to get them more marbles on such an occasion, and he obliged. So picking the marbles themselves from trees reflects a certain amount of independence from Daddy, the ability to get what they want with their own resources. Marbles are also often a sort of currency among children, and the expression 'money doesn't grow on trees' could have been reformulated by the dream as 'but maybe marbles do'.

This is speculation. But what does come out quite clearly in the dream is Carl's feeling that his sister gets more than he does in a competitive situation. While in the shopping centre, their Daddy is in charge of deciding what will be bought, and we may assume that supplies for both children are about equal. But when on his own, competing directly with his sister, Carl feels at a disadvantage. In an equal situation, his sister ends up with more than he.

Another child's dream shows us how clearly and impressively a dream may portray the emotional situation a person is in. This dream was told to me several decades after it was dreamed, but the content was verified independently, because the little child who had the dream insisted on its being written down at the time:

> *I was on the ocean, floating in the bowl of a big spoon. The spoon was tied with a long string to a boat and my mother was in the boat but I could not see her.*
>
> JOHN W., #2.

This is an anxiety dream. The feeling in the dream stands out most strongly. Some of the imagery can be traced to poems with which the child was familiar, Edward Lear's 'The Owl and the Pussycat' and the mysterious 'runcible spoon'. But this throws little light on the dream, which has made use of imagery familiar to the child in its own way, for its own purposes.

The feeling of insecurity and aloneness stands out in the dream. Mother is somewhere, but she is not visible and she cannot be communicated with, although it is her boat that is pulling the spoon along and, therefore, determines the direction the child takes, and, also, the speed of his movement. The child feels life to be like an ocean, an analogy that appears in the dreams of many people. The feeling of the imagery is quite frightening: floating on the ocean in the bowl of a spoon, unable to direct it in any way, totally at the mercy of an unseen parent; a feeling that life is very precarious, and the child unable to do anything about it. The importance of this dream came through to the child, who demanded that his mother write it down from dictation, something the child was not in the habit of doing. Incidentally, John apparently felt that his mother was safe enough — she was in the ship.

The question of symbolism first comes up in regard to the ocean. It is difficult to hold back and not to say, 'Oh, the ocean, that means . . .' It is also very difficult to reach agreement on what the ocean represents in such dreams. When we ask about the spoon, matters are a little easier. A young child is usually fed with a spoon, and the spoon is used when the child feeds itself. So it is tempting to say that the spoon, with its associations of eating, gives in this dream the feeling of a hiatus in the nourishing qualities of the mother for her growing child. This impression is strengthened by remarking that she is invisible in the ship, totally away from the sight of John in the spoon. The assumption probably could be justified that it is emotional nourishment, i.e. the feeling of emotional warmth and security, that the spoon represents.

Various other interpretations of the spoon are also possible and more or less equally plausible. The principal problem is that it is difficult to give an objective validation to any particular interpretation of the spoon. I suggest that the feeling of the dream be taken at face value, without the introduction of symbol interpretation. Obviously, the dream cannot be taken literally as a statement of objective fact, in the sense that a real spoon and a real ocean are meant. But the feeling imparted by this particular imagery is such that it could not be reproduced by any more prosaic means. To attempt to 'interpret' the 'symbols', in this instance, would be to run away from the emotional meaning of the imagery. If it were a modern poet who used the imagery, instead of a pre-school child, we would not hesitate in acclaiming it a very powerful image. By all this, I do not mean that symbols are not used in dreams, nor that their interpretation may not be justified, even necessary. But I do mean that, much of the time, the emotional impact of an image can slip away if we run too quickly for the symbols dictionary. We are reminded of Jung's statement: that a real symbol is an image that conveys a feeling that could not be as adequately expressed in any other way. This places dream language in rather the same group as non-representational art such as Kandinsky's, emotive sculpting such as Henry Moore's, expressive music such as Béla Bartók's, or the unique blend of pictures and words in William Blake's creations.

Why then do analysts speak of interpreting dreams? In part, because there are many aspects of dreams that we have not yet investigated in these pages; and in part, because it is therapeutically helpful to relate the content of a dream to experiences in the dreamer's life.

Obviously, anxiety dreams such as John's by no means dominate our sleeping life; they do, however, tend to be remembered more easily than other types of dreams, often because we wake up at their conclusion. One way of coping with a frightening dream is to awaken and be able to say to ourselves, 'Well, that was just a dream, it isn't real so there is no cause for alarm'. We need to go into the question of why we have dreams, and this is something we will look specifically at in Chapter 4. For now, we are assuming that there is some point being made that is important for the dreamer. I am setting aside, temporarily, the idea that dreams may serve a unique purpose simply in allowing the expression of emotions that are tabooed in daily life, though this does seem to be the purpose of many dreams. In John's case, we can argue whether, as a little child, he was experiencing in the dream a feeling of anxiety and insecurity too overpowering for him to allow to come out during waking life. The fact that he felt it so important to dictate the dream to his mother and insist that she keep it may lead to the conclusion that he was also trying to communicate this sense of ultimate anxiety and insecurity to her in the only way he knew how, by means of imagery. As a message remembered through its imagery in his daily life, John may have been keeping alive the realisation of the fundamental insecurity of his existence. Seen in this light, this dream parallels John's dream that was narrated and discussed at the beginning of the chapter, the dream of the rubber shoe-laces. We may at least contemplate that the feeling of existential insecurity remained so powerful that John was unable to see that it was he himself who was impeding his progress through life, through his feeling of deep anxiety, and that the supposed hoodlums of the outer world were not the real threat.

Reassuring dreams, though, are just as powerful and important as anxiety dreams, and in the next chapter, we will encounter dreams that attempt to resolve issues that the dreamer feels uncertain about. If any generalisation is to be made at this point, it is that dreams can help to find equilibrium, by focusing on situations, attitudes, and relationships that can help the dreamer to centre herself/himself emotionally, if they are taken into account. This appears to be a valid generalisation even for nightmares, as is discussed in Chapter 5. But dreams can sometimes be a way of crying for help, especially if they are being recorded or discussed in the context of psychological therapy. In John's childhood dream, both reassurance and the cry for help are found: reassurance in that the spoon actually is floating on the ocean and is being towed by a secure ship, even though only by a string; the cry for help in John's reaction to the dream, which was to tell it to his mother and insist that she write it down to be kept.

Let us turn, finally, to a dream that will lead us directly into the second phase of our investigations, the dramatis personae of dreams:

I was with a group of college students. There was a lot of noise and foolery. One boy in particular was fond of me but could only show it in a juvenile way. Everyone then went their separate ways. Then I was going to the beach to lie in the sun and read. I was then standing on a

*high parking area—there were people and cars everywhere. Dr W.
[science teacher] was there and we were talking. He was very sympathetic and I could communicate with him at an adult level. Joyce then
appeared. She was going canoeing—I was a bit worried as there was a
strong wind. They were taking the ferry route. A young man then
carted her off in a familiar manner. They each got into their own cars
and off. Someone reminded me about the lad that was interested in
me and that he would like to take me to a party. I was crossing the
highway and Ann was calling out and criticising me. I told her that I
minded my own business, etc.*

MARY E.

As we have seen with previous dreams, this dream has a mixture of real
and invented persons. It has taken an everyday situation, a class in college,
but the story that emerges is quite unique, and portrays directly Mary's
conflicting feelings.

The science teacher, Dr W., and the fellow students, Joyce and Ann, are
real. Joyce is a woman with whom Mary has a friendly rivalry in regard to
grades; Ann is a friend who does not compete intellectually. Dr W. is a
science teacher to whom the dreamer feels quite close. He seems to be the
one teacher who can understand her concerns and give friendly advice, as
well as a friendly shoulder to cry on. The juvenile-acting boy and the
young man who goes canoeing with Joyce are dream inventions.

It is pretty clear that the dream can not be very well understood without
some reference to the real characters and interactions of the real people
involved in the dream. But even so, an appreciation of the story-line is
essential in order to fit these references in.

The ages-old conflict between studying and enjoying life is very apparent in the dream, as is Mary's need for reassurance. Everyone goes their
own separate ways. Mary goes to the beach, which, to judge by the number
of cars in the parking lot, is quite crowded so that Mary cannot get the
relaxation and enjoyment she wants. Joyce goes out canoeing, presumably
with her young man. Ann? We don't know what she is doing, but she is
critical of Mary, perhaps jealous. Mary feels left out and has to be reminded that there is a fellow interested in her. She also has the ability to
carry on a meaningful discussion with Dr W., which is true in real life, too.
It is a reassuring dream, reminding Mary that she does know someone to
whom she can talk on her own level, and of a potential love life about
which she need not feel ashamed. There is a criticising voice, Ann's, but
Mary retorts quite rightly that it is her own affair and not for someone else
to judge.

In everyday life, Mary is carrying on an affair with a fellow student,
and it may be that Ann's voice of criticism reflects her own self-judgment
and perhaps a sense of neglecting her studies in favour of her boy-friend.

Ann is, after all, not intellectually gifted, and has to study hard for grades
that come easily to Mary. But Mary also studies hard, and Ann's criticism
may indicate a doubt concerning the propriety of spending time with her
boy-friend at the risk of getting less than an A. Ann's criticism does seem
to personify Mary's inner conflict between the goals of academic pursuits
and the pursuit of a love life. Mitigating this is the fact that the real-life
boy-friend is taking the same classes as Mary, and much of their time
together is spent in helping each other with their studies. As far as the
dream goes, the real decision that Mary has to make is whether to go off to
relax in the sun and read (probably study) or to follow up the possible love
interest with the young man. These are not really mutually exclusive, as
said, but we feel that Ann somehow represents a guilt feeling, through her
criticism.

The fellow whom the dream invents for her is the topic early in the
dream and then again near the end of the dream. It is much as if the
dream were trying to say, 'Joyce has her young man as well as her high
marks, why not you?' It may not be easy sailing, so to speak. Joyce may be
headed for stormy weather. But she and her young man are taking a well-
proven route, one used by the ferry. The geography in this dream is fairly
realistic. The ferry boat crossing is in the heart of the city, across the Swan
River in Perth, a very attractive scene when viewed from the parking area
in Kings Park which towers above the river on high cliffs. But as the dream
reminds her, Joyce's path and Mary's own are their own personal concerns,
not to be entangled with one another. The temptation to tangle them
comes from Mary's scholastic rivalry with Joyce. Academic rivalry can
easily be supplemented by emotional rivalry, and then one's own individuality runs the risk of getting lost. The dream addresses itself to this concern.

There is an intriguing question brought out by this dream text: why, if
the dream means to speak of Mary's love life, does it use an invented young
man instead of her real lover? Also, what is the significance of her discussion with Dr W.?

The short answer to the question of the young man is probably that the
dream is concerned not so much with this particular romance, which may
well fade out in time, but with Mary's right to have a romance at all. The
early part of the dream says that the boy 'was fond of me but could only
show it in a juvenile way'. Since it is not a real person who is represented
here but a dream invention, we might speculate that Mary's own romantic
interests seem juvenile to her, that she is not really taking the idea seriously. When she finishes her degree, she and the real man in her life will
indeed go their separate ways, and Mary may well be telling herself that it
is only a kids' romance, which then makes her feel envious when she sees
the serious romance going on between Joyce and Joyce's young man. The
alternative, that her romance might turn into a serious commitment, is a

prospective that Mary may not be ready to face at the moment. It requires some serious discussion before it can be resolved.

The conversation with Dr W., the science teacher, may be briefly considered. Dr W. is the only teacher in the college whom Mary finds understanding and sympathetic. The possibility of a romance with him is probably not far from Mary's mind; he is with her on the high parking area, which may refer not only to the real car-park in Kings Park but to the heights of romantic imagination. It must remain imagination, at present, because Dr W. has shown no romantic interest in Mary. But he is contrasted in the dream as 'someone I could communicate with at an adult level' with the boy who 'was fond of me but could only show it in a juvenile way'. He is an older man, more to Mary's taste, it may be, than the younger student, and certainly better equipped to help her academically than any of the students.

We have been moving into a new area, that of the meaning of the various persons who turn up in our dreams. More and more it has become clear that, while the story-line of the dream is absolutely essential to understand what the dream is all about, the individual people in the dream contribute a great deal of the detail of the dream's meaning, and must be investigated at length. Dreams such as John's childhood dream which involved only him and his mother are relatively rare. The more common, every-night type of dream involves both the dreamer and a variety of other persons, real and imagined.

Chapter Two

THE PEOPLE IN OUR DREAMS

In Chapter 1, we examined the way in which dreams cast their messages in story form. In the process, we discovered some very interesting facts concerning the people who turn up in our dreams: we found that dreams both invent people for their stories and use real people. The same can be said for the geography, buildings, and general environment in dreams. The real people may be persons who are actually connected with the dreamer, or people once connected with the dreamer in the past, or celebrities and other people known of by the dreamer. There have been two principal ways that dream researchers have viewed the appearance of real people in dreams.

The first, which may be called the subjective viewpoint, holds that all of the people in a dream represent aspects of the dreamer's own personality. Dream inventions are most easily fitted into this slot. We have seen how they can be taken to represent attitudes that the dreamer has, inner feelings, emotions, experiences, interests and concerns. When real people turn up in a dream, the subjective viewpoint holds that they personify personality features of the dreamer. For example, the dreamer's child may represent the part of her/himself that still feels like a child; the dreamer's parents may represent the influence those parents have had on the dreamer's life and, specifically, personality; and often, it is held that they represent the instinctual expectations with which we are born of the role to be played by the mother or father — Jung's concept of the mother archetype and father archetype. These expectations may be compared, implicitly or explicitly, by the dream with the real mother or father. Other real persons may be described and characterised by the dreamer during discussion, or by the dream itself. Their characterisation may fit some features of the dreamer's own personality, such as impatience, laziness, tender-heartedness, worry, helpfulness or other aspects which the dream has cause to represent. The dreamer's sister/brother, wife/husband may represent the dreamer's innermost soul in the sense of emotional centre; they may represent the dreamer's contra-sexual qualities, the masculinity in a woman or the femininity in a man.

The subjective viewpoint holds that real people, as they turn up in dreams, exemplify some particular features of the dreamer in a specially clear form. Real people and dream inventions are treated in the same fashion; sometimes, it is held, the dream inventions are patterned on real people in order to show how those people have been internalised by the dreamer as an integral part of her/his personality.

The other principal viewpoint, which is the polar opposite of the first, has been termed the objective viewpoint. This holds that real people in the dream represent real persons in the environment, and, especially, the relationship that the dreamer has with them, or, at least, how they are viewed and felt about by the dreamer. According to this viewpoint, dream inventions reflect relationships that are important to the dreamer. For example, an older woman may reflect the dreamer's feelings about a relationship with her/his mother. Dream-invented people represent people in the dreamer's real life, or sometimes types of people encountered by the dreamer in waking life. Real people in the dream represent actual people, and the dreamer's need to come to grips with them, even sometimes symbolically. For example, the Queen or President might stand for the way the dreamer views her/his mother or father, at times. According to the objective viewpoint, dreams can give us objective information about other people and about the situations we are in.

Thus, the two viewpoints clash. The objective viewpoint claims that dreams can give us objective information about other people. From the subjective viewpoint, dreams can only tell us something about the dreamer, though that something may be extremely valuable information. On looking back over the discussions in Chapter 1, readers will find that I have used both viewpoints in working with the dreams, although, on occasion, I have explained why I took one viewpoint or the other, without naming them.

In the pioneering work that was done on dream research in the early part of this century, Freud's name is largely linked with the objective viewpoint, and Adler's with the subjective. Jung straddled the line, taking an intermediate view, holding that sometimes the one and sometimes the other viewpoint works best with a particular dream, while occasionally, we can get still more understanding of a dream by using both viewpoints. It was Jung who gave the two viewpoints their names. As a rule of thumb, he suggested that, when the dream involves real people with whom the dreamer has some connection, we should, whenever possible, take the dream objectively, as being concerned with our actual relationship with those people and the information that the dream can thus provide. On the other hand, when the dream deals with dream-invented people, or with real people with whom the dreamer does not actually have any connection, we should view the dream subjectively, as being concerned with inner qualities, attitudes and concerns of the dreamer, and perhaps with the dreamer's ways of approaching life. If in doubt, or if the dream involves both real and invented people, we should test both viewpoints and see what eventuates. Since Freud, Adler and Jung propounded their ideas, many writers have made use of these approaches: sometimes choosing just one, sometimes mixing them.

My own experience is that Jung's approach on this point is very helpful. I am not sure that the two approaches are quite as opposed as they appear at first glance. There seems to be no particularly good reason to deny that dreams can portray an objective reality, and give the dreamer information about other people and events involved in the day's waking life. ESP dreams give very strong support for this. But all of us, at one time or another, have mislaid something and subsequently dreamed where it is, or discovered that a friend, who in a dream is pregnant, really turns out to be pregnant, although we had not given the matter any conscious attention. The mind is constantly sorting out input and coming to conclusions about people and events during our waking period; there is no reason to suppose that the process stops once we are asleep. On the other hand, if we hold that a dream is perfectly capable of portraying real people and events, there is not much justification for assuming that a dream-invented person represents someone else. But it is equally true that dreams are often more perceptive than we give them credit for. They are particularly skilled at not only telling us about other people's reactions to us, but also our re-actions to other people.

The dreamer's relationship to life is the most profound theme running through dreams. Relationships with other specific people are portrayed by interaction with those people within the dream. From this standpoint, the dream can give extremely valuable information about other persons and the dreamer's relation to them. Attitudes towards life — typical ways the dreamer has of relating to the events and people encountered during waking life — are represented by dream-invented persons and situations. These may be deeply ingrained in the dreamer's personality structure, or be more casual, spontaneous reactions to particular situations.

It is clear that I feel that dreams are something important to us. They are, only semi-metaphorically, a voice within us that does not merely reflect what has gone on during our waking life, but contributes a new way of relating to life. More than one writer has called dreams the 'forgotten language', meaning that dreams are a way of bringing to our conscious attention ideas, feelings and emotions that we did not consciously know, whether about ourselves, about other people, or about situations we are in. They stem from the unconscious, knowledge of which can expand and enrich our lives. This point is so important that I have devoted all of Chapter 4 to its discussion.

We should take care, however, not to over-emphasise this. An individual dream rarely has such far-reaching import. The typical dream, such as constitutes virtually all of our dreaming time, contributes only a little towards the overall picture our dreams form in the long run. The mountain is made out of countless grains of sand.

In the practical approach to dreams, the principle that we found valu-able in Chapter 1 needs to be kept carefully in mind: to attempt, as far as possible, to keep within the framework of the dream story itself.

When it comes to discussing the various persons in a dream, we frequently are forced to supplement the dream story with information about these persons, simply because the dream does not characterise them much. It is rather like watching one segment of a serialised television programme, where knowledge of what has happened before and who the people are is necessary in order to understand the story. Even so, often the significant features are brought out in the episode or dream itself.. What we want to avoid as much as possible is the danger of reading into a dream our own presuppositions, which run the risk of missing the point the dream wants to make.

The little boy, Carl, whose dream of the marble trees we looked at in Chapter 1, dreamed the following at age eight:

> *Daddy had found his treble recorder and had started playing some tunes he knew. I wanted to play too, so I found my plastic treble but I wanted to play the tenor. I found the bottom to the tenor. I searched for hours for the top part, and then I lost the bottom part and found the top part.*
>
> CARL N., #2

Recorders are members of the flute family, and are usually dismantled when not in use. Generally they come in three parts. The treble recorder, which has a higher tone than the tenor, is smaller and easier for a child's small hands to play. The dream reflects a real life situation: Carl owned a set of plastic recorders, and his father, wooden ones. Both were very accomplished musicians on the recorder.

The story in our dream is pretty simple, and the cast of characters is small, making it a good example to look at first in our discussion of the people in our dreams. The subject of the dream story is the relationship of Carl with his father, and Carl's difficulty in equalling his father. Both could, in real life and in the dream, play the treble, but Carl wants to play a different instrument, thus making a duet in which he and his father complement one another. The dream is, then, a 'growing up' dream: the boy's search for his own individuality distinct from his father's, but co-existing with it. He has not yet found his own distinctness, but the desire is there and also the feasibility. As the dream puts it, he possesses the various parts of the tenor, it is a matter of getting them all together at one time.

In contemplating this dream, most of us would like to go on and ask about details, some of which inevitably involve symbolism. The choice of treble and tenor is fairly obvious, in that the sound of the treble is high-pitched, like a boy's voice, while the sound of the tenor is an octave lower, like a man's voice. Both are adults' instruments, in the sense that most children are taught the much smaller and still higher-pitched descant recorder, and generally only the most serious of child musicians take up the treble and tenor. Carl and his father were equally skilled on all three instruments, so the frustration in the dream over not finding all the parts of the tenor at one time makes sense — Carl has the capacity to do what his father can do, but somehow cannot get all the component parts together.

Most readers who have some background in dream work will probably suggest a sexual interpretation for Carl's dream; in fact, in Chapter 6, I return to the dream to discuss this possibility in more detail. A sexual interpretation is made plausible by the point that I have already mentioned, the difference in pitch of the two instruments. If Carl's unsuccessful search for the tenor reflects the change of voice that will come only a few years later, at puberty, the two instruments may concern the sexual characteristics of the boy and man, and it is not terribly difficult to move from that to think of the treble as representing the boy's small penis compared with his father's large penis — this may be the point of Carl's not being able to find all the parts of the tenor at one time.

We do not need to go far to understand why the dream may have chosen the recorders instead of penises. Music is the primary way our culture has chosen for the expression of emotions. Sexuality involves not only penis size, for a boy, but a whole flock of emotions as yet foreign to him. Some of Carl's favourite music was the Beatles, most of which does best on the descant or tenor, and the Beatles' music is, by and large, sexually oriented, although much of it is social commentary. Thoughts about penis size were certainly not alien to Carl, to judge by comments he made about his own erections from time to time.

Still, to take the dream as having a sexual message, which would run, more or less, 'Carl, as yet your penis is only small, but it has the potential for becoming big and one day you will have one as big as your father's', is very speculative. The interpretation is plausible, but there is nothing in the dream that demands it. It rests upon a premise that a treble and tenor recorder must mean something other than what they appear in the dream. In using that premise, we are stepping outside the framework of the dream story, about which I cautioned earlier.

Without prejudicing the sexual interpretation, then, is there a way of looking at the dream that does not step outside its framework? The first thought about this, which appears extremely plausible as an answer to why the dream has selected musical instruments to portray its theme, is that Carl has genuine musical talent that now rivals that of his father and is likely to surpass it. From this point of view, as well, the dream is pointing Carl towards future development. That is, he can equal his father now, indicated in the dream by the fact that both are playing the treble recorder. But is just a matter of time until he can make his own contribution, to be in duet with his father and not only imitating him.

We must not, in any case, lose sight of the frustration in Carl's dream: that, while wanting to play an instrument his father is not playing, he cannot find all the pieces together. He has one part or another, but the dream ends without his finding and putting together all three parts.

A third suggestion about the relationship between Carl and his father as portrayed in the dream rests upon the idea that playing music is expression of emotion. Perhaps Carl is moving away from the stage of reflecting his father's moods to a stage of having his own, independent moods. The realisation of this is not yet complete, but under way.

We are not really in any position to make choices between these and other possible interpretations at this point in our investigation of dreams. But they do lead us to consider what the significance of the dream might be for Carl. In each of the three suggested interpretations, there is a common theme: that of Carl's coming to equal and then differentiate himself from his father.

That three possible interpretations have been proposed for the same dream brings up the particularly difficult question of how we know when an interpretation is the right one. I have stressed the importance of keeping within the dream story, and to avoid, as far as is humanly possible, reading into the dream our own preconceptions. Obviously, it is not possible to keep out our own ideas completely when discussing a dream. But we can try to tune our ear to what the dream is saying, and it may well be that the basic message of the dream has a number of equally plausible applications.

When the dreamer is available to discuss the dream and the possible applications, we have a bit of help, in that the dreamer can comment on our suggestions and react to them. In the long run, about the only way an interpretation of a dream can be accepted as 'right' is when the dreamer hears or helps make the interpretation, and feels that it clicks, that it evokes an emotional feeling of being 'right'. This is, obviously, a very subjective process indeed, and it is not only possible but everyday experience that several experts interpreting a dream will come up with quite different interpretations. When this happens, we must ask two questions: are the interpretations contradictory, or do they all make different applications of the same dream story theme? And, do any or all of the interpretations feel right to the dreamer, do they bring a sense of recognition of some emotional experience or discovery in the dreamer? Dream interpretation cannot be a hard science, because the human mind does not work according to the principles of the hard sciences. But a dream interpretation can be 'true' in the same degree that an interpretation of a picture or drama can be 'true', i.e. hold meaning for both the creator and the interpreter.

Fortunately for this book, and especially for the sample dreams and interpretations in the Appendix, I have had the opportunity to discuss almost all of the quoted dreams with their dreamers, and work out the most plausible interpretations with them.

The further we venture out of the framework of the dream story in our interpretation, the more unverifiable our interpretation becomes. With this in mind, we can feel both a loss and a gain. The loss is that it is virtually impossible to interpret a dream without the active help of the dreamer. The gain is that there is real hope of finding a way to apply your dream, if you can find a friend or someone who knows you well to help point out features of the dream that you might otherwise miss.

One point that stands out in working over dreams is that the inter-relationship of the dreamer with other persons in the dream serves to portray a growth situation. A glance back at the dreams in Chapter 1 will make it clear that this is quite a regular feature. The situation portrayed may be a reassurance to the dreamer, or it may indicate an area to be developed. Probably, most dreams serve, in one fashion or another, to promote the growth of the dreamer. Some do it more obviously than others. In the chapter on nightmares, we examine this point closely, because it infers that dreams do not merely reflect events, emotions or experiences in the past, but have a purposive nature, bringing to notice facts that can promote the dreamer's welfare.

This can be illustrated by a rather long dream, in which the people who feature play a double role, portraying the dreamer's relationship to another person and pointing out how his emotional growth can be enhanced. It comes from Alfred M., whose dream about the *National Geographic* was examined in Chapter 1. In that dream, Alfred's difficulty in relating to women was the theme. In the following dream, some of the bases of that difficulty appear:

> *I am waiting at the bottom of the library stairs for Joanne, having arranged to meet inside actually, but she was late so I waited outside. She appears and dashes up the stairs (worried at being late?) and goes into the library. I follow her, amused at her concern and relieved to see her. She beats me inside and down the stairs to the patio area where we had arranged to meet. On the way, I meet a young guy, Robert, and we chat, then there is a scene of another young chap who I know and who is alarmed at being recognised by another guy I do not know. They meet and a confrontation looks likely and I am distracted, feeling I should see there is no trouble and wanting to follow Joanne. The issue sorts itself out after some time and I go on, but my mood has changed, feeling down. I go through into the seated area and notice Joanne seated at a table with friends, chatting away. I am not going to see her alone and feel as sulky as a child. I go up to the table, reaching her side and saying hello quietly to her in a self-conscious and subdued tone. Just as I say this, she says, in conversation to the other people, 'my husband', and they laugh. I see the coincidence of my arriving just at that moment but feel myself to be the object of a joke. I then go to get a chair, at first a deck chair, but,*

*realising I cannot sit around the high table like the others, I take a
chair from another table to place by Joanne's side. For some reason,
she has to go somewhere, because of her two children; the news of the
children, along with the husband, depresses me very much. I reach
for an old sandwich and walk along with Joanne and a woman friend
of hers while the kids run ahead. I am sulking along quite happily but
Joanne doesn't take any notice of me (nor was she surprised when I
turned up at the table). My bag had been left at a table earlier and I
pick that up. As we walk, the kids skim a lid or flat object across the
fish pond then, laughing and playing, run round the other side to pick
it up. Everyone seems to be having a great time except for old Mr
Sulks. I say to myself that if I act like a spoilt child, how could I have
coped if it had been me that was Joanne's husband and father of two
children.*

ALFRED M., #2

In working over this dream, we will find it helpful to examine it from
several aspects, as we did with earlier dreams. With such a long dream as
this, it is helpful to diagram the content according to the persons who turn
up in it. Let us give careful consideration to their roles:

Joanne:
> has arranged to meet Alfred in the library,
> is late for the engagement,
> passes Alfred without noticing him,
> sits chatting with friends,
> speaks of her husband,
> must leave because of her two children,
> walks with Alfred and another woman,
> ignores Alfred as they walk.

Robert: chats with Alfred after Joanne passes by.

Young chap (a dream invention):
> is known by the dreamer,
> apparently is about to fight another fellow,
> is alarmed at being recognised by the other fellow.

Guy Alfred does not know: seems ready to fight Robert.

Joanne's friends:
> prevent Alfred from being alone with Joanne,
> laugh when she says 'my husband'.

Joanne's children: play with a frisbee and enjoy their play.

Joanne's woman friend: walks with Joanne, Alfred and the children,
> thus preventing Alfred from being alone with Joanne.

Alfred:
> has a date arranged with Joanne,

waits for her outside instead of inside,
follows her when she passes by him,
chats with Robert,
has conflicting feelings: to follow Joanne or to deal with the likely
    conflict between the two guys,
enters the library feeling depressed,
feels sulky when he finds he will not meet Joanne in private,
speaks to her self-consciously,
feels she is making fun of him,
finds a suitable chair and brings it over,
is depressed by her reference to a husband and two children,
takes an old sandwich,
walks with Joanne, another woman and the children,
picks up his bag,
sees everyone having fun except himself,
criticises himself strongly.

Starting with the portrayal of Joanne, we can see in Joanne a semi-real, semi-invented figure. The real woman, Joanne, has sparked off a long dream fantasy. To understand her significance in the dream, we need to know something about the real Joanne.

Alfred is a college student; Joanne, a fellow student whom he glimpsed but whom he does not know. It is in his mind to ask her for a date, but at the time of the dream, he has not yet done so. About Joanne he knows nothing whatever, except that she is an attractive young woman whom he has seen on campus. The dream portrays his forebodings of what might happen if he were to arrange a date with her. It portrays some of his hopes and many of his fears about Joanne, and in so doing, it tells us a great deal about his trepidations and inner fantasies. The dream is fairly typical of youths, and some not so young, who are at the beginning of forming heterosexual relationships. It is perhaps not so typical of a young man in his twenties, except that, in some important emotional ways, he is still an adolescent.

The dream also portrays typical features of a highly introverted person, for the introvert has a way of imagining all the things that could go wrong in a social situation. Introversion is a normal, quite healthy personality feature, which has a bad reputation in our highly extroversion-oriented society simply because it does not correspond to social ideals and the 'norm' that is frequently set up for us. A highly extroverted person has her/his own difficulties in forming relationships, which are different from but no easier to bear than the introverted person's. One of Alfred's particular problems is in getting up the courage to meet people. Thus, his dream imagines that he has made a library date with Joanne, and then his mind runs through all the things that might go wrong. Joanne might pass him by without noticing him; she might be busy with other friends and not be interested in giving him some of her time alone; she might be married, the mother of two children, even; she might make fun of him. It is an introvert's way of preparing herself/himself for a possible rejection, since that is the typical introverted way, to look at what might go wrong rather than what might go right in a social situation.

Thus, the dream represents Alfred's frame of mind, rather than external events. And it states its own answer to the inner fantasy: 'I say to myself that if I act like a spoilt child, how could I have coped if it had been me that was Joanne's husband and father of two children?' It portrays the start of the hoped-for situation, a date with Joanne, goes through all the things that could possibly go wrong, and then it comments on Alfred's way of reacting to the failure of his hopes. It allows his fantasy to present its forebodings, then it gives its own reflections on them.

Of course, the neat answer at the end of the dream may be more a half-waking or just-wakened rumination rather than an integral part of the dream. There is no way to tell. But I hold that such ruminations are directed by the same emotional framework as that that motivated the dream, and complete or fulfil the point of the dream. A real, conscious reaction to the dream would more likely be 'What rubbish! Why do you imagine such things when you don't know anything about her?' Instead, Alfred's account gives us 'What a baby you are, you cannot bear the thought that your hopes might not be fulfilled'. The rumination assumes that the situation in the dream is correct, and that Alfred just doesn't like to look reality in the face. The evaluation by an outsider is, instead, that Alfred jumps the gun and assumes the worst without giving the hoped-for date a chance.

This way of viewing a dream — that the final form of the dream, complete with half-waking reactions, contains the true character of the fantasy — is in direct contrast to Freud's assumption that dreams and the mental processes taking place during the period of wakening distort the content and message of the dream. Freud held that the imagery in dreams as they are remembered is a distortion of the original dream content. He distinguished between the latent, i.e. original, content of the dream and the manifest, i.e. remembered, content. Much of the interpretative work in Freud's *The Interpretation of Dreams* is devoted to tracing back from hints remaining in the dream to what the latent content was. Jung held that the remembered dream says what it was intended to say. His stand was that what is important for the waking mind to remember at the time is, in fact, what is remembered. This coincides with my own experience of dreamers and their dreams.

We have been taking the subjective viewpoint in dealing with this dream. Although Joanne is a real woman, she plays no role in Alfred's life, but merely serves to pin his hopes and fears on. Since we are dealing with an entirely imaginary situation in this dream, it becomes clear that Joanne represents more the dreamer's hesitations than she does the real woman. The sight of the real Joanne sparked off an inner dialogue that took the form of a dream. The dream-Joanne does almost everything Alfred could fear might happen. But when we look at the descriptions of Alfred's own actions, we can see that he provokes, or at least makes no attempt to change, the dream-Joanne's actions. He decides to wait in a different place than the one agreed on, so that she, intent on what is to happen inside the building, might not see him. When she passes by without seeing him, he does not call out to her. Neither does he hurry directly into the library to meet her, but instead, pauses to solve a quarrel that has arisen. He does not ask whether her 'joke' about her husband was, in fact, pointed at him, and whether it really was a joke or not. He is not at all surprised at her nonchalant attitude toward him, despite the fact that she had made the date with him.

There is something to indicate that Alfred has encountered this sort of situation before, in that he takes an old sandwich to eat, as if he were used to the taste of rejection. But again, we are struck by his lack of self-esteem; was there really nothing better to eat? Is this sort of fantasy the only kind of nourishment his soul has to help to grow, just the same old sandwich time and again?

When we look at the list of persons in the dream and to the actions that Alfred takes, we see his customary reaction to the situation of meeting a woman. The dream story is, as it were, a sort of test case. It says, 'Look, Alfred, this is how you go about things, no wonder you have had so many failures!' Some of Alfred's actions in the list are usefully examined briefly: he has conflicting feelings, whether to follow Joanne directly into the library, or whether to stop and deal with a likely conflict between two fellows, one of whom (in the dream) he knows and one of whom is a stranger to him. Both are actually imaginary characters, but for the dream's purpose, he knows one and not the other. What there is between them we are never told, only that a conflict is brewing. There is a conflict in Alfred, and it manifests itself in his hesitation to follow Joanne in entering the library for the date. This delays him further, since he has already stopped to chat with Robert. Joanne has hurried into the library, presumably so as not to be later than she is already, but obviously arrives at the patio area only to find that Alfred is later still; we could hardly blame her for being cold towards Alfred at this point, but whether she is we do not know for Alfred does not give her a chance to say.

Alfred assumes that Joanne is making fun of him, with no justification apart from his depressed feeling. He expects to be made fun of, he does not feel he meets her expectations, which is imaged by his first choice of a chair. It is a deck chair, too low to reach the table, as if he were saying to himself, 'I'm not big enough for her, she is too high above me'. Only on second thought does he bring a chair from another table and sit down at Joanne's right.

Joanne's friends represent distractions that Alfred feels would keep her attention turned from him. But what stands out is that, unlike his own friends who fight, her circle is having a good time. A bit later, her children, when they turn up, are playing happily, and she does not seem to notice his sulkiness. But he does not try to join in the fun.

We can legitimately ask whether the dream's entire function is to portray inner doubts and hesitations, or whether it has a more positive motive. From the very dramatic portrayal of the whole scene, including the larger-than-life portrayal of Joanne's actions and Alfred's, we can conclude that the dream also functions to try to correct the inner doubts and hesitations. It magnifies them out of all proportion, so that any discussion of the dream would inevitably bring out the fact that Alfred is responsible for them. The point of the dream really is not 'Don't sulk because of your disappointment', but 'My God, man, you never even give the girl a chance!'

As I have remarked before, dreams by no means always portray what is wrong in life, they often serve to give courage and reassurance. A very simple-looking dream from a six-year-old girl can illustrate this fact nicely:

> *I am sitting on something and a woman is sitting beside me. I push my curtains apart, and notice that the woman, instead of doing the same, is putting pretty designs on the curtains.*
>
> ANNE G.

The little girl's mother, who relayed this dream to me, filled in the situation in which the dream took place: the child and her family were on an ocean voyage coming from Italy to Australia. The cabin was small and cramped, the bunks had curtains that could be pushed open. This part was exciting to Anne, who had never been on a ship before. But the crowded ship, the noise, a very limited understanding of where they were going and why, and the limited but real culture shock already experienced on board made Anne feel very anxious as well as excited. The prospect of going to a new country where things were very different, and people spoke queerly, was daunting for the six-year-old.

Anne's dream has only two characters in it: herself and a grown woman. The grown woman is a dream invention, and we need to examine this dream from the subjective viewpoint. If we were to try to take it 'objectively', the only candidate for a grown woman in the situation would be Anne's mother. But if Anne's mother were meant, why would the dream not say so, as many of the girl's other dreams did? We have no good reason to suppose that the dream figure is substituting for a real person. Who, then, is she?

Anne and the grown woman are sitting side by side, apparently on the same bunk. (Anne had an upper bunk, and it was very exciting to climb up and down the ladder.) Anne is presumably about to get out of the bunk, or perhaps she just wants to look around the cabin, so she opens the curtains. To her surprise, the woman does not help in opening the curtains, but decorates them instead.

It is a fair guess that the woman is an older version of Anne. A very long sea voyage is tedious, and when it is part of moving to a new home in a new land, it is not surprising that it would be frightening. The woman makes the cabin bunk pretty, turning a possibly dismal situation into something cheerful and attractive. The woman takes on the character of wisdom beyond Anne's years, her grown-up self. She is giving Anne reassurance that the trip can be a beautiful undertaking rather than a frightening one. It is not at all unusual for an older figure, invented by the dream, to do or say something reassuring, personifying the dreamer's innate wisdom, which goes far beyond her/his years.

The 'old wise woman' or 'old wise man' is a typical dream figure isolated by Jung as a recurring motif in many people's dreams. The distinguishing of such figures, and the interpretation, are based on the study of quite a few thousand dreams of children and adults alike, which anyone can do with enough patience and time and material. I have found this older man or woman motif to be quite widespread among the dreams that I have examined.

Apart from some typical figures, such as this one, each individual person's own dreams, when viewed as a sequence over a period of years, have their own figures familiar to the dreamer. When possible, the most fruitful approach is to examine the people who turn up in a long series of one person's dreams, to understand the meaning they have for that person. When working on your own dreams, an index to the dreams, emphasising the people who turn up in them, will frequently give clues as to what these people mean for you.

In Anne's case, we do not have such a long series of dreams. We have only the one dream that her mother retold to me. In our explorations, consequently, we must draw on our knowledge of typical figures in dreams in general in order to understand Anne's dream.

What would Anne's dream be doing by bringing in this motif of the older woman at this time? If we understand the woman as representing the latent adult understanding lying still nascent in Anne's personality, parallel to the 'child' that continues to live on in each of us after we are grown up, then we can see the dream as trying to compensate for the little girl's fear by saying 'You are able to hold out despite the emotional stresses placed upon you; you can be a woman, able like your parents to take this change in your life without being destroyed by it. These bunk curtains can be turned into a thing of beauty, and this transition into a pleasant experience instead of a state of fear.' It is, implicitly, giving a 'pep talk' to Anne, though, of course, she would not experience her dream that way. From her viewpoint, the dream is saying 'Don't worry, Anne; your mother and father may be away behind other curtains, but there is a woman right here who will take care of you and make your situation beautiful, that woman is right inside you.'

This emphasises that the 'invented persons' in our dreams represent what is inside us, and these dreams bring to our attention the fact that these 'people' are there in us, and we must pay them heed. They may be frightening facts about ourselves that we would rather not know, or they may be reassuring features within ourselves, the awareness of which may help us in our difficulties. They may also be features of our personality that need to be linked up with our awareness in order to be more complete, not necessarily frightening or reassuring, but just facts about ourselves we can find it helpful to know.

Alongside the older man or woman, there is a very prominent typical dream motif of a child. I am not discussing here the appearance of a real-life child in a dream, but the dream invention of a child. This dream-child represents the childhood experiences and the lasting impressions they made upon us that have gone to form our personality. The appearance of a real-life child can sometimes play a similar role in a dream, but generally, it is important to examine the relationship of the dreamer with that child to see just what is being said.

A third dream of Alfred's can illustrate the appearance of a dream-invented child and the way the image can be tackled. It also brings up some interesting points in regard to the question of why Alfred's first dream emphasised the distant past.

I am swimming in a river with companions when an old man disappears. I begin searching under water (though there is no great sense of loss) but fail to find him. However, I do see the body of a little girl (perhaps five or six years, though she gets continually younger) wedged below water level in the branches of a sunken tree. It seems that a few people have come to grief this way. I decide to bring her body back and have to tug quite hard to free it. Having done so, I call out to people across on the opposite shore that I have found a body, emphasising that the child is dead so as not to cause panic or excitement. I have a companion with me in the water, though he/she fades out of the picture. I swim over to the bank, the people do get excited for it seems they have been searching for a child. They are not willing to accept it is dead, despite my holding the body up in the air with one hand. Then, to my complete surprise, the body begins muscular spasms and comes to life in my hand as I reach the shore. A woman comes running up to take the child: it is her daughter, as she and the others had believed all the time. Now it is me who is overwhelmed,

realising I have, unintentionally, saved the child's life. I am overcome
and break down and cry.

ALFRED M., #3

The story in this dream begins with a tragic scene, but instead of leading
up to a nightmarish ending, the reverse happens. What appeared at first to
be a tragedy becomes a drama of reassurance.

To understand what this dream is all about, there is quite a bit of personal history we must look at. But before that, we may take a quick look at
the principal features: an old man disappears, presumed drowned. The
body of a five- or six-year-old girl is found, also apparently drowned,
wedged in a sunken tree. Alfred rescues the body, convinced that she is
dead. As he brings the body to the surface, two things happen — she
becomes younger and younger, and she comes to life. The emotional impact of all this is overpowering.

This dream was brought up in a dream discussion group, and it aroused
considerable interest. Anticipating Chapter 3 a bit, we may ask about
Alfred's swimming in the river. Diving under water is a fairly frequent
dream motif, which often refers to delving into one's own depths to find
what is lying under the surface; in other words, to look at feelings,
thoughts and experiences that lie buried deep down inside. A similar motif
is that of digging in the earth to discover what is hidden there, which we
will see when we examine George Fox's vision in Chapter 3, and two of June
T.'s dreams in Chapter 4. The essential point is to discover what is underneath and bring it to the surface. This means finding what has been hidden by the accumulation of years, in the case of discovering what is buried
inside the earth. In the case of Alfred's dream, the drowned child means
something in his life that once was alive, but which became snagged and
lay dormant under the surface until found and brought into the open air
again.

Alfred is swimming in a river with companions, an image that fits the
fact that he is participating in a dream discussion seminar, where everyone
is in the swim and discovering their own under-the-surface realities. An old
man disappears — apparently, he had been one of the swimmers. He is a
dream invention, and he may play the same role for Alfred that the woman
played for Anne G. In Anne's case, as we saw, the woman figured as the
maturity latent within herself; so, too, the old man in Alfred's dream may
represent the accumulation of wisdom that ought to come with the passing
of years, though Alfred himself is far too young to qualify as 'an old man'.
In going in search of this wisdom, if that is what the old man represents,
Alfred makes the tremendous discovery that is at the heart of the dream.

I asked Alfred the child's age at the end of the dream. He said about two
to three years old. This recollection of ages then spontaneously reminded
Alfred of some turning points in his life. The girl is aged five to six when

first discovered snagged by the sunken tree; she becomes progressively younger as she is brought to the surface and ends up at about the age of two to three. These ages hold a special significance for Alfred. At age three and a half, he had rheumatic fever, as a consequence of which his testicles retracted into the body. At age seven, he underwent an operation to rectify this condition. The operation was emotionally very traumatic for him, and he suffered from the emotional effects and after-effects of the operation for many years. When, in the seminar discussion, we asked about the significance of ages five to six and two to three, he spontaneously commented that they were the ages immediately preceding the hospitalisations. Sexually, they hold a great deal of meaning for Alfred. To restore life to the two to three-year-old is to undo the illness at age three that made the operation at age seven necessary. To get hold of this emotional effect, he has to get back first to the state of the five- to six-year-old, the age just before he 'died' emotionally, or rather, his sex life did.

Two major elements are available to his conscious awareness at the time of the dream: the memory of all that went on up to the evening before the operation and after the return home from the operation, but a complete black-out for the hospitalisation and the operation itself; and a persistent feeling of weakness in the part of his body that was cut by the operation. There may be some relationship between this early trauma and Alfred's difficulty in forming relationships with women at the present time.

There is some reason for the timing of the dream. Just before the dream, Alfred had become interested in an unpublished thesis about the psychological effects of operations for undescended testicles, a thesis available for him to read at a local university. So as he attends the discussion seminars and has this dream, the topic is very much on his mind.

There is a sort of rejuvenation motif in Alfred's dreams, if we accept that the little girl is the child he once was, who early on had rheumatic fever and later on underwent the operation. The question arises about the sex of the child. Can the little girl represent Alfred as a child with this exclusively male condition? In answer to this, there is an observation by the author of the thesis, Sally Smyth, that the children, when asked to draw themselves before they underwent the operation, portrayed themselves as boys; but after the operation, when asked to draw themselves, they largely portrayed girls, indicating that emotionally they felt the operation as a castration, despite the visual evidence that it was not.

There is still another dimension to the portrayal of Alfred as a girl. A dreamer's contra-sexual qualities are generally portrayed by a dream figure of the opposite sex to the dreamer. Thus, the feminine components of a man's personality are portrayed in his dreams by women; and the masculine components of a woman's personality by men. Jung spoke of these components as the anima (feminine components in a man) and animus (masculine components in a woman) and we will have occasion to discuss them in greater depth later. There is a tendency for real people to draw these traits out into the open for someone, through relationships. Thus, a relationship with a woman will often draw out a man's feminine features; and a relationship with a man will often draw out a woman's masculine features. What exactly is to be regarded as feminine or masculine is determined by the culture and sub-culture in which the person has been reared, as well as by family and parental presuppositions.

In Alfred's two previous dreams, a woman featured: the first time, a dream-invented woman, whom we considered as his emotional framework of relating to a woman, determined by his past; the second time, a real woman who drew his fantasies out into the open. Each time, the dream was concerned with Alfred's difficulties in getting along with the feminine world. Now, in this third dream, a little girl serves to give him reassurance: that a part of himself that had died (been submerged) after age six has been restored to life but with a much younger age, giving him the chance to grow again without the emotional trauma.

Such a dream comes when a deep emotional issue has been brought to the surface. The emotion is not necessarily hidden from the dreamer's conscious mind, though that may be the case. Since sex plays a very important role in people's lives, we should expect any major sexual incident to leave its traces in dreams, especially if the incident was felt by the body as mutilation in some respect. Alfred says that not only does he still feel the place where the incision was made to be tender, though the operation was many years ago, but he still has a feeling-memory of a testicle being ripped out of his body, even though, intellectually, he knows this was not the case.

As we discussed this dream, there was an unexpected corroboration from a woman in the seminar, who also had experienced an operation as a sexual assault.

> She had had an ovarian cyst removed and, for some time after the operation, she dreamed of being the victim of a pack rape, a dream she had not previously experienced and which did not recur afterwards.

> HELEN I.

Operations are regularly felt by the body as an attack, even though, consciously, the person involved knows that it was a curative measure. In Helen's case, the intensity of the experience of the operation is reflected by the multiplication of attacks in the dream.

In yet another instance, persons and events involved in a real incident years earlier reappeared in dreams, though the original incident had long been pushed out of the dreamer's conscious awareness:

> After very intensive psychotherapy, John began to dream repeatedly

of scenes of being sexually assaulted, of being hung, of being cut down, until eventually, these fragments joined up into one horrific dream, which repeated itself over and over again until he remembered the entire incident which actually took place when he was a young child.

JOHN Z.

After full conscious memory of the event returned, John ceased to have the nightmare, although other serious problems took its place.

From these dreams, we can see an attempt by the psyche to assimilate and come to terms with a traumatic event, sometimes many years after it occurred. It appears that the event, in all three cases a sexual trauma of one kind or another, was not emotionally registered as over and done with, nor in the first two instances that it was a helpful operation rather than an attack. Alfred's operation left emotional scars that lasted for many years and that, apparently, affect his life still now. In his dream, it is felt as if a child-part of himself died and now has to be brought back out of the depths of oblivion and returned to life. Helen's operation was also felt as a dangerous and frightening experience, put by the dream into terms her body could understand. In John's case, the event was a real, life-threatening assault, one so vicious and intolerable that it was wiped from the boy's mind and remained eradicated from his conscious memory until psychological prodding brought it back, first in the form of nightmares and then as true memory.

Thus far, we have been examining dreams in which it has been fairly obvious whether the events and people are drawn from real life or are representative of parts of the dreamer's personality and outlook on life. It is not always easy to determine, when a specific child is a key figure in a dream, whether the child refers to a still child-like feeling that persists in the dreamer, the subjective viewpoint; or to the real child, the objective viewpoint. A dream can illustrate the difficulty:

I am getting married to Sonya—located in older house like Sturk Street. We don't seem to have a ceremony and I suggest that we have a rest—but it is in separate beds and no copulation. She has brought me presents, also says that she found them in the garden at home. They are half-empty whisky bottles etc., which she has used illicitly through an older system. During the afternoon, we are to go and see my parents to celebrate the wedding. I feel uncomfortable about things and I can just hear an argument in the next door house.

ROGER H., #1

Roger's family situation was troubled, and he found himself closer to his elder daughter Sonya than to the other child in the family. The memory of the dream, though vivid, was not altogether clear, particularly in respect to the whisky bottles Sonya has acquired in the dream. There is no hint of alcoholism in Roger or his family, which makes the reference to the whisky bottles rather difficult to understand.

How are we to take Roger's daughter Sonya as she appears in the dream? We could take her literally. It is by no means unknown for a father to have a sexual interest in his daughter, though the dream does specify that there is no copulation of the father and girl. Freud, and many researchers after him, held that the memory of a dream may censor it to remove the more unacceptable references, a point we have noted before. I consider this aspect further in Chapter 6, where we re-examine this dream from the viewpoint of sexuality. But before we move into that question, let us consider what the dream could be getting at in the form in which memory presented it. Our first task is to examine the figure of Sonya and see what sort of person she is.

As the elder child, Sonya felt displaced by the second child. Her jealousy of the other child is very marked. She is a very strong-willed person, very independent, very capable of taking care of herself. Roger said he could identify very readily with Sonya's temperament. Perhaps for this reason, Roger finds it easier to get on with Sonya than with the other child. Sonya was still a schoolchild at the time of this dream, and living with the family.

The mention of the house in Sturk Street takes us back to the time before Sonya was born, to an earlier phase of Roger's life. We can see in this a nostalgic wish that the hands of time could be moved backwards. This also brings up, however, the image of Roger's parents, which is disquieting to him, and also rumblings from next door.

The dream story is fairly simple: Roger is marrying his daughter Sonya, in a house in which he once lived years ago. There is no ceremony, they go straight to bed, but separate beds, and there are no sexual relations between them. Sonya has brought along some half-full whisky bottles that she found in the yard back home and that she apparently has been drinking. It is afternoon. They go to see Roger's parents, but he is uneasy about his situation, and he hears a fight going on next door.

Looking at this story as a synopsis of a short play, what is striking? Roger feels very close to Sonya, presumably closer than to his wife or his parents, but he is marrying Sonya in a house in which he once lived years ago. It goes back in time, keeping the daughter from the present time, even though the location is from the past. Roger would like to keep his one-time pre-family situation but to marry Sonya in it. Does that mean that he wishes he had married someone with Sonya's character back then? Or does it mean that he wishes he had been more like Sonya back then, independent, strong-willed and on his own? Is he uneasy because he feels that there is something wrong about marrying his daughter? Or because it seems to be a sexless marriage? Or because he fears his parents will frown upon the marriage? Or is it because he would like to recall the past but that would mean bringing in his parents again, and he would not like that — much as Sonya wishes she could be independent of her parents?

What about the whisky bottles Sonya brought her father as a wedding gift? As said, there is no evidence that Roger used alcohol to help him forget his troubles. And there is nothing to suggest that Sonya drank on the sly. So we are forced to take the whisky as an image: that the dream — Sonya tries to drown her sorrows in drink, and proposes the same to her father-husband. Roger's dream says that Sonya has used the whisky illicitly through an older system. What can this mean? Does the old system mean that whisky was available in her dream-invented family situation? Was she in the habit of drinking heavily, perhaps to numb herself against the unhappiness at home, and now Roger, via the dream, considers the same thing himself? She used the whisky illicitly. Because she was under age? Or because it is an illicit way to forget her troubles?

We must not, however, overlook the central motif of the drama: Roger is marrying his daughter. They sleep separately, and there is no sex, but Roger still feels uneasy about the situation. And he hears rumblings from next door. It is certainly not unknown for fathers to be sexually interested in their daughters, and vice versa; that this is a repressed idea during the waking hours merely means that it comes out during sleep, via dreams. Another father was quite astounded to dream that he was fondling his fifteen-year-old daughter's genitals. The dream came as quite a shock to him. For several weeks following, he felt a violent pain in his penis, as if his erect penis had been broken in two. Medical examination revealed nothing abnormal. It seemed to be a body reaction against the incestuous desire, a kind of self-punishment for the no longer repressed idea. So the fact that Roger's dream involves the same double motif — of marrying his daughter, of whom he is very fond, while at the same time, precluding sexual relations with her — is not so surprising.

In one way, Roger fell into the famous Oedipal situation, of the fantasy of father marrying daughter. In another way, his guilt feeling (revealed by the statement that he felt uncomfortable about the situation) led to placing them in separate beds and with no copulation. We are used to viewing the Oedipal situation from the child's angle, the daughter's desires to be her father's mate, or the boy's desires to be his mother's lover; but it works the other way around as well, the parent's desire to be maritally intimate with the child. This often does lead to real incest. In Roger's case, however, an inner feeling stops him from carrying out the incest. It is a convenient shorthand to say that his superego prevented his carrying the fantasy out to its full conclusion; in other words, that his superego said, 'marry Sonya, OK, maybe; but copulate with her, no!'

There is an argument audible from the next-door house, presumably the house next door to where he is with Sonya. In the context of viewing this dream story as a drama, it would mean that Roger hears a conflict going on within himself, 'next door' meaning 'next door to his conscious thoughts', the conflict of guilt feelings and desire. But 'next door' means a bit more than this; it implies neighbours, society's attitudes. If the drama were a narration of a real-life event, we would probably suppose that the neighbours are incensed at what is happening between Roger and Sonya, and in conflict whether to denounce him.

The incest taboo that stops sexual relations between parent and child from being acted out in real life is partly an internal, psychological pressure; but it is also a social pressure placed upon us. The internal psychological taboo is apparently not strong enough in itself to prevent incest. There are many cases in which incest does occur, and for every formally reported case, there are multitudes that go unreported. The social scandal that ensues is often so great that the lives of both parties are ruined, while hushed-up instances of incest are a frequent cause of deep-seated emotional difficulties for the child, from which it may often never fully recover. Sometimes, this is true also of the parent involved.

The dream does indicate that Roger did have some such fantasies. We have no indication that he did, in fact, act upon his fantasies. In this particular case, the fantasy may have been a pre-genital one, that is, the fantasy of a small child who has not yet grasped the genital sexual implication of marriage but sees the marital state as a social institution; in which case, Roger's fantasy would trace back to a regression to an emotional state long lost in the mists of time of his early life history. But, as suggested, it may cover up a real sexual interest. We will return to this in Chapter 6.

In the process of examining Roger's dream, we have looked at it from both the subjective and the objective viewpoints. Seen subjectively, the marriage with Sonya represents Roger's 'marriage' with Sonya's qualities, that is, his identification with them: her independence, her abilities, her self-sufficient attitudes, and along with this goes an attitude of self-intoxication to block out relationships with the rest of the world.

Seen objectively, there is the parent's inner desire for marriage with his child, which may well be reciprocated — or even precipitated — by Sonya's desire to marry him, an oft-repeated feature of childhood. There may well be a real sexual desire for his daughter, and perhaps vice versa, which is repressed but uneasily felt nevertheless and which comes out in the dream.

We are in no place to be able to decide between these alternative views. Quite possibly, both are true. For why does Roger's fantasy turn towards his elder child? Perhaps because her personality reflects his to the point that she is a living example of how he would like to conduct his life, and thus provides an attraction for his sexual desires, something we would find normal and expected if she were an adult woman, and repelling only because she is a child and also his daughter.

It is easier to decide which viewpoint to take when the dream makes it

clear that the situation portrayed is a feature of the dreamer's own psychological state, with little to do with other persons. As an example, we can
examine a third dream by John W., whose dream of the rubber shoe-laces
in Chapter 1 indicated that inner factors were holding him back, and
whose childhood dream examined earlier in this chapter indicated a very
profound sense of insecurity from an early age:

> *A male friend of mine has been interested in a woman and she has*
> *rejected him. He wonders why. Jan gets her on the phone and then in*
> *person. The woman talks a long time with Jan. Jan cannot answer a*
> *question and turns to me for an answer: the woman says she has had*
> *daily bleeding for the past week. I ask her whether she is on the Pill.*
> *She says no. I say she should phone my family doctor and ask her*
> *about the bleeding.*
>
> JOHN W., #3

This dream contains a mixture of real people and dream inventions. The
male friend and the woman who rejected him are both dream inventions.
Jan is a real person — she is John's wife — and the family doctor is also a real
person.

What we have, then, is an imaginary situation: a woman who complains
of what she thinks is abnormal bleeding, and who has rejected the advances of John's (imaginary) male friend. John's wife, who, oddly, asks
John about menstruation, is unable to answer the woman about her bleeding, and seems to think John will be an expert on the subject. For some
reason — perhaps breakthrough bleeding is in his mind — John asks the
woman whether she is on the Pill; and, finding that she is not, suggests she
phone his real family doctor, a woman, for an opinion.

The image of an imaginary woman bleeding is not an unusual one in
men's dreams. In this dream, she seems to be having a heavy menstrual
period. According to our hypothesis that people invented by a dream refer
to the dreamer's own personality, we are led to an interesting suggestion:
that the menstruating woman represents something in John's psychological
make-up. Men do not menstruate physically; is there a sense in which it
can be said that they do so psychologically?

The suggestion of cyclic swings in men is not a new one. It has been frequently proposed, most popularly in the theory of biorhythms. What has
spoken against these suggestions is, I think, a tendency to assume that the
cycles must be absolutely regular. But the dreams use the imagery of
menstruation, and menstruation in an individual is not absolutely regular,
and the length varies considerably from individual to individual. We
would expect that, if there were male cycles, they would vary similarly.

In the dream, John asks the bleeding woman whether she is on the Pill.

The suggestion of breakthrough bleeding was his suggestion for explaining why he asked this question. The dream-woman is disturbed by what at first appears to be a natural phenomenon. It makes sense, if we pick up on Jung's anima concept, that a dream-invented woman may refer to the feminine traits in a man's personality. Although these traits may be suppressed, even buried completely out of awareness, they nonetheless remain an active part of the man and can be observed at close hand by his acquaintances. Emotional menstruation might mean, in a man, a periodic, though irregular, mood cycle that is beyond his conscious control and of which he may be only vaguely aware because our society has denied such variations in men.

The conclusion, then, would be that John, at the time of his dream, was undergoing a low point in his mood cycle; in dream imagery, the 'woman within' was menstruating.

When we tackle the other figures in the dream, we are at first perplexed about the male friend whose advances are rejected by the dream woman. There is one feature of John's personality that would be most affected by his emotional swings, and that is his persona, his public face. More than that is affected, however, namely his relationships with everyone as well as with himself.

Jan is a real person, John's wife, and she embodies for him those feminine aspects that lie still undeveloped in himself. She is the store of feminine knowledge for him, and the long conversation between the dream-invented woman and Jan represents the 'conversation' between John's own feminine side and his wife. She draws out his hitherto suppressed femininity and brings it into the open. By holding this 'conversation', she enriches John's own personality, making it more inclusive and complete. By turning the question about the bleeding over to him, she is forcing him to recognise that his own inner self has moods and cycles that he must become consciously aware of.

It is often said that there is a natural opposition between a man's anima and his persona, that is, that a man attempts to keep his public face always the same, never varying, regardless of his inner feelings. It usually takes a real woman to diagnose for such a man just what his inner feelings and moods actually are, and to force him, almost, to take cognizance of them instead of keeping up a front. This is how I would take the opening of the dream, in which it is said that 'a male friend of mine has been interested in a woman and she has rejected him'. His inner mood, personified by the dream-woman, rejects the external show that he attempts to present to the world.

This phenomenon is not restricted to men, of course. Inner feelings may need to be portrayed, in a dream, for a woman; the more cut off she is from her natural roots, the more the conflict between inner feeling and conscious intent will be. We return to more of John W.'s dreams later in this book. Let us now look at a woman, Margaret J., whose dreams we will also follow in subsequent chapters:

I am walking in a tea-house lot, in an oriental setting. The trees have been cut down. It is mostly an uphill walk. I meet an old oriental man who says, 'I am going to die today. I'll show you how to die.' He is very friendly. I disbelieve him, he seems healthy and strong, though old. He takes me to the eight-sided tea-house. There is a bed in it, and four male friends are there. He serves us all tea, which is delicious, there is a feeling of agape [fellowship]. He looks at the sun and says, 'It is my time to die' and he lies down on the bed.

MARGARET J., #1

Much of this dream anticipates the discussion of symbols in the next chapter, but the dream story can be taken at face value and discussed as it stands.

The tea-house, the old oriental man and the four male friends are all dream inventions. Margaret is the only real-life person in the dream. Let us take the dream as if it were a miniature stage play that included the dreamer among its cast of characters. We see the motif of death twice: first in the trees that have been cut down, later in the old oriental man's preparation for dying. Margaret is to be taught the art of dying.

The setting is oriental. The tea-house is a well-known oriental tradition for furthering the sense of relaxation, fellowship and relief from the cares of the world. We think of *The Teahouse of the August Moon*, a play known to Margaret. All these themes are implied in the religious term 'agape', which also involves the sense of pure love between God and human being, or between two fellow human beings.

There is beauty in the old man's death. There is no panic, no fear, simply an acknowledgment of death and preparedness to die. The dreamer has strong religious feelings and it is not far-fetched to see a point of similarity between the old oriental man and Christ in their preparedness for death and recognition of the time to die. This parallel is borne out by the reference to the eight sides of the tea-house and the four male friends, eight and four being traditional symbols of spiritual wholeness which, in Christian tradition, is seen at its epitome in Christ.

The location of the tea-house, however, is a bit disturbing. The trees have been cut down, nature has been interfered with. This suggests to us that the point of the dream story is to regain a link with nature, that the dreamer has an uphill walk ahead of her is understandable, in that light. (I am assuming here that the dream in its imagery is giving concrete expression to a verbal metaphor: 'an uphill climb' = a very difficult procedure.) But there is an old oriental man who belongs to this tea-house. From his appearance in the dream, he embodies natural wisdom, the wisdom that:

There is a season for everything, a time for every occupation under heaven:

A time for giving birth,
a time for dying . . .

ECCLESIASTES 3: 1–2
Jerusalem Bible

This leads us to think of Freud's introduction of the concept of the death instinct. Part of the rough going that Freud's concept has had is because of the general assumption that it must be a destructive, even pathological, urge. But as Freud envisaged it, death is a natural process just as life is, and has its representations in our dream world. To relate the dreamer with the natural cycle of life and death, or, metaphorically, in terms of the life and death of interests or occupations, is the main thrust of the dream.

Why is the old man oriental, why is the setting a tea-house? Margaret is familiar with oriental religious thought as well as with Christianity, in which she was reared. Death in Christian thought is seen as an evil caused by disobedience to divine commandments, and life beyond death, a divine gift. In oriental thought, death is part of the rhythm of nature; it is not final, for all that dies springs back to life again, whether it be vegetation, or human destiny via reincarnation. Margaret, then, is being initiated into this rhythm by the events in the tea-house. And the old man is the portrayal of this natural rhythm, in particular, of the fact and 'instinct' of death.

Why this dream, though? Margaret was not near death, and she survived the period of this dream without any hint of actual death appearing. It must be a metaphorical death that is meant. If the significance of the old oriental man is what it appears to be, then the emphasis is on the cycle of growth and decay. It could be a death to an old personality that is meant — this would fit in well with Margaret's subsequent life history — and it is in keeping with oriental religions, which emphasise the theme of being a part of the cycle of nature, a death to the feeling of apartness. Jung's reference to the 'two-million-year-old-man within us' is a good characterisation of the fact that we are a product of nature, with millions of years of evolutionary development behind us. In our artificial civilisation, we are apt to forget our natural heritage, and we may need to be reminded of it from time to time, especially when crises arise. The dream can come to point out the path that we need to follow. In this specific instance, a radical reorientation to the natural environment and to Margaret's re-formation of herself.

This discussion of Margaret's dream brings us back to the vital point that dreams are not merely reactions to events taking place, or residues of experiences, but have a purpose and a goal. We examine that thought in some detail in Chapter 4. But it is as well to repeat, at this stage, that our discussion of dreams has had the tacit premise that each dream has a meaning and a purpose.

A final dream for this chapter may lead us to a survey and summary of what we have found so far, and clear the ground for our next topic, the subject of symbolism in dreams. The following comes from an adult woman:

> *Jim and I have just found out that I am pregnant. We are quite happy about it, though I'm a little reluctant to relax straight away. He makes a joke about my being shy even now, and puts his hand on my stomach. It seems to swell as he feels me. I've been cooking as we're talking about how I already show. Some friends come—suddenly I'm very conscious that there are no clean dishes and have to rummage for mugs.*

> JOAN L., #1

We see another dream of Joan's in Chapter 5, the chapter on nightmares. Fortunately, this dream is no nightmare but a very different sort of matter.

Jim is Joan's husband. With this dream, we move from an image of dying, the old oriental man, to an image of new life, pregnancy, although, of course, the two dreamers are very dissimilar. Joan was not, in fact, pregnant at the time of this dream, nor did she and Jim at that time contemplate a pregnancy. For that matter, she did not become pregnant within a considerable time of the dream, so that it cannot relate to a physical pregnancy. The pregnancy, then, must be a symbolic one. Setting that to one side for the moment, the dream reads as a simple, straightforward account: happiness in pregnancy, the feeling of shyness, the arrival of friends for dinner and the lack of clean dishes. There is some interesting imagery in the dream, especially the mention that she has been cooking as they were talking about the pregnancy, since cooking is an age-old folk image for gestation; to 'have buns in the oven' comes to mind as an example.

This dream played a special role in Joan's and Jim's lives: it is an 'initial dream', that is, one of several dreams that Joan had immediately after her first session of analysis with me, before her second session. It portrays a reaction to the undertaking of starting a new life in her soul. It is, as we see in Chapter 5, a very different dream from the nightmare that preceded her first session with me, and that proclaimed her fears about what might come out in analysis.

The personnel in this dream are quite limited: the dreamer herself, her husband, some friends. These people are all real. Joan can rejoice with her husband that something new is taking place within her. Jim can relate to the situation. But Joan is less prepared for her friends. The child within her, her own self-renewal, is the important thing. This motif of self-renewal is particularly important. The dream came at a time of doubts, hesitations and worries, to give reassurance. The child, this time still *in utero*, points to new life for Joan; and, what is very important, indicates that Jim is happy with the new situation.

The last bit of the dream where Joan realises that she has no clean dishes, and must rummage for mugs, is very symbolic, and one that is familiar in various forms from many persons' dreams. The basic point is that not only must Joan 'cook' (prepare a new life for her own soul) for herself and her husband, but she must be able to present the results to her friends. Clean plates, like clean laundry, indicate a new setting with which to meet people in the outer world, a new way of giving them nourishment from one's own stock of emotion-filled 'food'. With this, we find it necessary to turn to a systematic examination of the realm of dream symbolism.

SUMMARY OF PRINCIPLES

From a simple reading of a dream, and knowledge about the people in it, it is possible to add a vast new dimension to our understanding of dreams. Knowledge about the people in a dream is usually something that only the dreamer can give. Sometimes, the descriptions in the dream are enough to understand their role; other times, the dreamer must give rather extensive explanations. It is hazardous to try to attempt the interpretation of a dream without the dreamer available to discuss it. Personal references often make a dream difficult to fathom if they are not explained. This is one of the reasons why books on dream interpretation cannot be enough to cater for attempts to interpret someone's dream. Nevertheless, the basic principles can be taught, and if applied by a second person with the help of the dreamer, they can bring considerable illumination to otherwise difficult or obscure dreams.

The basic principles uncovered so far in regard to the people who inhabit our dreams are to:

1. list the people who turn up in the dream;

2. characterise each person in the light of how that person is described in the dream;

3. when the person is a real one from the dreamer's environment, consider the dreamer's interaction with that person as the dream describes it, and compare or contrast this with what is known of the relationship in waking life with that person;

4. when the person is a dream invention, consider how the characterisation of the person fits as a characterisation of some trends in the dreamer's own personality or situation;

5. fit what is discovered about the people in the dream into the dream story, to round out the drama that the dream story portrays — it is helpful to think of the dream as told as if it were a description of a drama that the dreamer has seen, and the characterisation of the dramatis personae as filling in a vital part of the course of the drama;

6. attempt to see how the dream story, with the description of the people in it, fits the life of the dreamer.

Not all dreams will be explicable in this fashion. While the principles given here will apply to a great many dreams, there are other aspects of dreams that we must investigate in order to get a balanced picture. But when this approach does fit a dream, it gives a valuable insight into the dreamer's life and personality, and, more than that, it helps to indicate how that life and personality can be enriched.

Chapter 3

DREAMS AND SYMBOLISM

As far back as written records go, there have always been handbooks on how to interpret dreams. These handbooks focus especially on symbol interpretation; that is, they take images from dreams and tell the meaning of each image. To do this, there is an assumption that the meaning of the images in one person's dreams will fit the images of another person's; that there is, in other words, a universal pool of images and meanings into which any individual's dreams dip. This particular concept continues into the present day, not only in popular handbooks, but also in much of the specialist literature on dreams.

Most readers are aware of 'Freudian symbols', which are largely known through Freud's book *The Interpretation of Dreams*. For the most part, 'Freudian symbols' have a sexual interpretation. In Freudian psycho-analysis, these universal symbols are used to enlarge the framework of a dream's meaning when the dreamer's personal information relating to the dream's images runs out or is insufficient. Jung, too, held that there are universal images in dreams. He spoke of archetypes, which are inbuilt patterns of making images and concepts. What most distinguishes Jung and Freud personally from traditional popular handbooks is their insistence that personal memories and experiences of the dreamer must provide the framework for interpretation, with universal symbols employed only as an adjunct. The specific meanings of universal images as interpreted by Freud and Jung are also different from those in traditional handbooks, although in recent decades, many of their ideas and interpretations have been incorporated into popular dream dictionaries and the like.

We have seen in Chapters 1 and 2 that it is possible to understand a great deal of dream material without resorting to interpretation of symbols. But we have also seen that, often, it is not possible to explain all of the images in a dream solely in terms of the dream story and of the people in the dream. Inevitably, we need the dreamer's own associations, that is, personal background and information relating to the images in the dream as the dreamer knows them. Personal associations do not relate only to the people who turn up in dreams. References to places, to specific events, to particular objects, etc., are frequent in dreams, and without knowledge of the explanation, which only the dreamer can give us, we would be severely hampered in working over a dream. For this reason, it is seldom possible to understand a dream fully without information from the dreamer, though an understanding of the story told by a dream can get us a part of the way and provide a necessary context for understanding the dreamer's associations. However, as we have seen in the first two chapters, images that cannot be explained by the dreamer are sometimes met, and there is a need to understand symbols and their interpretation.

Unlike popular dream handbooks and dictionaries, which generally treat dream symbols as the most important or possibly only avenue to the understanding of dreams, my emphasis has been quite different. I have taken the approach of looking at each dream as a story that can be taken in its own terms; when personal references have been made, we have looked to the dreamer to supply the personal information. Only then do we come upon the need to consider symbolism. When we come to that point and add non-personal information about the dream images, we enlarge the images by bringing in material that is not directly mentioned by the dream. This process, often called amplification, is a very delicate matter, because our imagination can run wild if we are not careful.

Traditionally, any dream image that cannot be taken at face value has been termed a symbol. Dream researchers have often narrowed down the definition a great deal. But why dreams should use symbols at all is a matter of considerable dispute. The most popular explanations are:

1. that a dream, or, rather, the dream-making process, filters out too explicit references, particularly to sexual matters, and replaces them with symbols, which are less explicit and thus are more palatable or acceptable to the dreamer;

2. that references are made in a dream that cannot be better expressed than through symbolic imagery;

3. that dreams lack the ability to use all of our mental functions, and, therefore, they must turn to imagery that hints at what is being expressed as the only way open for the dream to give its message.

These explanations do not necessarily conflict with one another, and more than one of them may be useful in considering dreams. A fourth explanation takes a rather different line than the first three:

4. that dream images mean what they say, in the same fashion as a poem or a drama does. From this point of view, what has been regarded as the need for symbol interpretation is really akin to the footnotes that may accompany the poems of T. S. Eliot or the plays of Shakespeare, explaining difficult passages by telling us what they relate to.

In line with the fourth 'explanation', it might be added that the comparison is perhaps better made by seeing many dreams as akin to the poetry of William Blake, where a mass of images has to be taken in its own light, with annotation that helps to follow the story rather than to interpret it. A similar comparison might be made between the imagery in dreams and that in the paintings of Marc Chagall. Again, this fourth 'explanation' does not necessarily exclude any or all of the first three.

As we have been seeing in earlier chapters, by no means do all dreams call for symbol interpretation; the larger share do not. But when it does appear necessary to discuss symbolism, what sources do we use to make the interpretation? First, the dreamer's own thoughts. Many dreamers have their own pet theories about symbols, and these need to be taken into account when discussing their dreams. For example, a dreamer well versed in Freudian psychoanalysis will tend to have a great many images that are to be taken sexually, having learned of them from reading Freud's and Freudian books. Similarly, what appear at first to be major archetypal symbols frequently turn up in the dreams of persons who have read a great deal of literature by Jung and Jungians. Most dreamers have their own familiar ideas of symbolism, and their dream 'symbols' must be taken in that light.

Secondly, when the dreamer's own stock of associations runs out, dream images can usually be understood in the light of the dreamer's cultural background: traditions, popular sayings, folklore, scientific and artistic knowledge, and literature all influence and determine the imagery that we find in dreams.

Rather than run the risk of providing yet another dream dictionary, which might follow if I were to present symbols systematically, I intend to illustrate the process of symbol interpretation by discussing specific dreams, showing how to go about the task.

A woman in her early thirties dreamed as follows:

> *I am being driven in a car by Jack. The car door on my side (the passenger's side) was wide open. We were driving alongside the sea, and the water was so far up that it lapped onto the floorboards of the car. At the bottom of the water, which was about a foot deep, I saw four gold pens.*
>
> JANE B.

Jack is a psychotherapist whose group therapy sessions Jane was attending. She was badly frightened in one of the group sessions, and this was still on her mind at the time of the dream. She offered the suggestion that the pens refer to her university graduate studies which she was undergoing at the same time. The car she identified as an FJ Holden, a car we have discussed in regard to Alfred M.'s dream in Chapter 1, that is, a car manufactured about the time of Jane's birth.

There is no suggestion of drowning in this dream. The four gold pens at the bottom of the water are reminiscent of Alfred M.'s dream of discovering something very important under the water, discussed in Chapter 2.

However, Jane's and Alfred's situations are very different in their dreams. Alfred dives into the water in order to find a presumably drowned man. Jane is worried because the car is being flooded. She does not get out of the car. The reason for the flooding is apparent: her (passenger's side) door is open. Presumably the car will cease to function soon, being flooded by deep sea water, and the situation is very uncomfortable.

Jane's reaction to the dream was that it had the same feel as what she experienced in Jack's group therapy session, which was that she felt herself being pulled into a catatonic state, that is, a feeling of complete withdrawal from the world and everything going on around her, so that, although she saw and heard what was happening, she was herself unable to move or utter a sound — a terrifying experience. She felt that she was going totally insane. To an onlooker, nothing seemed wrong, except that she did not move, and Jack did not recognise the state she was in and therefore made no attempt to pull her out of it.

It seems clear that the motif of being flooded in Jack's car refers to Jane's experience of being overcome by a psychological state that she was completely unable to control. Control, in both the therapy session and in the dream, was in Jack's hands. That the passenger's door was open and thus let the floods pour in is an image of not being protected against the uncontrollable experience. But we must be cautious here: there is no suggestion in the dream that the open door was Jack's doing. And there is no suggestion that Jane will be drowned. The water is only about a foot deep, and just laps over onto the floorboards. There does not seem to be any grave danger represented in the dream. About the only consequence, from the dream's point of view, would be that Jack's car might totally cease to function, in which event Jane could wade out into the water, retrieve the pens, and go her way. (It is unclear in the dream whether Jane is in the front seat beside Jack, in which case, to get out she must wade through the water, or whether she is in the back seat and might simply open the other door and get out. The implication seems to be that she is in the front seat next to Jack, being driven by him but easily able to get out.)

The water is shallow and the car is from the time of her birth; there seems, thus, to be a suggestion that the way of proceeding that she has adopted is one that goes back to earliest childhood. This is quite probable, since Jack lays special emphasis on the reliving of childhood experiences, with special attention to the experience of being born. Jane eventually became familiar with Jack's 'rebirthing' techniques, and found them very helpful. At the time, however, it was all new to her.

The catatonic state that Jane described is somewhat similar to the state of a young infant: able to perceive what is going on, but unable to control its movements or vocal expression. However, this analogy must not be taken too far. The infant is able to scream, and this, Jane was struggling unsuccessfully to do during her catatonic state. The description 'catatonic', I might add, was one Jane used in discussing the experience she went through in the group session. It is used here, not as a psychiatric diagnosis, but as an expressionistic word Jane used to describe how she felt.

In the context of all this, the dream story seems pretty clear and enough has been said about Jack to explain his presence in the dream. Jane, in the dream story, found herself out on a car ride, being driven by Jack; her door was open and they were travelling on the edge of the sea so that water lapped the floorboards. She saw four gold pens in the water, which was shallow. It is a very expressive snippet of a dramatic scene, indicating how Jane felt. It is saying, in effect, 'In Jack's session I felt like he was driving me along the seashore and my door was open so that the water came in'. The climax of the dream lies in its final sentence, that Jane saw four gold pens underneath the foot-deep water.

Although the bulk of the dream story feels satisfying without any greater interpretation than referring to Jane's experience during Jack's group therapy session, this discussion is not yet satisfying. We wonder just how the pens fit into it all. And we are naturally curious whether the car, the water and the gold pens have any special meaning.

Cars are one of the most frequent dream images in the present day. Other modes of transportation also feature frequently, especially bicycles, trains and airplanes. All of these vehicles have one thing in common, they are modern inventions, with no prototype except for the horse and carriage in earlier centuries. It is very difficult to make a case that these vehicles in themselves represent as dream images any particular symbolic meaning. We will see bicycles, trains and airplanes in later dreams in this book and discuss them there. But there is no empirical basis on which to state that any of these vehicles — in this instance, cars — have a fixed meaning.

Cars have had different social connotations from time to time. Many older people still remember the time when owning a car was a status symbol, but generally speaking, that connotation of a car has disappeared from general usage now that cars are almost universally owned. A car may mean many things to many people. And this is precisely my point: cars have neither been around long enough, nor do they have a general emotional connotation, for them to have developed symbol status. I am deliberately including in my discussion the Freudian interpretation that takes cars to be sexual symbols, usually (since we sit inside them) symbols for the uterus. This interpretation presupposes firstly that the symbol must be sexual, and secondly, that any enveloping container is representative of the womb. To my mind, this is a prior assumption for which I can find no justification or supporting evidence.

For an individual dreamer, of course, a car may have many personal associations, and these must be taken into account in working with that person's dream. But as a generalisation, to the question 'What does a car represent?', we must answer, 'A means of transportation, which an individual person, who is often the only passenger as well, drives, and the direction and speed of which are under that person's control, and which is self-propelled.' This is mostly a definition of a car, rather than a symbol statement. There are some popular phrases connected with cars, among which 'to be taken for a ride' = misled by someone, is very common. This particular phrase seems apt for the feeling in Jane's dream: Jane is being taken for a ride by Jack, i.e. chauffeured by Jack, thus, metaphorically, in Jack's car. In the process, she finds something frightening taking place.

When we come to the sea, we have a different situation. The sea, or ocean, is an ages-old part of the natural environment, and it plays a very definite role in the life of the 'two-million-year-old woman' inside Jane. Put more prosaically, while our evolutionary adaptation over the past couple of million years does not extend to cars, which are too recent an innovation for evolutionary changes within ourselves to take place, it does extend to the sea, which has been part and parcel of life, not only for ourselves, but for all living creatures — plant and animal alike — since life began. We can cogently argue that we have an evolutionary development in relation to the sea, if not to cars.

The sea, and, in variations, expanses of water of various kinds, such as rivers, lakes, ponds and pools, is one of the most widespread and familiar images in dream life. The motif of being flooded is one of the most frequent dream motifs. We have a large number of popular expressions that not only indicate the prevalence of the sea as an expressive image, but characterise it as well: 'in between the Devil and the deep blue sea', 'to be drowning in work', 'a sea of worries', 'to be at sea', 'half seas over' (= drunk), and many more. The common factor in these phrases is that the sea is viewed as a danger, in which one feels hopeless and helpless. The basic concept is 'to be out of your depth', i.e. in a situation beyond your control.

The sea, and its variations as a lake, river, etc., can lay very cogent claim to being an archetypal image, that is, a common experience of all life, not only human, from the earliest single-celled creature to modern *Homo sapiens*, to which all life has adapted in one manner or another (generally, by living in it, swimming in it, or shunning it). Because of this, we have an evolutionary relationship to bodies of water, and that is, succinctly, what Jung meant by an archetype.

The 'sea' that is outside Jane's control is her being sucked into states that incapacitate her. The water in this dream, then, represents her unconscious (= not consciously willed or controlled) openness to such states. The word 'unconscious' is really necessary here, even though I have taken effort to avoid terminology that is not common currency among the major psychological schools of the present day. It refers to events within the personality that overpower the consciously-willed state, no matter how desperately she/he tries to prevent it happening. In analytical literature, it is common to say that bodies of water symbolise the unconscious. It is more accurate to say that, in this particular dream, the water represents a process of feeling a threat of being overcome by some uncontrollable experience. But, at the same time that the dream expresses this sense of threat, the dream image also says that the felt danger is not so great. The water is only a foot deep, not enough to pose a serious life-threatening situation.

The four gold pens at the bottom of the water require a special discussion. There are several motifs involved here: the number four, gold, pens, under the surface. Jane's suggestion that the pens relate to her university graduate studies may be taken as a basis for discussion. Why are there four of them, why are they gold, and why are they submerged in the sea, albeit a very shallow part of it? The last question is most easily answered. The dreamer was able to give the principal point: her university studies were submerged, the victim of the condition she was feeling, not only the catatonic state but her more general feeling of being unable to cope and to concentrate. Her pens were captive, so to speak, under the sea of her despair, though still visible. She was fighting a losing battle to keep on with her studies at that time.

Gold emphasises the value Jane placed on her university work. If, to follow the image, she does her university work with a set of gold pens, this means it is supremely valuable for her. Gold as supreme value is a very ancient concept in most of the world's cultures, including our own. There is another, symbolic, use for gold in our literary tradition. Gold as the symbol for conscious understanding and goals is a major item in western symbolism. This meaning fits in well with the dream: the goal of her conscious striving, a post-graduate degree, has been submerged in her feeling of being emotionally flooded. Yet, the dream implies a reassurance at the same time: being only a foot deep in the water, the gold pens would be easily retrieved.

We are left with the number four. We came upon the question of the meaning of this number in the tea-house dream in Chapter 2, in which it referred to a set of male friends who were companions of the old oriental man. Now, in a very different dream from a very different person, we find a set of four gold pens. The number four turns up much more frequently in dreams than would be warranted mathematically. Explicitly as a set of four persons or objects, or implicitly by being the number of persons in a dream, this number is extremely frequent in dreams. In popular tradition, the number four constitutes a full set: the four corners of the earth, the four phases of the moon, the four seasons, the four suits in a deck of cards, etc. The tea-house dream concerned the need to be integrated into the rhythmic cycle of life and death; the four companions of the old man can be seen as representing the full cycle, which the old man personified. In the present dream of the four gold pens, we can see the number as representing the whole problematic theme of Jane's university studies, which were submerged at the time of the dream. That they were golden indicates the value she placed on them.

Jane's dream portrays for us the fact that a discussion of symbolism can enrich our understanding of a dream, though it does not necessarily provide a key to the understanding of it. Dreams that require little symbol interpretation are much more frequent than those that do. Even very bizarre dreams may prove to require less symbol interpretation than would appear at first glance. The little boy, Carl, whose dreams we looked at in the first and second chapters, has provided us with a very strange-looking dream indeed:

> *You [his father] and me were walking on a winding path seeing different plants and dolphins. I soon got lost in a dark alley with a railway track at the end. You went into a shop to buy something, and when I found you coming out of the shop, you were riding a bike. So you got a bike for me to ride and we stopped at a miniature house and I peeked into the little door. What I saw was very small clocks and they all looked green from a laser light. There was a clock like a pen-watch, only the time was in a mouse's mouth at the end of the watch, like a cuckoo-clock. We went home again, and a couple days later, I went back to look at the clock house and everything inside it was exactly the same as before.*

CARL N., #3

This story is so bizarre that the reader might be justified in wondering whether it is a true dream at all, or a story invented by the nine-year-old child. I have no reason to doubt its authenticity; it was told as part of a series narrated by Carl to his father. But if it were not a dream but a fantasy-invention, I suspect that much the same procedure could be applied to it as to a dream. We will proceed to treat it as a real dream, and see what comes out of the examination. What at first hearing sounds utterly bizarre does, in fact, make a kind of sense if we look into the background of the references in the dream.

There are quite a few associations to various parts of this dream:

Dolphins: Carl had been watching slides of dolphins performing tricks, taken by his father. The dolphins had been trained to leap into the air, jump through hoops, etc.

Railway track: there was a suburban train station at the end of the street where Carl and his family lived. The track has been transposed to the end of a dark alley, in the dream.

Bike: Carl was an avid cyclist, though his father was not.

Peeking into the little door: this is a scene that comes up in *Alice in Wonderland*, with which Carl was very familiar. Alice sees a tiny door in a hall-way wall, but it is so small she can only peer through it.

Laser light: Carl's father had taken him to see a display of laser lights and holograms shortly before the dream. Carl had these two confused in his mind, so that laser light meant, for him, not only a spectacular type of lighting but also the quasi-miracle of holograms.

Pen-watch: while shopping not long before, Carl had seen a pen-watch on sale and wondered at it.

Cuckoo-clock: Carl said that this reminded him of the floral clock in a nearby park. The floral clock vaguely resembles a cuckoo-clock because of a little enclosure housing the mechanism, at the top of the clock. His father added to that the observation that there was a cuckoo-clock in the kitchen.

Mouse: Carl had bought a Mickey Mouse electronic game with money he had saved up.

As can be seen from these associations, virtually everything in the dream has some connection with experiences or objects in Carl's life. In order to get some clarity into the dream, let us dissect out the skeleton of the dream story:

1. Carl is out walking with his father.
2. They see plants and dolphins.
3. Carl gets lost in a dark alley, with a railroad track at its end.
4. He finds his father coming out of a shop.
5. Carl and his father both ride bikes.
6. Carl peeks through a little door into a miniature house.
7. He sees tiny laser-green clocks.
8. He sees a pen-watch with a mouse at the end of it.
9. Carl and his father go home.
10. A couple days later, Carl returns, there has been no change.

Two things stand out immediately when looking at this dream: Carl's companionship with his father, on whom he relies; and the question of the passing of time, an emphasis on clocks and the changelessness of things. In Carl's earlier dreams, discussed in Chapters 1 and 2 — the dream about the marble trees and the dream about not being able to find all the parts of his recorder — his father also figured prominently. One feature those two dreams share with this one is that Carl's father initiates an action (going shopping; playing the recorder; taking Carl for a walk and later providing him with a bike) but Carl then, on his own behalf, undertakes something (picking marbles, looking for his own tenor recorder, peering into the

miniature house and later returning to see if it stays the same). This is a
'growing up' dream, a type very common among children, in which Carl
receives his basic support and way of proceeding in the masculine world
from his father, but then, on his own, sees that there is a passage of time
(= the clocks), although nevertheless he can rely on his experience of
reality to remain unchanged.

Looked at in skeleton form, much of the dream falls into place. Exotic
things can be experienced by Carl when with his father: there are dolphins,
strange animals that breathe air yet live in the sea, and that can be taught
to perform spectacular feats; everyday things like plants are accompanied
by the mysterious and wonderful — the dolphins, laser light and holograms,
even the miniature house has a background in connection with this. At the
laser light and hologram display, there was an exhibit of a giant hologram
that gave a three-dimensional image of a complete living-room (though
this room was life-sized, a phenomenal feat of holography). Viewers were
invited to peer behind the hologram and to view the room from all different angles. The dream is saying, 'With your father, you can experience
quite extraordinary things', and it makes it clear that both real life and
dream life are included.

At this point, perhaps, I should say that the reason Carl wrote down this
dream to give to his father was that his father had told him that I was looking for children's dreams to use in this book, and Carl volunteered to make
a collection of his own dreams for me to use. I talked directly with Carl
about the dreams, later, and got his associations for the dream images,
and also with his father to clarify other references in the dreams. After I
worked up the first draft of the commentary, I let Carl read my comments
and he was able to correct me on several points. So, by this time, dream life
was one of the 'extraordinary things' that Carl could discover with his
father's initiative and by moving into the subject himself.

The theme of competition is important in Carl's dreams, though it is
somewhat muted so that it can escape the reader at first. In the first
dream, the competition was with his sister, in picking marbles. But in the
second and third dreams, it has been with his father. He receives guidance
and help from his father in this third dream, but the emphasis is on Carl
doing his own thing. He learns from his father, as for example in playing
the recorder, but he strives to find his own place in the world, which
involves adding on those things his father does not do, such as (in the
dream) playing his own, wanting to play a different recorder or looking at
a scene his father does not see, and returning to it later to check on its
reality.

The railway tracks serve to orient Carl, both in real life and in the
dream. By taking an image from real life — the rail tracks at the end of the
street — and transferring them to the end of a dark alley where Carl feels
lost, the dream says to Carl, 'You can find your way, even when you feel

you are in the dark and have lost your way in life; the old familiar railway
is there at the end of the alley to help you find out where you are and how
to get back to familiar ground'. For a child of this age, that kind of support
is what the child needs, and it is this support that the dream is giving, a reassurance. It is saying, 'Your father is able to lead the way, and is available
as a refuge and help when needed, so that you can safely explore life, and
he will be there when you feel lost'.

The bicycle is a means of transportation that Carl is familiar with. He
can ride his bike and be accompanied, rather than driven, by his father. In
the context of this dream, the bicycle for Carl is a representation of his
equality with his father, despite their difference in size and age, an important thing for a child to learn. The same point came up in the dream of the
recorders.

The miniature house and door, which are a direct steal from *Alice in
Wonderland*, are important. In *Alice*, not only is the little door that goes
off the hallway important, because it gives Alice a goal (she sees a wonderful garden the other side of the door, and it remains her goal to get to this
garden throughout the story), but so, too, is a miniature house. The miniature house in *Alice* belongs to the White Rabbit, and Alice enters it when
she is very tiny in size, but, while in the house, she grows to enormous proportions and blocks the door so that the Rabbit cannot come in. The problem for the Rabbit is, then, how to get Alice out. The door is a view onto a
wistful goal seen as unobtainable. The house is a feeling of being trapped
in a situation that has been outgrown. In Carl's dream, the little house and
door serve to give him a glimpse into the passage of time, represented by
the clocks.

The clocks are green from a laser light. Not only does life have much
ground for him to cover that he is unfamiliar with, it also abounds in the
mysterious. The passage of time is coloured by new ways of viewing the
world. At present, Carl can get only a small glimpse of this (= the door is
very small) but, in a sense, it is only through play at the moment. The
miniature house is like a doll's house, with which to play at being an adult.
But more still, the miniature house resembles the structure that hides the
mechanism of the floral clock, and resembles the traditional appearance of
a cuckoo-clock, two features with which Carl was well acquainted, the
cuckoo-clock from daily life.

One clock looks like a pen-watch, except that the time read-out is
enclosed in the features of a mouse's mouth attached to the end of the pen.
It is similar to a cuckoo-clock in that the cuckoo, which proclaims the
time, is housed in a little space in the attic of the clock-house, so that if you
were to hold the pen-watch upright, the time would be in the mouse's
mouth like it is in a cuckoo's in a cuckoo-clock.

So far we have seen little, in our examination of the dream, that would
qualify as a 'symbol'. But with the pen-watch, we must be careful. Why

should it be a pen-watch that draws Carl's attention? If the clocks represent the passage of time, what is there in the passage of time that is best represented by a pen-watch? It is much the same question as we asked of the recorder dream in Chapter 2: why a musical instrument and why specifically a recorder? A sexual suggestion was made there, and is re-examined in Chapter 6. I rather suspect that a sexual theme is also portrayed by the pen-watch, this suggestion being based on the point that the pen-watch mouse is long and barrel-like, and would be held upright in order to make use of it. Extra support is given to this suggestion by the fact that it is in the company of his father that Carl sees the pen-watch. This would mean that Carl's glimpse into the framework of the passage of time includes also the mystery of the erect penis, which, like the pen-watch, is a barrel-shaped object with fluid in it.

Although a sexual interpretation of the pen-watch is quite plausible, there is nothing in the dream that demands it. We may prefer to use a variation of Occam's Razor (that explanatory theories should be kept to a minimum) and symbolism should not be read into a dream more than is absolutely necessary. The pen-watch may simply be a curiosity of the past few days, something that Carl wishes he could have, and the mouse's head at the end may be a merger of two electronic marvels — the computerised, hand-held electronic Mickey Mouse game and the computerised, miniature time-reckoning mechanism in the tiny space of the end of a pen-watch. In other words, while a symbolic interpretation of the pen-watch is possible and plausible, it is not required by the content of the dream in order to satisfy the criteria for meaningfulness.

An interesting question can be raised in regard to the green light. There has been a running dispute for many decades, now, about whether dreams are in colour. Many people vehemently deny that their dreams are in colour, yet others are surprised by the suggestion that colour might be lacking in dreams. The key to this confusion might be that dream reports rarely mention colour. Since dream images are not distinguishable by the dreamer from real-life events, and are confused with daily life by young children and very occasionally by adults, natural colour is a normal part of dream imagery. When a colour is specially mentioned in a dream report, that is, presumably, because the colour has some special role to play in the dream. A house full of clocks bathed in green laser light would certainly be extraordinary, and worthy of mention in reporting a dream.

The fact that the colour is green may cause us to pause. A 'green light' is an internationally used traffic signal that means 'go ahead', and perhaps this is the significance of the green laser light that colours the clocks green. This would be a 'symbol' in the sense that the dream is using an image from daily life to portray an abstract concept — the passing of time while growing in life.

What we have seen so far is that, for the most part, a dream can be taken in its own terms, and very little symbol interpretation is necessary in the sense of substituting one image for another, or using an image to represent something unrepresentable. This by no means signifies that symbols are not used in dreams; just as they have an important role in poetry and drama, so they also have a major role in dreaming. But before jumping to the conclusion that an image is symbolic, we do need to investigate whether it is meaningful in its own right. There also always remains the possibility that the same image may have a meaning in itself and be symbolic as well.

It has become quite clear that there can be no mechanical substitution of a standardised 'meaning' for standard dream images. Each proposed symbol interpretation must be examined separately in the context of the dream story in which it appears. What may be symbolic for one dream may well be metaphorical in another dream, and to be taken literally in yet another.

Still, it should not be difficult, if symbolism is, in fact, used by dreams at all, to find some dreams to illustrate symbol usage, and I have chosen two brief dreams of Robert M. for this purpose:

> *I saw a big soup-spoon. My son was sitting in it. I tried to move it, but hadn't enough strength.*
>
> ROBERT M., #1

> *I was in a house that looked square. In the middle was a big, square hall with a lot of people. On every side, there were apartments. A woman, who was said to be a little queer, rushed through the hall. Later I saw her cleaning her apartment windows. I got a photo of her in my hands, taken some years ago. It was said that she was worse then.*
>
> ROBERT M., #2

We see two more of Robert's dreams in later chapters. The two preceding dreams bring us up against the problem of the meaning of dream imagery, and they relate us back to Chapter 2, 'The People in Our Dreams'.

There is an interesting similarity of images between Robert's soup-spoon dream and John W.'s early childhood dream discussed in Chapter 1, and it is rather interesting to compare the interpretations of the two spoon dreams.

Robert, at the time of dream #1, was having great difficulties with his small son. We can, therefore, take the dream objectively, and we will do this first before looking at it from the subjective viewpoint. Robert's relationship with his son was indeed 'in the soup'. That Robert is unable to budge the spoon with his son in it reflects his feeling that his relationship with his son was too much for him to handle. He expresses this in his dream by making a picture image of a slang expression, 'to be in the soup'. Such visual imagery for spoken expressions is fairly common in dreams. This is, indeed, a symbol. Both the visual imagery and the slang expression mean something other than appears if they are taken literally. They express a kind of feeling, one difficult to put into direct imagery or words. We may suppose that Robert was attempting to move the spoon by holding its handle, and might surmise that the image is saying that his problem with his son is too much for him 'to handle'.

Why should this dream come up, then? Surely Robert was well aware of the difficulty in his relating to his little son. The answer would probably lie in the fact that this, too, is an initial dream. In this instance, it was one of several dreams brought to the second session of analysis. We will see, at various points in this book, that when the dreamer is in analysis, the dream may frequently—some would say always—be a communication to the analyst, so to speak, dreamed for the analyst. This dream could be a communication to me, to tell me that Robert's problem with his son was the most pressing issue to be dealt with. There is a great deal to commend this interpretation. Robert had great difficulties in relating, a point that will come out much more strongly in the discussion of his second dream. One way of approaching Robert's problems would be to take a very specific relationship problem, namely that with his son, and deal with it in depth. This would mean that the relationship with his son was to the exclusion of dealing with his relationship with his wife, and his many problems at work, all of which were very pressing. But it could be a message to me: 'Take the situation with my son first, I feel he is in the soup and I cannot get anywhere with this problem'.

Seen from the subjective viewpoint, the dream takes on quite a different character, in that it is more of an appeal for help than the designation of a specific problem. As mentioned in Chapter 2, a dreamer's child may represent the dreamer's feeling of being still a child inside, at least in relation to some part of life. The child is, then, also a symbol, not to be taken as referring to a specific child in the dreamer's life but to an emotional state of the dreamer, one that says 'I feel like a child when faced with life right now'. This dream would be saying: 'I feel like a child, in the soup, and I just don't have the strength to alter the situation'.

There are quite a few life circumstances in which this held true for the dreamer. He was in an extremely deep depression, to the extent of being incoherent during his first session with me, and the feeling of being in difficulties from which he could not extricate himself would be very well imaged by this dream. As said, his relationship with his baby son was extremely bad. His relationship with his wife was no better. He was bound by contract to a new job that now felt beyond his capacities. He was unsure of his ability to communicate his problems to me, but had come to me because, quite a few years earlier, a psychoanalyst had been of very great help to him in the problems he was then experiencing. He hoped this would also be true of me in the present predicament.

Yet again, the dream is a communication to me, as seen from this subjective viewpoint; it is an appeal: 'Help me! I feel like a child in the bowl of a soup-spoon, and I am so stuck that I cannot even budge it!' What I have actually done is to give a very slight paraphrase of the wording of the original dream. This is in line with the view that a real symbol is best expressed as is, without translation. It speaks directly from one soul to another.

How would we decide between the two interpretations, the objective and the subjective? As they stand now, they complement each other. The objective viewpoint simply gives a specific problem to be dealt with, while the subjective viewpoint here is more general and conveys more feeling. In handling this dream in practice, it would be worthwhile to look at it from both viewpoints, and then talk about one, while keeping the other at hand to supplement the discussion.

Robert's second dream makes no sense unless seen from the subjective viewpoint, and its interpretation leads us to feel that the subjective interpretation of the first dream is likely to be most valuable. This second dream makes considerable use of symbolism, as we will now see.

In this dream, we come upon one of the most frequent dream images, that of a house. Apart from representing a real house, which is the preferable viewpoint in some dreams, it may embody a symbolic meaning, namely the feeling that the body is a house for the soul or spirit. The old pop song 'This Old House' uses this connotation very vividly, by describing the singer's body as a house in a state of decay, which will soon disintegrate altogether and release the imprisoned soul to heaven ('I'm getting ready to meet the saints'). In the Bible, we are familiar with a similar usage. The body is the temple in which the Spirit resides, in one of the apostle Paul's expressions. Jesus speaks of a house built on rocks as contrasted with one built on sand, to express the quality of one's life — here, the meaning has shifted from the body to the life quality that characterises the body. We can unite all these various usages by a single concept, that the house symbolises the framework of a person's relating to the world within and without.

The framework in which a person relates to the people around her/him and to her/his own inner life is really vital. We may view the house in this dream as representing Robert's own person, his psyche, as that term has been presented in this book. It surrounds Robert on all sides in the dream. The dream emphasises its square shape. Because Robert had a very intensive religious background, which appears in a later dream of his, we may be right in bringing in a biblical reference; the new City of God that was to be a perfect square (Rev. 21: 16), and which was to be God's dwelling place, his house. (This reference occurs also in regard to John W.'s dream of the Emerald City discussed in Chapter 4.) This gives a sort of divine quality to the dream-house. According to Robert's own conviction, his soul is the residence of God, and the dream-house, a representation of the practical framework in which his soul finds expression.

The square within a square makes us think of cloisters, also in keeping with Robert's religious background. We can take the internal courtyard as the centre of his psyche, and the many people there as the many facets of his life: on the one hand, the many roles he had to play in the course of relating to other people, but on the other hand, also the many attitudes and convictions that he had adopted from other people. This idea is suggested by the many apartments in the enclosed portion of the house, that is, compartments of his personality.

The woman who rushes through the hall and into her apartment is reminiscent of the anima figures discussed in Chapter 2, and which we first met early in Chapter 1. As an anima figure, she is a representation of feminine qualities, both as possessed by Robert himself and for which he searches in specific women. In this particular instance, the task is to get the windows clean so that the woman can see out. This suggests that Robert was closed in upon himself, unable to find the meeting point between his own inner qualities and those of the people about him — in particular, his wife and (from the first dream) his son. He had indeed gotten a picture of this situation years before, when he first encountered psychoanalysis.

There are various ways in which we can formulate these points. We can say that the house symbolises the basic, he would say 'divine', structure within him, and cleaning the windows symbolises his attempt to see the world more clearly. But we must go further and say that these images are to be understood in the context of Robert's life, experiences and problems. To Robert, it makes all the difference in the world whether his dream is interpreted abstractly, off the cuff, so to speak, or whether a specific context in his life is found in which to place the dream. This is the biggest argument against lists of dream symbols and their meanings, not that the meanings are always 'wrong', but that they are inadequate.

Thus, Robert's two dreams need to be taken on a concrete level, as a lead into discussing his relationships with his son and his wife, and any other women that may be or have been involved in his life. That is where the objective viewpoint is usually most helpful, in pointing out specifics to be considered at length. It is also why it is better, if at all possible, not to turn to symbolism as a first resort, but rather as a last resort. It is more helpful to consider Robert's relationship with his son and his wife, than his 'stuck' son inside him or his anima, not because the latter are wrong but because they tend to be too abstract.

The combination of symbolism with real people in dream imagery is common, and a brief example will show how valuable symbol interpretation can be for the understanding of dream imagery:

I see my girl-friend; she is four people, with me in the centre.

DON C.

Don explained that his girl-friend appeared four times simultaneously,
thus:

O   O

X

O   O

We need to know something of the relationship in order to understand this
rather unusual dream image. Don had split from his wife quite a while
before, and was now living with a girl-friend. From examining the
diagram of the dream image, the thought occurs that he 'only has eyes for'
his girl-friend. The fourfold multiplication of the girl-friend indicates that
she is over-emphasised. He is placing too much emphasis upon her in his
emotional life, to the exclusion of the impact that separation from his first
marriage had upon him.

Don was well read in Jungian theory, so that he recognised two frequent
dream symbols: the mandala and the anima. The mandala is a circle (the
word 'mandala' is Sanskrit for 'circle') used in Hinduism and Buddhism for
a special type of contemplation; in psychological usage, it has come to
mean any circular image, especially one that is combined with a square-
form, that appears in dreams and art in times of emotional crisis. It represents an attempt to hold yourself together in the face of severe emotional
stress.

Don's description of the positioning of himself and the girl-friend in the
dream, as the diagram shows, had him in the centre, with the girl-friend
appearing in the four corners around him. This sort of squared circle is
typical of psychological mandalas, and, along with other information
gleaned from Don directly, indicates that he was, indeed, in a severe emotional crisis. The crisis intensified and not long after, he and the girl-friend
split up.

The division of Don's girl-friend into four persons surrounding him is a
very intriguing feature. I have already discussed anima figures several
times, and they reappear repeatedly in this book. If the girl-friend in the
dream image were a fictional character, we would find it easier to say that
Don's own femininity and his relation to the feminine world in general

(both inside and outside himself) were suffering from a serious split. The fact that the dream girl-friend is a real person, with whom he was having a relationship at the time of the dream image, complicates the matter considerably. What tends to happen in such a situation is that in 'only having eyes for' one person, the man tends to see everything he has experienced and fantasied about feminine figures in the one woman. She is not seen for herself at all, but only as a walking, talking embodiment of the man's fantasies. One intriguing piece of support for this conclusion is the fact that Don never called or spoke of his girl-friend by name, but used the rather curious nickname 'Lady' as a proper name.

If the girl-friend in the dream were an imaginary woman, it could be said that this dream image was asking him to consider his way of dealing with femininity, if he is to preserve his sanity. But what comes out of the fact that the girl-friend is a real woman is that he is attempting to hold himself together emotionally by seeing everything he knows and fantasises about women in her. This places an intolerable burden on the woman, because Don then sees in her everything negative as well as positive: he sees her as a promiscuous prostitute; a chaste nurturing madonna; a reincarnation of his mother who used to both boss and comfort him; highly intelligent but stupid; reliable but a liar; loving but cold; devoted to him but uninterested in him; and countless personal qualities that really feature in his own personality are attributed to her. What the dream image is trying to say, by expressing the mandala motif with the girl-friend as the circumference and himself in the middle, is 'You are self-centred, the woman is peripheral to you, and you see a number of different women in her. Your relationship is an illusion because all you see is her, but you never see her as she really is; and you are relying on her to keep you from falling apart'.

Obviously, it is not only a female figure who might serve in such a dream, but the girl-friend was the most important figure in his life at the time. There was a relationship going between Don and his girl-friend. But real people can turn up in a dream in a purely symbolic role, too, portraying different aspects of the dreamer's life and personal features. It is not always easy to know just what a particular person stands for in a given dream. Jung's rule of thumb is helpful here: if the people in a dream figure in the dreamer's actual relationships, they need to be taken as referring to the relationship. But if people from the distant past turn up, people with whom the dreamer has had no contact for a long time, they need to be examined for their symbolic significance as characterising parts of the dreamer's own personality. This does not mean, of course, that people from the past are always *only* symbolic; their lasting influence on the dreamer may be meant.

Let us examine how this works in practice, by looking at a dream from a middle-aged university teacher in the midst of arranging a divorce and also of delving into his personal history:

Leading a tour to Tasmania. I take a group up through the under-
graduate building to view the Acropolis of Hobart. A party starts, at
which drugs are to be taken. I leave and meet James S., who tells me
about the performance of his new Ford Cortina. I meet another
group, including Professor L. and Professor M., and start leading
them upstairs to join the rest of the group. They get into the two small
elevators to go up there, and there is no room left for me and a few
others, so we go up the stairs.

THOMAS O., #1

The references in this dream require a fair bit of explaining, and as we
look at each one, let us consider its relevance to Thomas' life.

Tasmania is an island located off the south-east coast of continental
Australia, and is one of the six States that form the Australian federation.
Thomas had been there at some time in his life, but it plays no particular
role in his life's history and experience. What might be noteworthy about
Tasmania for this dreamer is that it is an island, because an island plays a
very important role in a nightmare of Thomas', which we will look at in
detail in Chapter 5. When an island functions as a symbol in a dream, that
is, not as an important factor in the dreamer's life but as a symbolic representation of the dreamer's psychic state, it tends to refer to an isolation of
oneself from the mainstream of life. We are reminded of John Donne's
famous 'No Man Is an Island', meaning that no person exists isolated by
herself/himself.

The tour to Tasmania is also fictitious, of course. In reality, Thomas
does no such thing. But he takes a group to the capital city of Tasmania,
Hobart, to view the Acropolis there. Actually, of course, an Acropolis is an
ancient Greek building. This has a symbolic meaning in dream work,
because it has frequently been noted that ancient places and buildings
often appear in dreams to refer to 'ancient history' in a personal sense, that
is, events that took place long ago in the dreamer's own lifetime. It sometimes refers to infancy, more often to childhood, occasionally to matters
that took place in adult life but are now over and done with. As I said,
Thomas was engaged in studying his own family history, and so 'ancient
history' has a special meaning for him, as his ancestral roots and his personal history, especially in childhood.

Thomas is, then, retreating into himself to work out his own history and
experiences. Who the people are that form the group he is leading is not
stated, but we do learn that there is a party at which drugs are to be taken.
Thomas would regard this as reprehensible. But if we see the drugs as a
dream metaphor for loosening of inhibitions and less concern about saving
face, then the dream applies quite directly to him, for his social attitudes
and opinions are all-important to him. Uninhibited enjoyment of parties
and festivities are the furthest things from his conscious mind. In the

dream, he leaves the party the moment it starts, and begins to meet colleagues.

James is, in real life, a man whom Thomas knows primarily by correspondence. His chief distinction, at the time of Thomas' dream, is that he had just obtained a divorce, and had thus been through what Thomas is going through now. Thomas looks to James, at least in fantasy, as a person who can serve as a guide in this new, mysterious emotional realm, that of becoming single again. James has a new car, not a luxury car but a Ford, whose performance is apparently remarkable.

Here we again have a car appearing in a dream, but in quite a different context and with quite a different meaning. In Jane B.'s dream, discussed earlier in this chapter, the car belonged to the psychotherapist, Jack, and referred specifically to the way he was driving her into becoming emotionally flooded, though only a bit, an event that terrified her. In Thomas' dream, the car is a new car James has bought — an everyday type of car, with impressive performance. In this dream, James serves as a model for Thomas in regard to obtaining a divorce and living as a single man again. Jim has a new vehicle for moving through life. Here, a car represents a mode of travelling the road of life. Vehicles have often served in folk tradition to symbolise an attitude to life. Thus, the two major groups within Buddhism are popularly termed the Mahayana and the Hinayana, words that mean 'Greater vehicle' and 'Lesser vehicle', respectively. Again, the specific image 'car' has no fixed meaning, but must be interpreted in the light of the dream story. James represents the divorcing side in Thomas, and his new car, Thomas' prospective new means of moving through life.

After talking with James, Thomas meets another group, which includes the two professors of history, with whom Thomas has little or no real contact. They represent in his dream the activity of doing intensive research on the past. Once his divorce is finalised, Thomas is going to have a major task before him: to work out how and why his marriage failed so irrevocably, and this will require research into his own life history, not just his ancestral roots, but his personal history from childhood up to the present.

The professors are part of a different group, which Thomas meets on the lower floor of the university building and plans to lead to the upper storey where the party is going on. But it appears that, while it is possible to get most of the new group into the elevators, Thomas and some others have to use the stairs. There is no suggestion of waiting for the elevators to make a round trip and take them up as a second load. In other words, what appears to be easy for the professors of history is an upstairs climb for Thomas. As a variation on the idea of an uphill climb, this would indicate that Thomas is not going to find it easy going, to do his own historical researches into himself.

The most important keys to understanding this dream are the brief characterisation of the people in it and a linking up of these characterisations with the dreamer: 'James = newly divorced', 'professors = research into history'. When we also add 'Tasmania = island', we have the essential nature of the plot mapped out for us. This can be phrased as a series of symbolic equations: to view the heights (Acropolis) = to get above everyday life and see from above, get an over-view; a party with drugs = to lose inhibitions and fantasise; new Ford Cortina = new, popular way to travel the road of life; upstairs = imagination, fantasy (slang usage: 'upstairs' = the brain); elevator = getting a mechanical lift (metaphorically: to get a lift = to feel 'high', light-headed); climbing the stairs = going laboriously. But this is a mechanical way of going about things, and while not wrong, can miss the point for all the individual details.

One thing is left unexplained: what is the purpose of this dream? After all the symbol examination, what does it have to say that was not known before? In Chapter 4, we investigate the premise that 'a dream has a purpose', but it is worth asking this question now, in order to see Thomas' dream in a wider perspective than simple symbol interpretation allows.

If we replace the 'symbolic equations' with an 'I feel like' statement, we get a very interesting result:

I feel like:

>I am in charge of a tour of the University of Tasmania, where divorce and looking through history are the regular thing;
>there's a party going on that uses drugs, and I am not interested in that sort of thing;
>Jim tells me all about the new car he has bought, what a contrast to my old thing!;
>others can go up easily, but I really have to climb to get where I want to go.

The end of the dream, about going upstairs, is the climax to the dream, and can be approached as if the dream were a little drama with a definite structure: an initial statement, 'I lead a tour to the University of Tasmania'; a development, 'I leave the party and meet up with James S., Professor L. and Professor M.'; a climax: 'When I want to rejoin the group, there is no room left for me', and 'With some others, I have to go up the hard way, on foot'.

This way of viewing the dream has a great deal more emotional impact than the approach via mechanical symbol equations. It also brings out the movement in the dream story: 'I take a look and I see that, while others find it easy to "join the party", for me it's hard'. The really crucial symbol interpretation for the dream is the placing of the real people mentioned in a context that is relevant to Thomas' life, that is, Jim = divorce, and the professors = study of history.

Before we leave the question of symbolism and Thomas' dream, there is an interesting observation to make. This dream, in common with many others, has a cast of characters of four. We have looked at the use of the number four in several dreams previously. It is a frequent, though so far inexplicable, fact that when dreams wish to portray several parts of a single personality, they tend to split the characters into a set of four including the dreamer. While only a generalisation, when the dreamer is in context with three other persons in a dream, it usually refers to the unconscious and conscious aspects of the dreamer's psyche.

So, in this dream we meet four persons, including the dreamer, in order to say 'This dream is about your personality'. The ending of the dream portrays the feeling of being squeezed out and having to take the hard way up, that life in this respect is an uphill climb.

A real person from everyday life may also turn up in a dream, representing a major problem, or type of problem, which needs to be carefully considered. In illustration of this, let us look now at the dream of a young social worker:

> *I had an image of myself as a very good social worker. However, this woman (a young girl who works in a shop and who had previously been my client) came to my office and told me that nobody she knew would come and see me any more, because I don't understand other people's problems. She said that I am too concerned about my own image and not enough about my clients. She said that she felt that there were many people in my area who are starving and living in terrible conditions but that they would rather suffer anything than come to me for help. I suggested the girl discuss the matter with my supervisor as I was not prepared to discuss it with her. I left her to get my lunch. I was stunned and very hurt by what this girl had said. The shop that I went to for my lunch was run by Roland S. [the funeral director]. An old lady was served before me. She ordered a continental cake which cost her $1.00. I ordered an anchovy sandwich.*

> RONALD P., #1

In Chapter 6, we examine two other dreams of Ronald P., in the context of which some further aspects emerge that will, in retrospect, shed further light on this dream. But quite a bit can be said about it now.

There are three real people in the dream: Ronald, the shop girl and Roland S., the funeral director. There is one person who is purely a dream invention — the old lady who buys the cake (a cup-cake).

Although two of the people mentioned in this dream are real people with whom Ronald has had some contact, there is reason to take them both, along with the old lady, as symbolic. The girl who criticises Ronald so strongly in the dream did not do so in reality, nor did Ronald have any reason to expect she would. She is portrayed in the dream as a critical

voice, and as such, she makes some devastating criticisms that certainly require to be taken up at length with Ronald. But that he puts the criticisms
into the mouth of the girl-cashier who once consulted him makes us want
to examine his relations with women in some detail, a matter which is
given considerable support by the two dreams in Chapter 6. The funeral
director has still more reason to be taken symbolically, in that, though he is
a real person, he does not really run a lunch shop and has no particular
connection with Ronald.

We may take it that the girl represents not merely criticisms that have
been levelled at Ronald, but also reflects a kind of self-criticism. Traditionally, in depth psychology such self-criticism has come from the mouth
of an older person in the dream and traces back to the parents of the
dreamer, and has generally been called the super-ego. The concept of the
super-ego is a very valuable one, and I wish to retain it. In this instance, it
has been combined with the figure of a real-life younger girl from Ronald's
recent past experience, and represents a much deeper and penetrating
voice of criticism than is usually found in super-ego dream imagery. The
girl makes extremely sharp criticisms, about as strong as they could
possibly be: that Ronald does not understand other people's problems, is
more concerned with his own image than with other people, and people
would rather starve than seek help from him. Ronald is totally unprepared
for such devastating opposition, and refuses to speak with the girl, telling
her to talk to his supervisor instead. Wherever these self-doubts have come
from, they are global in their negativity and, one would think, represent a
tearing to shreds of himself by himself. Not so surprising, then, that he is
not only stunned but goes for his lunch to the funeral director's! As if the
bread of death was about all that was lacking to him.

It would be putting it too mildly to say that the girl represents Ronald's
doubts about his suitability to be a social worker, and the heavy burden he
feels in carrying the responsibilities of his job, but that is what it boils down
to. The burden he felt and his feeling of incapability had two sources: the
feeling of any professional person taking up a first position since becoming
qualified and being shouldered with responsibility for the life and health of
other people; and a very big chunk of feelings of inferiority, which have
little to do with the job and a lot to do with an overall sense of inferiority.
He has serious doubts about his qualification at all. Initially, he had applied to enter the social work programme of a local university, but failed to
get into its quota. Since he felt social work to be his true vocation, he
turned to the local Institute of Technology, which also has a social work
programme. In practice, the degree from the Institute of Technology is
more highly regarded in professional circles, since the university degree is
more theoretical and less oriented towards actual work qualifications. But
in terms of prestige, Ronald holds that a university degree is infinitely
superior to one from the Institute of Technology, precisely because it is

more philosophically oriented and less concerned with mundane things. Ronald's view of himself is that he is 'not good enough for a real degree' and, therefore, has only a second-rate degree from a second-rate institution, in his opinion.

The funeral director actually plays a double role in this context, even though it is only his lunch shop that appears rather than Roland S. himself. As said, it is a fitting climax to the tirade of the shop girl's that he goes to get his nourishment from an undertaker, an emotional feeling that all he is fit for now is death. But there is a prospective side to the image also: that it is time to put 'paid' to this particular kind of life. As the girl represents self-doubt and the sense of being unfit and unable to cope, so the funeral director represents the theme that this life must end, not literally but symbolically, e.g. by a deep reappraisal of the nature and conduct of his job, the differences between his expectations and the realities, and his conviction that he is less capable than others at meeting the needs of the job.

Of the old lady, we know almost nothing, merely that she is there before Ronald, and that she buys a cup-cake for $1.00. Ronald, in contrast to her, buys an anchovy sandwich. It is not evident in the dream what the significance of the two snacks is, but Ronald told me that he views the 'continental cake' (i.e. ornate, creamy cake) as bourgeois in contrast to the 'working class' anchovy sandwich. Ronald has strong leftist leanings, and for him, Marie Antoinette's famous 'Let them eat cake' is associated with the old lady in this dream.

We have, then, two types of symbolism used in this dream: one of the type discussed in Chapter 2, related to the subjective viewpoint in viewing the people in our dreams; and one that is of the more traditional type of symbolism concerned with the meaning of objects and imagery.

Ronald's dream probably had some reason in using the real girl to illustrate feelings of self-doubt and inferiority. Some of this might be ideological, that the shop girl represents the working class, while he has — in his view — sold out to the Establishment; he does feel a pang of resentment at the laws, rules and values he is expected to promote as a social worker employed by the social services division of the community. Others of his dreams, not discussed in this book, indicate not merely a resentment towards the Establishment, but a very strong pull towards the alternative society culture. He may have picked up some deprecation of the Establishment's values in the way the real girl treated him when she was his client.

Symbolically, she is an anima figure, representing the values he has had to suppress because of his job, and accusing his conscious self of not really heeding the needs of people. As we have seen in several dreams now, and will see further in other dreams, the anima figure is a classification, not a thing. In other words, an anima figure is a classification we give to female figures who in a dream conflict with the dreamer's conscious values and striving, while incorporating the dreamer's attitudes toward women and feminine values generally. What an anima figure represents is frequently not by any means negative, although the dreamer may well feel it as nega- tive because it represents precisely what the dreamer has eliminated from conscious goals and ideals. This may relate to sexual problems, and often does. Ronald's later dreams, which we look at in Chapter 6, indicate quite severe sexual maladjustment. But it extends beyond the realm of sexuality, as we generally conceive it, to the whole feminine world, which society has judged unsuitable for a man, or — increasingly — for a woman either.

Roland S., the funeral director, and the old lady who eats cake, are also symbolic figures: one representing the need for funeral rites to bring about the burying of old attitudes and values and the survival of life-fulfilling values; the other, the Establishment's values so beautifully summed up in the figure of Marie Antoinette and her disregard for the masses.

This is seeing the people in the dream as symbols, and quite often that is their role. The more traditional conception of symbols views symbols as objects, rather than people, that represent something: in this case, the cake and the sandwich, where the key to their meaning lies in Ronald's political ideology.

Perhaps the most frequent people to turn up in a person's dreams are the dreamer's parents and close relatives, rivalled perhaps by the dreamer's spouse and children. Generally, they too are symbolic, that is, they repre- sent attitudes and viewpoints absorbed by the dreamer from the real per- sons or the real situation with them in the past or present. Let us turn to another bewildering-looking dream to see how to make sense of it. It is another dream from John W., whom we last saw being consulted on men- struation, in the dream in Chapter 2.

> *It is going to be a birthday party for Grandmother (or perhaps it is Christmas) who is bed-ridden upstairs. Mother and I are arranging it, mostly Mother. She gets many Christmas decorations. One problem is gifts for Grandmother. One is to be a piano, how to get it upstairs, and I notice that, as an added complication, the stairs make a sharp turn half way, so I wonder about space for the piano. Another gift is a new fridge. How is that to be taken upstairs too? I suggest we call pro- fessional movers to do it, and Mother agrees.*
>
> *I go out and talk with a woman musicologist who is getting ready with her friends to go somewhere. I ask her about hearing frequen- cies, and she cites a book which I have already read, that implies that the power of suggestion greatly affects how we hear. I say, 'So it is just suggestion that makes me think that I hear a difference between a 16,000 hertz and a 14,000 hertz tape recording?' She says no, but seems not to answer the problem. She then says it is time to go and invites me, but I tell her I have a stage show to put on tonight.*

I go back downstairs. The inner doors are locked but open easily with the key(s) left in them. Inside, Mother says that she has finished the preparations. I say it looks beautiful, even though to me it looks like a mess and no better than when I left it earlier. She has also, I think, summoned the movers to move the piano and fridge upstairs for Grandmother.

JOHN W., #4

This very bewildering dream yields quite a bit of meaning, if we follow the procedures I have outlined earlier. The story-line is as follows:

1. A party is arranged for Grandmother upstairs.
2. Mother has the major task in preparing the party.
3. Worry about how to get the gifts, a piano and a fridge, up the stairs, and decision to use professional movers.
4. Conversation with musicologist about hearing frequencies.
5. John cannot go with the musicologist, because he has a stage show to put on tonight.
6. Mother says that she has finished the preparations.
7. The preparations don't look any different than before.

So the whole dream summarises into three dramatic scenes, a tendency that Jung noted long ago in regard to long dreams. They are:

Scene one: preparations for the party and worries about it.

Scene two: discussion with the musicologist.

Scene three: the original scene revisited, there seems to have been no change.

Clearly, the story-line and the schematic portrayal of the dream in three scenes are not enough to understand the dream, though they go a long way towards it. We need to look next at the people in the dream.

Grandmother: had actually been dead for some years before this dream. In the dream, she features solely as the recipient-to-be of a party.

Mother: was actually on her death bed at the time of the dream.

Musicologist: A personal friend of John's had, in fact, once exclaimed in reference to cassette decks that 16,000 hertz is beyond the range of hearing. It is this specific woman who appears in the dream. One important feature of hers, relevant to the dream, is a strong belief in life after death.

Yet again, we find an elaborate dream with a cast of characters of four. The symbolism of four people, as we noticed in earlier dreams, seems to be that the foursome represents the total personality of the dreamer, the other three characters representing attitudes, feelings or influences that colour the dreamer's personality.

Grandmother is, in reality, long dead. In the dream, she is still alive, but bed-ridden and the very heavy and elaborate gifts are to be carted upstairs. We may wonder at why a piano is chosen as a gift for the bed-ridden woman, though perhaps the fridge might be valuable in keeping food ready for her meals. The key to all this is that it is a death-dream. 'To go upstairs' = to die, in popular speech. The gifts then fall into place. It has been an age-old custom among virtually all peoples to include grave gifts along with the body of the deceased. This seems to have reached its peak in ancient Egypt, where all sorts of things were buried with the body, to serve the departed soul in the after-life. A piano for Grandmother's entertainment and a fridge for keeping her food is thoroughly in line with this tradition. I do not mean that John or his mother had any such conscious beliefs, but that the dream is expressing an ages-old theme of providing for the dead.

The mother, who is also actually on her own death bed, in the dream wants to hold a birthday, or more likely a Christmas party, for her deceased mother, and this involves 'going upstairs' (dying) also. A birthday represents the birth of an individual into this life. But Christmas is a symbol that celebrates the birth of a saviour who guarantees eternal life. As the dream proceeds, it becomes more and more apparent that a Christmas celebration is meant, in other words, a celebration of life beyond the grave, for which preparations are being made, not only for the (in reality, dead) grandmother but also for the dying mother.

In the first scene, the suggestion is made that professional movers should shift the piano and fridge upstairs. In the context of a death-dream, the movers would represent (some would say, symbolise) the undertaker and the minister/priest/rabbi who officiates at the funeral and burial, and — as popular speech has it — speeds the soul on its way. John is unwilling or unable to help shift the piano and fridge. The likelihood is that he is unable, since, in the dramatic context, he and his mother could hardly handle such massive objects. But he may also be unwilling. In reality, John, who was not at all fond of his grandmother, felt no concern at her death, and even told his grieving mother that he felt no particular need to send consolation cards to his grandmother's survivors, since he was feeling quite pissed-off at both of them.

The second scene, the episode with the musicologist, looks like an extraneous scene, hard to link up with the main currents of the dream, except in so far that musical frequencies and the piano to be shifted upstairs do seem related. Actually, though, this scene moves the dream drama onwards. The discussion in the dream is a quite realistic one, it could be a mundane report of a real conversation, except that it is not.

One discovery in working over many thousands of dreams is that the dreamer herself/himself generally reacts to the premises and basic events in the dream as in a similar situation in real life. It is, for all the world, as if the dream presents a situation and plot, realistic or not, and says to the dreamer's ego: what are you going to do, what are you going to say, what are you going to feel, in this situation? As we investigate dreams, we see that the dream-figure who represents the dreamer's waking ego uses judgment while interacting with the other characters in the dream. The essence of what I am saying is that the dreamer does not shut down conscious psychological functioning during dreaming, but that this functioning remains active, accepting the dream personnel and plot as the environment in which to interact.

The traditional statement, then, since Freud, that dreams are products of the unconscious, is not quite correct. Rather, dreams are a product of the interaction between the unconscious and the normal, waking self. This is one major reason why the investigation of dreams is so important, because the dreamer's unconscious is inter-relating with the dreamer's ego, bringing it new understanding and new perspectives. I am indebted to Alfred Adler for this viewpoint, although he phrased it differently.

John's discussion of hearing frequencies with his musicologist woman friend takes on meaning when we stop to think about it. The issue in the discussion is a fairly technical one. In music, the actual notes played have a fairly low sound-frequency, easily handled by cheap, non-precision instruments such as a portable transistor radio or cassette player. But each note played on an instrument sets off vibrations of a much greater sound frequency, and it is these 'overtones' that give the colour and flavour to music; it is their absence, which is the case with the portable machines, that makes the music lover shudder, because it is the musical equivalent of a black and white photo compared with a three-dimensional colour hologram. But hearing ability for the higher frequencies diminishes with age, so that, on the average, a late teenager may be able to hear frequencies of 20,000 hertz or more, which is beyond the range of virtually all commercial hi-fi systems; but by age thirty, the average listener's hearing ability has dropped to a maximum of about 12,000 to 14,000 hertz, which is well under the performance ability of true hi-fi equipment, and about the range of the average commercial hi-fi system. In this context, the dreamer asks a technical but quite meaningful question: 'Does that mean that when I claim I can tell the difference between 14,000 hertz and 16,000 hertz, I don't really and merely imagine that I do?'

If we transfer the discussion out of literal music and take the matter symbolically, it makes sense. If we take the discussion of hearing frequencies as representing the ability to hear the overtones of other persons' feelings, then the provision of a piano for the dream-grandmother would be the capacity to tune in to her feelings. In other words, for the mother in the

dream, the piano would be a movement of her emotional framework from
life in this world to the realm of the dead. Popular thought has regularly
attributed music-making to the dead, as in the image of angels playing
harps. John is confronted with the question: How far are you able to attune
yourself to your mother's and grandmother's emotional framework? Can
you go along with the musicologist who believes in life after death? Can you
tune to her feelings, or she to yours? In the dream, his answer is no, he cannot go along with her. But the reason he gives is somewhat odd: he has a
stage show to put on.

Stage shows and movies are very common dream motifs. They often
represent the dreaming process itself: the movie you watch or the play you
see and in which you act, during the night. From the context of this
dream, it would seem that the dramatised interaction of John and his
mother constitutes the stage show, for which John forgoes accompanying
the musicologist. This can be seen as the dream's attempt to force John to
come to grips with the emotional fact that his mother was dying, rather
than to continue theoretical discussions about death and dying.

The gist of this dream is, then, to attempt to make John face the fact of
his mother's impending death, and to accept that her preparations for it
are different from his own, and are her own responsibility.

The task of realising that every individual has her/his own responsibility
for facing the fact of death and preparing for it is difficult, but the end of
the dream indicates that, though to John it looks like his mother's preparations are a mess, and no better than when he last looked at them, she is
satisfied, it is her style and he has no call to judge it.

Discussion of this dream with John found a responsive chord when this
interpretation was offered. The emotional side of accepting his mother's
impending death, together with fears about his own eventual death (in the
dream, he is partly involved with the piano and fridge), stands out fore-
most. Like the tea-house dream discussed in Chapter 2, this dream is concerned with the question of death. But whereas the tea-house dream was
concerned with showing its dreamer, Margaret J., 'how to die', integrating
the rhythm of death and life, this dream is concerned with accepting the
dying mother's apparent unpreparedness for death — unprepared, that is,
from John's own point of view. All this made sense during the discussion.

From the topic of death, we will turn to life, and this involves some fairly
obvious sexual symbolism. The purpose of the following dream was not so
much to tell its dreamer something, but to inform me:

> *I dream I am sitting on a toilet. It is a primitive outside toilet and I
> can see the ground outside from under a big crack between the
> bottom of the floor and the door. A small snake crawls under the
> door. It looks a bit like a fish as well. Although I don't believe it is
> poisonous I nevertheless thrust it under the door with my foot. I feel a*

bit guilty as I do this. Then I see it dragged into an ants' nest. I look down into the nest and know that the snake will be eaten as I see a whole colony of white ants. There is a feeling of power that has no consciousness—nothing you can reason with—following the powerful drive of their instincts as they carry the snake away to be eaten.

MARILYN Q., #1

Marilyn told me this dream at her first session with me, but was not able to get very far with working on it. She failed to turn up for her second session, and for several months, I heard nothing from her. Then she unexpectedly made an appointment and told me, at the session, that the reason we had been unable to get anywhere with the dream was because she had been withholding a piece of vital information, namely that, at the time of the dream, she had been having an affair with a married man, and she was afraid her own marriage might break up. She had recognised the sexual theme of the dream and was afraid to follow it up at that time, for fear that I would disapprove of her actions. Now that the affair had ended, she felt safe enough to discuss it.

Let us look at the bits of the dream one at a time as they come:

I am sitting on a toilet. This is a primitive, outside toilet such as might be found at an old-fashioned farmhouse. Toilets have many connotations. 'To get the shit out' is an expression that means getting rid of a burden of guilt and shame. Toilets also have a sexual connotation. They are a very primitive aspect of sexuality; toilet jokes and curiosity about toilets fascinate children. We still usually segregate toilets for men and women in public places, sensing an uneasy sexuality about them. Both ideas coalesce in this dream, where sexuality and guilt are mixed. Dream toilets are also frequently an image for discussion of one's 'filth' with an analyst, so we should take note that this dream immediately preceded Marilyn's first consultation with me.

A small snake crawls under the door. It looks a bit like a fish as well. The snake is one of the most common animals to appear in dreams. In folk tradition, they are common as an image for unexpected danger (e.g. 'a snake in the grass'); for pure instinctuality; for sexual energy (the Kundalini snake); for wisdom and knowledge (good and bad alike, as in the story of the Garden of Eden); and most of all, for male sexuality, specifically the penis. Since Marilyn linked the snake up with sex, we can take it that the snake is a sexual image here. But why a snake instead of a straightforward sexual scene? Possibly because sex is portrayed as a potential danger. In her dream, Marilyn knows that the snake is not poisonous, but she pushes it out under the door anyway, just in case. It looks a bit like a fish as well. Fish are something doubtful; when something 'smells fishy', it means that there is an intuition that something is wrong. Marilyn does not view her sexual affair with the other man to be straightforward, she cannot come out into the open with it, it must remain hidden, and feel shitty and foul instead of enriching and spiritual, as it should be.

I nevertheless thrust it under the door with my foot. Since this dream was immediately before Marilyn's first session of analysis, and was, therefore, so to speak, dreamed for me—and since we know that, in the actual session, she brought up the dream but avoided discussing what she knew to be its antecedents—the kicking of the snake back under the door may reflect her resolution to hide the sexual affair from me. This is cogent if we accept the common use of the image of sitting on a toilet as referring to the analysis session. In this respect, we should take note that Marilyn was by no means unfamiliar with analysis and its demands. She had consulted another analyst in the past, and a subsequent dream of hers, which we examine in Chapter 4, is concerned with her divided loyalties between the previous analyst and me.

Then I see it dragged into an ants' nest. The ants, or rather termites as they turned out to be, are said to be acting purely by instinct, devoid of all reason and consciousness. Instead of bringing the sexual affair out into the open and discussing it honestly, it is kicked back under the door and delivered totally into the hands of blind, instinctual force, which is designated by the dream as like termites, destructive creatures that destroy the fabric of a dwelling from the inside, leaving an appearance of strength and firmness to the woodwork that collapses about as soon as it is touched. Though the snake is said to be probably harmless, this is not true of the termites. Instead of being brought into the open for discussion and integration into her understanding of herself and her life as a whole, Marilyn's 'secret' was left to decay and destruction in the world of instinctual acting out of impulses that can eat away the fabric of life without even being noticed.

In dealing with this dream, I have followed fairly closely the symbol world of its dreamer. Marilyn's own study of symbolism had influenced the imagery used by the dream. The symbol interpretation used in this discussion is partly derived from her own concept that snake = penis, corroborated by the frequent use of the snake in Australian folklore to represent the penis, especially in Aboriginal folklore and ritual. The equation that sitting on the toilet = bringing out 'filth' in an analysis session is based on my own observation of the use of toilets in dreams of patients. Neither of these symbol interpretations can be generalised. For instance, a snake may represent many different things, depending on the cultural background of the dreamer, while a toilet pretty certainly means something different to a person who is not discussing personal matters with an analyst.

Having looked at the symbolism, let us go back and rephrase the dream into an 'I feel like' statement:

I feel like:

> I am sitting on a toilet, getting the shit out;
> I see a snake crawl in under the door;
> though it isn't poisonous, I want to shoe it away;
> I am guilty when I do this;
> I can see the snake being destroyed by termites;
> termites act by blind, instinctual force;
> they have a power without consciousness.

This 'I feel like' statement is intelligible once the symbol equations have been made that snake = penis, and toilet = analytical session. When dealing with a rather bewildering dream such as Marilyn's first appeared, it is helpful to rephrase it into an 'I feel like' statement, and then to understand what the key images mean. Generally speaking, the dreamer herself/ himself must provide the basic information that makes sense of those key images.

Since there are no fixed symbols, with every dream you must look at the imagery afresh. Usually, the dreamer has an intuition of what the dream is related to, and this can provide a starting point. Even when the dreamer has no intuition of what the dream is all about, she/he will almost always have something to say about individual images within the dream, and these can lead to a wider discussion. Symbolism need not always be sexual. On the contrary, any important facet of the dreamer's life may be the subject of symbolism. Let us look at another apparently 'difficult' dream to see how this can work.

> *A bicycle trip in Britain? Going to an English town. I want to go on a gondola trip from one part of the town to the other—this involves changing from the upper to lower level of a river. The trip starts with gondolas moored inside a kind of cage. The town is an old walled town and I know it well.*
>
> *Later I am going down an English country lane with a guide. There is very rich farmland all around (red earth) with strange cattle in the fields (buffaloes?) and which sometimes block the lane. A train comes and goes across a level crossing, making me jump and just missing me. I remark how Australia is not fertile like these fields. I am aware of being in a specially well-known fertile part of England. I also wonder if the farms are still small or if they are now combined into large efficient holdings.*
>
> ROGER H., #2

Roger is originally from England, though he has been living in Australia for many years. This dream, like the one we just discussed, was brought to me in the first consultation. Dreams in this circumstance usually reflect the dreamer's anticipations about what will emerge from the consultations. Generally, this is because the analyst is consulted because of some major emotional crisis, and the approach to that crisis is one that has been under way for quite some time, and hopes about what the analyst will do about it, or fears about what the analyst will feel about it, permeate the dreamer's mind. This calls forth a dream that is concerned with the very important new event, namely the discussion with the analyst. Obviously, the same is true in any situation where a great deal of emotion has accumulated and some major new step is about to be undertaken. One of the very important goals in working with such dreams is to come to an understanding of what they are saying, because they do not merely reflect what is already known, but have something to be communicated that is important for the dreamer, and in this case, the analyst, to know.

In Roger's dream, the English countryside is imaginary, though it is based on various bits of England with which Roger is familiar. The dream tells him to look at his English roots. To a certain extent, this will be a solitary excursion (as indicated by the bicycle and gondola), though there is also provision for a guide. This guide is probably the analyst, who will be expected to do more than merely show an interest in the English roots, he will be expected to guide Roger through his feeling-memories that come from England. I am making this interpretation partly on the basis of the imagery in the dream and the situation, but also partly on the basis of later dreams that Roger brought, in which English memories featured heavily along with imaginary English scenes.

The dream is concerned that the dreamer get in touch with his English past. He, in turn, remarks in the dream on how much more fertile the English fields are than the Australian. This reflects his conscious conviction that the Australian countryside feels alien to his soul, in contrast to the English countryside where he grew up. It also says that Roger's English background will prove a more fertile area to explore than his Australian life to which he moved as an adult.

This is the gist of the dream. Now we can begin looking at individual images more closely:

The bicycle: We have already looked at the use of the image of a bicycle in Carl's dream earlier in this chapter, and some of the same comments apply here. A bicycle is a vehicle that is powered by the rider, just as a gondola is, in contrast to a car. The exploration of England that is to be undertaken is one that depends on Roger's own motive power. This has some meaning, because Roger might legitimately expect that what needs to be investigated is his life now, and the dream is saying that his British past is the terrain in which to get started. Since I could hardly act as a guide without knowing the details of this English past, the first parts of the journey depend on Roger's own individual observations and memories.

The image of a journey, and, more specifically, a journey on water, is one of the most frequent images in dreams to indicate an exploration of the unknown, whether some new field of interest or work of the dreamer, or the discovery and mapping of the inner self. Indeed, a person's narrative of her/his life sounds to the listener like a sort of travelogue, and this has caught the attention of many people. Bunyan's *Pilgrim's Progress* uses the image of a journey to portray the exploration of one's own soul, a fact that led to the use of the title *Journey Into Self* for Esther Harding's memorable commentary on Bunyan's book. In our present dream, the journey is to begin as a solitary one, though soon to be joined by a guide.

The goldola trip is reminiscent of Venice, a city that is slipping below sea level. The journey on water is still a favourite image in modern people's dreams as it has been for thousands of years. Water voyages can be dangerous and require a great deal of skill if the boat is a small one. There is the ever-present danger of capsising. Fortunately, there is no hint of disaster in Roger's dream, but difficulties are encountered: the need to change river levels and the task of getting the gondola out of the cage. Changing river levels could mean going from one level of feeling-memories to another; following the flow of feeling-memories from a superficial $=$ (upper level) to a deeper level. Even to get started, the barriers ($=$ cage) that we build around our painful memories of the past have to be opened.

The walled town: Since the dream is concerned with a look at the English countryside, the fact that the trip through England begins with an exploration of a walled town very familiar to the dreamer (though a dream town, not a real town that he knows) implies that the walled town is an image for Roger's personality itself. I have already mentioned the use of the biblical New Jerusalem to represent the dreamer's own personality. The image lives on in modern folk feeling as well. Roger has built a wall around himself, as have we all, to defend himself against intrusion. We are reminded of Pink Floyd's highly successful *The Wall.* This core of Roger's personality has to be explored before the surroundings, i.e. events and experiences, can be examined with the aid of a guide.

The guide: Now the guide joins Roger, once Roger is out of the walled city. The whole point of coming into analysis was to get the services of a guide for the journey of inner discovery. The guide would be any person to whom Roger turned for help — in this case, me. The English land is said to be very fertile, much more than in Australia.

The land: This is the fertile soil in which crops grow. Roger's life when he had this dream felt stagnant; worse, it felt stifling. The dream directs him back to the past to a time when life was more productive, more fertile.

The train: In marked contrast to the bicycle that began the dream, the train is highly impersonal, and Roger is not in it. A train is a social vehicle, and one that presents imminent danger in the dream. To be more precise, it refers to an event in Roger's life in England in which he was severely threatened by events and personality responses that might have led to death. (These were referred to in later dreams.)

The farms: Life comes to us bit by bit; it is only through memory that we connect up the bits into large wholes. Here, the dream presents the questions: is the English background to emerge as a mess of unco-ordinated memories and feelings, or is there some amalgamation of these that can form areas that can profitably be made use of? In other words, are the memories to be discovered merely to be bits and pieces, useful only for uncovering the past, or are they a fertile part of the dreamer's personality, able to serve for new growth and spiritual nourishment? Many people think that dwelling on the past is of little benefit. The question is raised in this dream whether examining the past may make life more fruitful.

In this dream, as with most, the specific imagery used is employed to support the story-line and to serve as a vehicle for what the dream is trying to express. To begin the consideration of the dream with the individual images runs the risk of losing the thread of the story, and it is this thread that we must grasp in order to understand the dream's meaning. Thus, it is pointless to ask a general question such as 'What does a bicycle mean in dreams?', or 'What does a gondola mean in dreams?', and the like. On the one hand, a bicycle or a gondola or whatever other image has no special meaning in dreams different from what it means in waking life. To the question 'What does a bicycle mean in dreams?', the answer must be, 'Well, what does a bicycle mean in ordinary life?' and, most of all, 'What does a bicycle mean to you (the dreamer)?'. For one person, as in this specific dream of Roger's, it may mean a vehicle used during youth. For another, it may be a vehicle used for fitness. For another, it may be a vehicle used for economy and to conserve the world's energy supplies. For another, it may be a vehicle that requires much personal energy to keep going. For another, it may mean recreation. For yet another, as also in this dream, it may mean solitary travel. All of this points to the fact that there can be no fixed meaning to which a dream image refers, it must always be investigated in the context of the individual dream and the dreamer's own personal life.

Yet, it remains true that some imagery is so familiar to us through metaphors, common experience or expression, that it needs little or no explanation, and sometimes loses its flavour when explained.

We need to link up what we have found with the ideas of Freud and Jung mentioned at the start of this chapter. In *The Interpretation of Dreams*, Freud devotes a great deal of attention to sexual symbolism. Eventually, this has lead to the compilation of lists of sexual symbols that, in general, can be divided into male symbols (referring to the penis and/or testicles) and female symbols (relating to the breasts, labia, vagina and/or uterus), and images for sexual intercourse. Quite often, in order to cut short the lengthy process of examining the content of a dream, people will jump directly to interpreting the images as sexual symbols. In so doing, they are overlooking Freud's point that the 'universal symbols' that he is discussing are a supplement to the thought and memories that a dreamer has of the particular images that turn up in the dream, and that personal associations to these images must take first place. Sexual symbols are real, though not as frequent as some interpreters would have us believe. It is not a matter of being opposed to or in favour of sexual interpretations, it is a matter of using sexual interpretations when they are appropriate, which they often are, as I hope to have shown, and discuss further in Chapter 6.

Jung introduced the concept of archetypes, which are patterns of thought or imagery basic to all of humanity because of the identical brain structure and nervous system that we all share. These patterns of thought are filled out by means of imagery taken from our personal experience. Thus, we do not find archetypes in a dream, but archetypal images, which means imagery taken from our personal life used to express universal themes. Archetypes are the 'mental' side of instincts, in the sense that instincts are patterns of action, while archetypes are patterns of imagery or thought. When some basic instinctual pattern is seriously disturbed or interrupted, dreams occur, which bring up images of this disturbance, and which have the goal of restoring mental equilibrium and wholeness to the psyche. Very frequently, these images portray sexual processes, since that is one area in which most people are disturbed at one time or another.

Archetypal dreams, that is, dreams that emphasise archetypal imagery, are relatively rare. They turn up most frequently in cases where there is some mental or emotional disorder at a very basic level. That is, an archetypal dream comes at times of severe emotional stress, and also in persons threatened by mental illness or suffering from it.

To illustrate this aspect of dreams, I will give one example, which comes from a young man, unmarried, who had undergone very powerful psychological disturbances:

I can't remember the first part of this dream, but I was called away from the activity there and made a long journey through the forest and across a river and into a hilly wooded area, where at last I came to an inn. It seems the time period was that of the American revolution and I was participating in it. In the main room of the inn were a

*number of men arguing and organised for some activity. I stepped
into the back room to get pistols and clubs to distribute, where I see a
snake with wings which I know to be very dangerous and poisonous. It
was a putrid green colour and vicious. But it held back from striking
me since I had the weapons in my hand. It actually followed me into
the main room but no one seemed to notice it. I didn't want to alarm
others about it and felt it was my responsibility to deal with it. I felt
the weapon to kill it with was a club which looked somewhat like it.
The snake was outstanding for its large number of teeth and its ability
to shrink to an invisible size and fly through the air. I left the inn
knowing it would follow me invisibly, waiting for my alertness to
slacken, when it would regain its full size and strike. I walked away
carrying the club in my hand, knowing I had to keep attentive to its
unseen presence for it could appear at any time.*

PETER R., #1

This dream is strikingly different from the others that we have looked at
so far. There is something of a fairy-tale quality to it. It is not just the
images that turn up in the dream — they have obviously been strongly influenced by childhood fairy-tales, American history and tradition, and, not
least, by very intensive reading in symbolism, particularly the works of
Erich Neumann. But when we discount the sources from which the specific
images were taken, we are left with a dream core that is palpably different
and unusual. Let us look at the dream story first:

1. Peter travels through forest, river and woods to an inn.
2. He is part of the American revolution.
3. He goes for weapons into the back room.
4. He sees a poisonous, repulsive, winged snake.
5. The snake follows him.
6. The weapon to kill the snake is similar to the snake in shape.
7. The snake can become invisible.
8. He must be ever alert, since the snake may strike at any time.

This, again, is an 'initial dream', that is, one that Peter brought with
him to his first consultation with me. It was a communication to me, in the
sense of informing me about his inner state.

We must investigate this dream as we have the others, though the
imagery in it is decidedly peculiar. There is quite a bit to be said about
most of the images, but we will limit ourselves here to the major motifs.

First, this is a somewhat unusual dream in that only Peter plays a role in
it, along with the winged green snake. Other people are mentioned, but
only in passing, they are merely something of a backdrop for the drama.
The time is, however, specially significant. It is the time of the American

revolution. We must take this dream from the subjective viewpoint, since there are no references to people or places or events in Peter's current life. This does not mean that the dream has no connection with outside events, but that it concerns Peter's state of mind in his relating to outside events. Peter is American, so the American revolution is, for him, his own war for independence. American history is pressed into service to express Peter's experiences and development. Another American image is alluded to in the opening lines of the dream, though not explicitly: 'Over the river and through the woods . . .'. The popular Thanksgiving song is put into visual imagery. The two momentous events of early American history, commemorated by the national symbols of Thanksgiving Day and Independence Day, form the setting for the dream. Its theme, consequently, is the achievement of freedom and independence. But it is not a peaceful scene, it is one of turmoil. Peter, we can be pretty sure, had been experiencing a lot of turmoil.

In the back room of the inn, there is a winged snake that is dangerous and poisonous, and of a putrid green colour. This is an archetypal image, or, rather, two archetypal images. The back room in a building, or sometimes a cave behind a main cave, is one such image. For the purpose of the interpretation of this dream, we can say that Peter is investigating the background to his personality. As mentioned earlier, houses and rooms often refer to the dreamer's own person. Here, in the deep background, behind the scenes, as it were, are the weapons needed to fight the battle for independence, and the deadly danger also involved.

First, of course, we need to ask what it is independence from. The answer, for Peter, is independence from his mother or, more generally, from his family. Just as the American War of Independence was for the purpose of setting up a new nation answerable to itself, so Peter's war of independence is for the purpose of establishing himself in adult life as an individual answerable to himself. In more detail, it emerged during discussion that this involved the establishing of relationships separate from the patterns that Peter's parents had set, and the working out of a relationship with a woman was, of course, a major part of the problem.

The winged snake is an image frequently found in use throughout the world in myths, folklore, religious devotion and simple decoration. Two examples will suffice as an illustration of this: Quetzalcóatl, the Aztec Indian god, who, according to Aztec myth, brought culture to the Aztecs and then eventually set sail off to the west. The name Quetzalcóatl means literally 'feathered serpent'. The other example is the Rainbow Serpent, found all through the continent of Australia among Australian Aboriginal folklore. The Rainbow Serpent is winged, like Quetzalcóatl, and the religious ceremonies concerning the Rainbow Serpent, conducted at the time when boys are initiated into adulthood, are among the most sacred Aboriginal rituals.

Peter was familiar with both the Aztec and the Australian winged serpent lore, and many other bits of folklore containing this motif. Consequently, his dream had at its command a rich mine of material from which to draw its imagery.

Peter drew two little pictures of the snake and of the club that he used to defend himself from the snake, and they are very reminiscent of pictures of a winged penis, a picture with which Peter was familiar. (A picture and a detailed discussion of the winged penis and its psycho-sexual meaning is to be found in volume 4 of C. G. Jung's *Collected Works*, ¶507.) If we put the two motifs together, the winged serpent and the winged penis, the threat to Peter that this dream portrays is an emotional one, the necessity to be able to withstand the threat to independence posed by his still too-close involvement with his parents, and the task of achieving a satisfying sexual life.

Snakes of the non-winged variety are a very widespread motif in folklore and folk practice. We have already seen their use in Marilyn Q.'s dream earlier in this chapter, where the snake was a simple, innocuous creature that Marilyn did not want to examine with me, representing her sexual relationships. For many people, snake simply means 'danger!' and certainly the danger element is found in Peter's dream image, for the snake is described as poisonous and a constant threat. Peter was also well acquainted with the lore of the Kundalini Serpent, a yoga motif concerned with changing levels of sexual energy. He was also familiar with Jung's suggestion that snakes can represent the autonomic nervous system, and that the appearance of a snake such as this one means impending danger of a psychiatric nature. Depending on which aspect we wish to focus on, all four of these themes are valid in the interpretation of Peter's dream.

The widespread use of (winged) serpent images is testimony to how basic a symbol it is. Peter's dream has availed itself of this basic symbol because it has something vital to convey to Peter and also to me: that when the hinter realms of Peter's personality are entered into, basic instinctual disturbances of a sexual nature are aroused after lying latent in the background.

There are, of course, many other images that could have been used instead of the winged serpent. This particular image was presumably used both because Peter was so familiar with it, and because it has a special nuance that other images would lack. In what sense, then, is the image of the winged serpent 'archetypal'? To call it archetypal is to say that this particular world-wide image is so extensively used because it conveys something of a basic instinctual nature in a unique way that could not be imaged with quite the same emotional flavour by any other image. For a full discussion of this, I refer the reader to Jung's discussion, as previously cited.

In very brief summary, it could be said that the special nuance of the image of the winged serpent is that it is at the same time spiritual, evidenced by the wings, and sexual, imaged by the penis parallel. The same image, i.e. the winged serpent, manages to cram together several themes at one time: the spiritual yet thoroughly sexual and frighteningly dangerous aspect of the penis, and, more widely, of male sexuality. The sexual urge is instinctual, and in so far as it is conceived of by the mind, it is archetypal. In other words, any image used to represent sexuality is archetypal. In what sense can the penis and sexual intercourse be called spiritual? Strangely, to most people, the religious cult of the penis was very widespread in the classical ancient cultures, e.g. Priapus, the figures of Hermes, and of course the lingam in India. The basic point is that 'spiritual' in a non-theological meaning refers to being in contact with the natural energies within oneself, in tune with one's own basic innermost nature. As for many religious traditions, 'God' is the term used for the innermost depths of the soul, so 'spiritual' refers to a relationship with these innermost depths, and sexuality is a part of those depths. In the Jewish and Christian traditions, this is expressed by God's command to newly created mankind: 'Be fruitful, multiply, fill the earth . . .' (Genesis 1: 28, *Jerusalem Bible*). This appeal to the religious importance of sexuality is particularly appropriate to Peter, who, having been brought up in a highly conservative Roman Catholic family, tended to think of spirit and sex as opposites, rather than closely connected.

Peter gathers up weapons to fight the winged snake with, and finally settles on a sort of homoeopathic weapon, a spiked club that resembles the snake. He realises that the snake may reappear any time, without warning, and he must always be on the alert for it. Because of Peter's previous experiences of psychiatric disturbance, it is inevitable to think of this winged serpent as representing an ever-present instinctual threat to his emotional balance and security. Unlike the harmless snake in Marilyn Q.'s toilet dream, Peter's snake is described as very dangerous and poisonous. We can see in it the possibility of being flooded by instinctual urges beyond his control; on the one hand, ineptitude in forming sexually-based human relationships, because of a serious sexual disturbance that undoubtedly has its roots in Peter's relationship with his parents.

These suggestions are, of course, going beyond the actual dream text at this point. They are a reading back between the lines of the dream of much that was discovered at later times from discussion with Peter about his life and his dreams. We have a very good opportunity to test out the validity of this 'reading between the lines' because the whole of Chapter 7 in this book is devoted to a series of Peter's dreams and their discussion.

Archetypal imagery, then, is characterised by a strange folkloric or fairy-tale-like, mythic flavour. It inevitably turns out to be a gripping type of imagery that has been found at all times and places. The specifics of the imagery — the details — vary from person to person, culture to culture, but the underlying instinctual theme remains constant.

It has often been asked whether there may be dream symbols that do not
come from the individual dreamer's experiences, but with which we are
born, that come from an innate stratum of imagery in the human personality. The answer to this is extremely difficult to give. It is known that
some, perhaps many, other animal species recognise images in a way that is
inborn. Thus, many bird species have an inborn ability to navigate by the
stars or by the position of the sun, and so do bees, implying that the image
of the star configurations and of the sun are present as inherited mental
images in those species. There is evidence that some, or most, primates in-
stinctively recognise a snake, even when they have been brought up in cap-
tivity and have never previously seen a snake. The evidence points strongly
to the likelihood that some images of the natural world are inborn in us
also, a product of evolution just as with other animal species. But this is
very difficult to prove.

Nevertheless, there are dreams that appear to use elements that are outside the realm of folklore, popular speech and other learned or experienced imagery, and which appear spontaneously and independently
among quite unconnected people. We have already seen the theme of finding a treasure under water, and it was promised that we would find the
theme of extraordinary things being unearthed. One such dream comes
from the religious pioneer George Fox, recorded in his *Journal* near the
middle of the year 1671:

> *And I had a vision that I had about the time that I was in this travail
> and sufferings, that I was walking in the fields and many Friends [i.e.
> Quakers] were with me, and I bid them dig in the earth and they did
> and I went down. And there was a mighty vault top-full of people kept
> under the earth, rocks, and stones. So I bid them break open the earth
> and let all the people out, and they did, and all the people came forth
> to liberty; and it was a mighty place. And when they had done I went
> on and bid them dig again. They did and there was a mighty vault full
> of people, and I bid them throw it down and let all the people out,
> and so they did.*
>
> *And I went on again and bid them dig again, and Friends said unto
> me, 'George, thou finds out all things,' and so there they digged, and I
> went down, and went along the vault; and there sat a woman in white
> looking at time how it passed away. And there followed me a woman
> down in the vault, in which vault was the treasure; and so she layed
> her hand on the treasure on my left hand and then time whisked on
> apace; but I clapped my hand on her and said, 'Touch not the
> treasure.' And then time passed not so swift.*

The Journal of George Fox.
Cambridge University Press, 1952, p. 578.

There is an uncanny resemblance between Fox's 'vision' and a spontaneous dream of Margaret J., whose tea-house dream provided much food for thought in Chapter 2. I will present her dream here, to illustrate the role of archetypes, but general discussion of the dream is reserved for the next chapter:

> *I was again at the temple in Memphis [Egypt]. There was a beautiful mosque with a key-shaped door. I was told to enter. Inside was a finely decorated black box buried in sand. A beautiful woman was sitting by it with a jar.*

MARGARET J., #2

In Fox's vision, there are three levels under the surface of the earth: a vault totally filled with people, covered by the earth, rocks and stones. After these people are released, digging recommences, only to uncover a second vault equally filled with people, who are similarly released. Finally, a third vault is unearthed that holds the treasure. A woman in white watches the passage of time, while another woman places her hand on the treasure, which Fox then forbids. This vision contains various motifs akin to those in folklore, but in such a way that it gives the tingling sensation of seeing a myth created before our very eyes.

The three vaults under the earth capture our attention. The nearest relative to this theme that I know of is the emergence myths of the American Indians, though in those myths, the theme is quite different. In the emergence myths, people are created far beneath the ground, then ascend, level by level, until they reach the earth's surface.

Something that seems very close to the imagery of Fox's vision is some modern postulates about the structure of the mind. Freud distinguished two layers below the conscious surface of the mind: the unconscious, which has an upper level of repressions; and a lower level, the id, which consists of the instincts and hereditarily acquired instinctual patterns. Jung used a three-part image that comes closer to Fox's: below the conscious surface of the mind lies the personal unconscious, which, as Fox's vision puts it, is chock-full of 'people', i.e. complexes that act independently in the unconscious, and, as we have seen frequently now, appear as people in our dreams. The second, lower layer he terms the collective unconscious, the hereditarily-transmitted realm of instinctual patterns that also tend to become personified in dreams, art, myths and doctrines, etc. A third, central layer is the self, the centre of one's individuality and uniqueness, often called the 'soul' by religious adherents, and often symbolised as a buried treasure.

In myths, literature, folklore and dreams, as well as in many religious customs, especially among the so-called 'primitive' peoples, there is a guide who leads the searcher to the treasure. In Fox's vision, however, the woman who accompanies him follows him instead of leading. In both Fox's vision and Margaret J.'s dream, there is a sort of guardian of the treasure, a motif also familiar in myths and folklore.

So it is not unexpected that Fox should see a woman, even two women, associated with the hidden treasure, for Fox was a mystic, and the realm of the inner world meant more for him than all the realms of the world around it.

It is intriguing that Fox should have two women in his vision, one in white who is watching how time passes, and one who touches the treasure, her touch determining how fast or slow time passes. The woman in white who watches the passage of time has a place in Plato (*The Republic* 617c). The other woman is more uniquely Fox's experience.

Yet, though we can find parallels to the motifs in Fox's vision, the whole is something uniquely Foxian. There is something special about this vision, in which Fox discovers and then protects his innermost treasure of the soul.

Much could be said to explain the background of Fox's vision. About two years earlier, in 1669, at the age of forty-five, Fox had married Margaret Fell. Does the vision imply a fear that a woman in his life might enter into him so far as to threaten his soul?

Deep dreams of this sort are not uncommon among people in their late thirties and forties. They belong to the 'mid-life crisis', meaning a breakdown in one's sense of values and goals, a questioning of the meaning of life, and sometimes a discovery of new meaning and value within oneself.

The vision of discovering buried treasure means discovery of the great value that lies hidden in the depths of one's own soul. Often, the mid-life crisis comes because there has been no recognition or awareness of this deeply hidden value. The 'treasure' is usually not something to be shared with the rest of the world indiscriminately, but with only a close few, if any at all. It is interesting to read what Fox himself had to say about his vision:

> *They that can read these things must have the earthy, stony nature off them. And see how the stones and the earth came upon man since the beginning, since he fell from the image of God and righteousness and holiness. And much I could speak of these things, but I leave them to the right eye and reader to see and read.*

In Margaret J.'s dream of the mosque, there is a similarity that strikes us as almost uncanny, not because it is similar to Fox's vision in any detail, but because similar motifs have been picked up and arranged. These motifs are archetypal. They become expressed in their own unique way in each dream. In Margaret's dream, we begin with a sacred ancient building, an ancient Egyptian temple, and we may easily understand this to be something that is far off in time as well as space. It is similar to Fox's third vault, the lowest in the earth in this respect, i.e. remoteness. In the temple,

though, is a mosque—something a great deal more modern than ancient
Egyptian temples, yet still remote in time and space and culture. To enter,
she must go through a key-shaped door, which is a fairly frequent archetypal image. It is called the image of rebirth. A similar image is frequent in
sexual slang: fitting a key into a lock = placing a penis in a vagina. In
sexual imagery, to go through a door into the holy room = to enter the
vagina or uterus, a reverse of the birth process. Mystics have long used this
image to express their idea of being reborn new. It has a biblical prece-
dent:

Jesus answered:
I tell you most solemnly,
unless a man is born again
he cannot see the kingdom of God.

Nicodemus said:
How can a grown man be born? Can he go back into his mother's
womb and be born again?

Jesus said:
What is born of the flesh is flesh;
what is born of the spirit is spirit.
Do not be surprised when I say:
You must be born again.

JOHN 2: 3–7,
Jerusalem Bible.

The imagery used by mystics as well as very frequently in dreams is that
spoken by Nicodemus in the dialogue: '. . . go back into his mother's womb
and be born again'.

Having entered the mosque through the key-shaped door, Margaret sees
a beautifully decorated black box buried in the sand and a beautiful
woman seated beside it. There, the parallel ends, though we shall see a
subsequent dream of Margaret's in the next chapter, and also return to this
one. But this wooden box is a treasure unique: in her discussion of it, she
named it as the Ka'aba, the most holy object in all of Muslim faith. The
most holy of holies is her treasure, and connected with this, as in Fox's
vision, is a woman. Who can this woman be? Like the woman beside the
child in the dream of the ship's curtain, this woman is a part of Margaret's
and Fox's innermost self, sitting by what marks, for them, the presence of
God. In religious terms, the treasure is the depths of the soul.

The need for such contact with the innermost depths can come in very
ordinary-looking imagery as well. A young man who could as yet see no
very bright perspectives for the future of himself and of his wife, dreamed

of an empty salt-shaker on the table. I involuntarily commented, 'So the spice has gone out of your life'. This sums up his particular outlook as it was at the moment: the feeling of having to give up long-hoped-for plans and goals because of the practical realities of gaining a living to support himself and his family. This realisation really hurt.

In the Bible, Jesus comments in the context of not doing one's best, 'You are the salt of the earth. But if salt becomes tasteless, what can make it salty again? It is good for nothing and can only be thrown out ...' (Mat. 5: 13, *Jerusalem Bible*). Flavourless salt, missing salt, where is the spice of life to be found? This is the question posed by the dream.

SYMBOL, IMAGE OR DESCRIPTION

There has been a lot of confusion among dream workers as to the use of the word 'symbol'. In this book, 'symbol' and 'image' have tended to be used interchangeably, meaning an allusion made by a dream without specifying or describing it directly. There may be numerous reasons why this should occur. It may be well to review some of the principal reasons here:

1. As in everyday conversation, the dreamer may find it rude or unacceptable to make direct reference to some matter, even in dream-thought.
   When this is particularly strong, it is known as repression. The same
   dreamer may find direct expression acceptable in some contexts but
   not others. Sometimes, it needs to be kept in mind that the wording
   used by a dreamer in re-telling a dream may have been edited or
   altered.

2. Everyday speech uses many euphemisms, particularly for sexual
   matters and also death. It is likely that the dreams of a person accustomed to using such euphemisms will employ them also: e.g. 'to sleep
   with' has become such a common euphemism for sexual intercourse,
   that a dream may use sleeping together for the same meaning. 'To put
   to sleep' = 'to kill' may be similarly used.

3. As in poetry and drama, an image may convey extra flavour and connotations that are lacking in a direct statement.

Chapter Four

A DREAM HAS A PURPOSE

Dreams have a purpose. They are not mere mechanical reactions to daily living, or pure repetition of emotional traumas of the past or present. Reactions to events of the day certainly appear in dreams, as do the emotional effects of past or present disturbances, but to focus exclusively on these aspects brings about a blindness to the fact that the dreams are communicating something important for the dreamer's psychic equilibrium and well-being. They often serve as a corrective when the dreamer is embarked on a course that is detrimental to well-being. Cumulatively, they bring out a direction that the dreamer needs to take. Even nightmares have a positive goal, as we will see in Chapter 5.

The question of whether it is possible to influence our dreams often arises. It certainly is possible to influence the content of our dreams. For that matter, whenever we look closely at a dream, this usually has an influence on the dreams that follow. But there is an important difference between a conscious endeavour to alter the content of our dreams, or to control the dream contents, and the natural tendency of dreams to respond to important emotional stimuli such as usually come out when we examine previous dreams. It is often possible to carry on a dialogue with one's dreams by closely examining the message of a night's dreams and responding to that message, which usually brings a response in the following night's dreams. This is why the content of dreams tends to follow the particular bias of the person undertaking the examination. When one particular theme is discovered and examined, the following dreams will usually follow up that theme. They will also frequently lodge a sort of protest if the examination of previous dreams has overlooked or manhandled the message those dreams conveyed.

The desire to control the content of dreams usually surfaces when there have been nightmares, in the hope that the fear may be dispelled. It also comes up in the hope that, if dreams can be controlled, then the whole mind can be under control. Both of these goals overlook the importance of the messages that dreams bring when they are allowed to flow naturally.

Often, however, what is taken to be control of dreams is actually something rather different. During the twilight state of falling asleep or wakening, there is often a short period of time when dream-type imagery appears even though you are substantially still awake. Some people find it possible, during this twilight period, to direct their reactions to the dream-type imagery and events, and in so doing, to take an active part in the outcome.

This is not true dreaming but a process called active imagination. Active imagination can be of tremendous help in consciously working with what would normally be unconscious material. Some people learn to prolong the twilight period and, thus, also prolong their active imagination. Also, some people learn to bring on this state more or less at will during the day. There is real value in this procedure, especially as a technique of psychotherapy or self-psychotherapy, but it is different in nature from spontaneous dreaming during sleep, which is beyond conscious control. The content of active imagination is palpably different from that of true dreams. For details of the procedure and the content of active imagination, the two volumes by C. G. Jung, *The Visions Seminars* (Zurich: Spring Publications, 1976) are valuable. So also is Rix Weaver's book *The Old Wise Woman* (London: Vincent Stuart Ltd, 1964). This is a real interaction of the conscious mind with unconsciously produced imagery. Variations on this technique have also been used with considerable success by psychotherapists who guide the type of imagery that is envisioned in the process, as well as in a number of religious medition techniques. But active imagination is a topic to itself. Our interest in this book is true dreaming, which we all experience whenever we sleep and is what is usually meant by the term 'dreaming'.

The first three chapters of this book have been based on the tacit premise that every dream is meaningful, and that it is possible to work out what that meaning is. More than that, however, has been my stated assumption that every dream has a purpose, and not just a meaning. Taken by itself, the meaning of a dream could be a fairly mechanical emotional reaction to the day's events, and the premise that the meaning of a dream is helpful could simply mean that a discovery of these emotional reactions can aid in understanding the dreamer's emotional and mental state. Freud's *The Interpretation of Dreams* is largely based on this premise. To state that dreaming has a purpose is to take the matter quite a bit further, and this statement has moved beyond the point where many dream researchers are willing to go.

That dreams have a purpose has been a popular idea as far back as discussion of dreams goes. Generally, it has been in a religious context, with the assumption that God (or sometimes the Devil) is the sender of the message. It need not to be as crude as that. Sophisticated theologians, such as Paul Tillich, have laid the groundwork for seeing dreams as an expression of the meaningfulness of existence for an individual person. That dreams express or carry a message of that that is Supreme is a widespread claim not only by adherents of organised religious movements, but also of many humanist thinkers who wish to retain the sense of meaningfulness of existence, but who are unwilling to carry it to the postulate that there is a Supreme Being.

It is not necessary, however, to place dreams in such a context in order to say that they have a purpose. Dreams can be viewed as a natural evolu-tionary development, like all the rest of our being. Support for this comes from the discovery that animals dream, not only *homo sapiens*. In the same way that the genetic code carries the blueprint for our physical struc-ture and lifelong development, we can presume that the same genetic code carries the blueprint for our psychological structure and lifelong develop-ment. Indeed, this is a necessary conclusion if we are to hold to the premise made at the start of this book, that there is no clear dividing line between mind and body, and the term 'psyche' encompasses both the physiological substrate for our mental functioning and the 'mental' processes themselves. Whatever 'mind' eventually proves to be, it seems inevitable that it will prove to be continuous with the physical body and not a totally separate entity. It seems a reasonable hypothesis, if not a justified conclusion, that what Jung termed the 'self is an expression of the genetic code to the same extent that the physical body is.

What seems to be verified by long-term studies of individuals' dreams covering a number of years is that there is a fundamental direction in which each individual's dreams are pointing, though that direction varies from person to person in its details. An individual's dreams do not seem to be random readjustments of emotional equilibrium, as might be supposed at first glance, but readjustments according to a pattern of psychological growth and development.

This conclusion in no way contradicts a religious or philosophical view of the origins or purpose of dreams, but it does emphasise that no such view is necessary in order to accept the meaningfulness and purposefulness of dreams. As far as is possible at the present time, it seems to me to be desir-able to place the study of dreams on as sound a scientific footing as we can manage, not because science has all the answers, but because much, much more collection of and research on dreams are needed before any but the most tentative conclusions can be reached about their nature, meaning, purpose (evolutionary or otherwise) and value.

The message and purpose of any individual dream may be very obscure. While it is usually possible to link up the content of a dream with daily life in some respect, finding a message or purpose in it seems often to be a very subjective judgment. But let us begin with a dream that appears, at least, to have a fairly obvious meaning:

> *Two men come to visit while I am having dinner with friends. I leave the friends to see the men and am delighted to find Jim B. and Robin G., my student friend and teacher, respectively. Robin has built a large 8' × 10' stretcher and is saying how necessary it is to build a solid frame to carry the canvas. I must be thinking of a similar-sized painting myself but cannot afford the heavier materials and wonder if it will be alright. We find ourselves looking at a painting of mine, a*

large yellow canvas. Robin asks me how I paint and I (somewhat dis-
paragingly) say with a casual gesture of the hand, 'oh, like Packson
Jollick' [a reference to Jackson Pollock]. Jim is enthusiastic and agrees.
I go on and say to Robin how I had spent too much time worrying
about being a 'painter'. He smiles and Jim backs my every word. I am
surprised and happy. We go on talking about the difficulty of estab-
lishing the means to paint and I say how I have only just now managed
to get this place. (I have just moved into a large enough area to have a
studio.)

HENRY S.

There are several points of contact with waking life in this dream. Jim and
Robin are real people, though a fair way back in Henry's life. Henry is a
skilled artist, and the American artist Jackson Pollock is one of his ideals;
Henry attempts to follow much the same artistic ideals as Pollock, though
he could not be said to imitate him. Henry would like to do very large-scale
paintings, similar to the 8' × 10' scale mentioned in the dream. In fact,
the dream could almost be a record of real life; we would know it to be a
dream only because Jim and Robin are people in Henry's past rather than
present, Henry would not confuse Pollock's name like that, and he would
not be likely to disparage his own work in the way he does in the dream.
This is one of those dreams that are so realistic as to make one wonder
where the dream-like quality is in them.

Virtually all of this dream is self-explanatory, when Henry's career and
situation are taken into account. Jim was a fellow student in art school
many years back. Robin was one of the art teachers. The question of style
receives its emphasis because of a problem that many abstractionists find
in art school, that Henry goes in for abstract expressionism, in contrast to
the prevailing current of intellectual abstractionism dominating at the
time. It took a lot of courage to persist with emotional abstractionism in
that atmosphere. The difference between the two currents lies in the goals
of the painting: is the artist painting in order to express her/his emotional
reactions to life, as Henry did; or is she/he painting in order to make a
geometrically or visually 'logical' statement? What the one regards as a
very good picture may be regarded by the other as a very bad picture.

Henry had gradually been moving to large-scale paintings, and it was
one of his goals to do wall-sized pictures, a point that comes up against the
practical questions of where would there be space enough to work on such
a gigantic scale, and how could Henry manage to pay for the materials
that would be involved, special canvas, large stretcher, vast quantities of
high-costing quality paint? The canvas must be special because an ordinary painter's canvas would tear under the weight of so much paint.

The yellow painting in the dream was not yet a reality. Henry had been
hoping to focus his next painting on the colour yellow. So the dream is a bit

futuristic, in that it has the trio contemplating the painting that, in reality, was yet to be painted, and discussing techniques. Jackson Pollock was a very controversial artist, whose pictures now command quite phenomenal prices, as much as a million dollars or even more. In Henry's eyes, Pollock was the very epitome of the use of colours and shapes to convey gut feelings.

In the dream, Jackson Pollock's name is scrambled, a sort of self-disparagement on Henry's part: he would like to compare with Pollock, but certainly does not say to others that he has such hopes. But to his surprise, both Jim and Robin support his style of art, a counterbalance to the discouragement he felt in art school.

Why the dream? On the premise that a dream has both meaning and purpose, where do we find the meaning and the purpose of this dream? The answer lies in those aspects of the dream that do not correspond (yet) to reality. The dream is a very encouraging one. If it were a summary of a real event, we would expect Henry to feel not only a lot of encouragement, but also a lot of satisfaction. Is the dream saying to Henry, more or less: 'Your project of a giant painting is quite realistic, your art teacher has even done one that size. And your idea for a yellow-based painting, that is really good too, you can pull it off all right, you'll see'? Let us look at the circumstances in which the dream took place.

The dream followed a long, dry spell, during which no major pieces of art were produced. It came at a time when Henry's outside commitments had eased and when he was contemplating a move to new living quarters. Different aspects of resuming active artistry have been shared out in the dream between Jim, Robin and Henry himself. From the subjective viewpoint, Jim and Robin represent aspects of Henry's own personality, because they are not persons with whom Henry had any link at the time of the dream or near to it. From the text of the dream, Robin represents the recognition of the technical difficulties in carrying out such a large-scale painting as this, and the reassurance that the feat can be done. He is the one who points out the practical necessities of the project, especially the need for a solid framework for the canvas. It is from his example and suggestions that Henry comes to consider the idea seriously and is led to think about the need for special heavy canvas. So, Robin = the influence of the art teacher, bringing his attention to practical details, and concerned about the procedure of actually painting the picture. Robin is a representation of Henry's asking himself: 'Is this project feasible?'; and also of his self-questioning, which every creative person experiences: 'Am I really an artist?'

Jim plays the role in the dream of being an admirer who is enthusiastic about Henry's comparing himself with Jackson Pollock, something Henry does not quite dare to do fully, so that he disparages himself by scrambling the name. Is this delusion? Or does an artist need to say to herself/himself that she/he is comparable with the greatest in order to get the courage to do the art-work at all? How can Henry know whether he is or is not comparable to Jackson Pollock until he tries? At the time of this dream, Pollock was best known among the public for his painting *Blue Poles*, which had sold for a cool one million dollars. Henry is contemplating not a blue but a yellow painting. Is he deluding or encouraging himself? If he had no artistic talent, he would be deluding himself but, then, he would never have graduated from art school. So he does have artistic talent — but does he have that much talent? Such would be the subliminal ruminations going on his mind; maybe he even asked them of himself openly. There is only one answer: do it and see what results.

The practical question of where to work on this enormous painting was a real question that Henry had been posing for himself. He was, in fact, looking for a place to make his studio large enough to accommodate the painting on the floor, since he normally did his paintings from various directions, standing at the side or at the top as much as at the bottom. The studio would have to be closed to outsiders most of the time, since the painting would have to lie stretched out on the floor for a long period, while being painted and then while drying. Then another practical problem: how to find a room big enough to hang the picture with enough space for the viewer (first of all, himself) to step back and be able to take in the entire picture at one time? That would require an immense hall, hardly to be found for use in finishing the picture!

But in the dream, this practical problem has been solved at the close of the dream. The affirmation that he has just moved into a large enough place for such a studio contradicts physical fact, but taken symbolically, it may well represent an emotional fact: that Henry has now found room within his feelings to allow for the painting to be achieved. After all, the whole dream seems to be about Henry's needing to be reassured about his ability to do the painting, and at the conclusion, he affirms that he is now ready and willing to start.

To round off the examination of the dream content, we may look at the beginning of the dream, where the dreamer has been eating dinner with friends but leaves them to be with Jim and Robin. The setting is one where social contact with others is set aside in favour of contact with the inner voices portrayed by Jim and Robin. Who are these 'others'? There are two possibilities, both equally plausible: that the 'others' are other commitments and concerns in waking life, which Henry needs to forgo in order to concentrate on his painting work; or that the 'others' are other inner voices, like Jim and Robin but concerned with other aspects of his approach to life. Either or both are possible, there is no way to tell.

As pointed out, the dream came during a dry spell in Henry's artistic career. How, then, are we to take the dream? Three viewpoints suggest themselves. It may be that the dream merely reflects Henry's thoughts and ruminations about his career. It may be an instance of wishful thinking: 'If I were given the opportunity, I could be as great as Jackson Pollock'. And, an encouragement: 'Henry, you're despondent, and it is because you have not taken up the challenge that is so close to your heart'. The positive mood of the dream is the dream's real message, and, we may reasonably speculate, its purpose is to remind Henry that he has something valuable to give to the world, and his soul will be incomplete without it.

The meaning and purpose of many dreams are much more difficult to find than in Henry's case. Before giving up on the idea, though, we need to look very closely at the text of the dream and follow up all the clues. As an example, I will present a dream that was so particularly powerful to the dreamer that he even gave it a title:

The Mouse that Cried

I see a mouse and catch it, either killing it or throwing it away, and am about to do the same to another one, probably its mate, when I see it begins crying. I am struck by the fact that the mouse has emotions and leave it alone.

There is an image of a guy on a bridge and a girl is also present, then the scene changes to a battle. In the battle, cannons are being fired, exploding in trees some distance away. It seems a contained conflict until suddenly some new cannons, perhaps being fired from Africa, begin shooting. The explosions from their shells are enormous.

The battle disappears and I am with other companions, one of whom picks up a piece of old corrugated iron to discover Don Juan beneath it—in the shape of a lizard, naturally. At first I am not sure it is Don Juan because I thought he looked a bit different, when a lizard. However it is him after all and he sits up looking around. The lizard notices a frog, actually Genaro I suspect, a little distance away and jumps up, swallowing the frog whole. He swallows it in a curious way, from the rear, and somehow seems to leave the outer skin, as though swallowing it from the inside out. As this is going on, a man, Mr Kafti, comes to a doorway but, seeing the lizard and the frog, backs away closing the door, looking through the glass pane. When the lizard has nearly swallowed the frog I see something fly from the frog and land on my shoulder, a bat's wing or the frog spirit. I had been fascinated by the whole process, calling my companions' attention to it.

RICHARD A.

There is quite a bit to say about this dream. The Don Juan and Genaro in the dream are the two men from Carlos Castaneda's books. In those books, Juan and Genaro are Carlos' teachers, though radically different in style. Carlos was very fond of Juan, but rather terrified of Genaro. Their aim, in the books, is to train Carlos to become a sorcerer (Indian witch-doctor). Richard was well familiar with the four Castaneda books that had appeared by the time of this dream.

Mr Kafti is the only other person referred to by name in this dream. He is from Richard's school-days. Younger than Richard, he appears to be outwardly more successful, a stereotyped business man and, incidentally, afraid of animals.

This dream is primarily concerned with Richard's relation to the world. There is a strange interlude while the human animal goes about its wars of destruction. The dream has picked up the emotional world of Castaneda's books, and has made that the essence of the spiritual experience Richard is going through.

As before, with such a complicated dream, it is helpful to outline the story in order to get the drama well in mind. We follow our basic principle, to treat the dream story as a report of something that has really happened, in order to see what the drama is all about:

1. Richard destroys a mouse, then sees its mate crying.
2. Surprise that the mouse has emotions.
3. A guy on a bridge, and a girl present.
4. A battle, African cannons being fired. Big explosions.
5. A companion discovers Juan in the shape of a lizard.
6. The lizard swallows a frog (= Genaro?) whole.
7. Mr Kafti comes to a doorway, sees the lizard, backs away closing the door.
8. Something flies from the frog to Richard's shoulder, perhaps a bat's wing or the frog's spirit.

There are three fairly clear-cut dramatic scenes in this dream: the opening scene of the mouse, from which Richard gave the dream its title; the battle; the lizard and the frog. There is nothing apparent to link the three scenes together. There is a sort of aborted reference to a fourth scene, that of the guy on the bridge and the girl, but it is not developed. The dream begins and closes with a scene from nature, although with human ramifications. The theme of killing is in all three scenes: the death of the mouse, the battle, the devouring of the frog. The human theme also runs through all three scenes, in Richard's destruction of the mouse, the battle, and the two men who have taken on animal shape for the drama.

In the first scene, the point seems to be that the mouse has emotional reactions, unexpectedly for Richard. It cries when its mate is dead, and perhaps it is crying out of fear for its own demise as well. Why should a mouse not have emotions? There is no particular reason for denying emotions to a mouse when we are well familiar with emotions in other complex creatures. In true Castaneda fashion, Richard is being brought to see that what he takes as a simple natural event, his killing of a mouse, has spiritual depths he had not suspected, just as in the closing scene he discovers spiritual realities beneath the natural cover. Even a mouse cries. Should he not cry too? Or is it that he needs to gain more insight into the depths of nature?

The second scene is similarly brief, but extremely vivid. Death and destruction are the central theme, of which everything else is an elaboration. Freudians would see a sexual reference here, the shooting cannons being penises ejaculating, and we cannot discount that possibility. Very frequently, dream images of cannons prove to be precisely that. Why cannons, of all the possible phallic symbols? They have an immensely aggressive connotation. If this is a phallic scene, then it is a very dangerous, aggressively painted one. The phallic imagery is hypothetical, we cannot be certain in this particular dream whether it is a correct interpretation. The aggression is quite overt, though.

We can bring in Adler's concept of the 'masculine protest' here, the self-assertive drive clothed in male sexuality, and aggressive precisely because Richard's self-assertion is overly weak and is over-compensated for. Adler's conceptions were highly sexist and need a great deal of reworking to become applicable to modern social concepts, but his point specifically in relation to Richard is probably accurate. Is Richard himself threatened by the battle? It is implied, but not explicitly stated. The 'contained' conflict gets out of control when the African cannons begin to shoot. Africa probably retains its feeling of being the 'dark continent' where nature is untampered with, popular in the fantasies of westerners. The outcome of all these deliberations is that Richard feels threatened by something that has got out of control and is highly explosive, Nature itself, and very probably, sexual Nature.

Juan and Genaro, in the form of a lizard and a frog, bring in the culmination of the drama. It is a simple, natural event, though with peculiarities all its own. A lizard swallows a frog and Richard feels the frog's spirit fly onto his shoulder. The peculiarities are that the frog is eaten inside out, and the escape of its spirit to Richard's shoulders. We must also consider what Mr Kafti is doing here.

In Castaneda's books, Juan is not imaged as a lizard, nor Genaro as a frog; this is a dream expansion of the portrayals in the books. Richard's dream presumably has in mind one of the larger species of lizards, which is able to swallow the frog whole. This is the mystique of Nature, the spiritual implications of Nature that Juan expounds so forcefully in Castaneda's writings. At the end, Richard inherits Genaro's spirit. Nature is life and death, the same theme we saw so beautifully expounded in the tea-house dream (p. 49), and we are a part of the world of Nature, Castaneda's major point.

What is Mr Kafti doing here? He comes to a doorway, sees the lizard and frog, backs away, closes the door and watches the events through the glass pane in the door. In Castaneda's books, Carlos is astonished to discover that Juan, the peasant sorcerer, is also a business man in Mexico City. He cannot comprehend how the two roles can be combined in one person. In this dream, when the sorcerer aspect is emphasised, the business man aspect retreats to the background. Mr Kafti is a successful business man, but he has no place for nature and its mysteries. Is this one of the major points of the dream, that the business perspective must retreat in favour of coming to grips with the spiritual character inherent in nature? Richard has no connections with Mr Kafti now; he remembers him only from school-days. Mr Kafti represents one of the directions Richard's life might have taken. Now he is bewildered, where should he be moving? Into a perspective where he can participate in nature and learn the eternal cycle of life and death that is nature.

But Castaneda's books are concerned with something more than seeing nature, though that is part of it. They try to bring to the reader an experience of 'another reality', a spiritual reality co-existing with our everyday perceptions. Their point is that the sum total of Reality is far greater than we are accustomed to supposing. Genaro's spirit comes to rest upon Richard's shoulders. In the books, Genaro is a trickster figure, one whom Carlos never quite trusts. Genaro is boastful, bombastic, fond of creating illusions, unpredictable. This unpredictability is one of the lessons Juan attempts to teach Carlos: to be at one with nature, and discover its hidden qualities, instead of eternally fighting it.

We are left with the guy on the bridge and the girl — it is not clear whether she is on the bridge with him, or not. This seems to be a kind of semi-symbolic linking of the first and second scenes. If we are correct in seeing the second scene, the battle, as aggressive sexuality, and the first scene as discovering that aggression can be hurtful, the guy and girl may represent the transition (bridge) from the animal world of natural aggression, for aggression is natural *between* species, to the human world of unnatural aggression, for death-dealing aggression within a species is unique to *homo sapiens*.

All in all, what have we done with Richard's dream? We have divided it into its natural formation of three parts, with a linking bit between the first and second parts, and we have seen the message each part portrays: from 'Animals have feelings, too', to 'Your (sexual?) aggression is absolutely enormous and is threatening to destroy you unless you take heed of it', to 'The spirit of nature is available to you'. In practical terms, how does this dream need to be followed up? First, by ascertaining whether the enormous aggression is acted out in daily life, or is kept pent up inside to the point where it will explode. Second, by linking the dream up with Richard's religious orientation, so as to incorporate the messages of the dream into a framework with which he is familiar and at ease. The purpose of the dream is to reorient Richard's attitudes towards nature, but the details of how this is to be done need to be explored. Following the hint of the possible symbolism of the cannons shooting, natural sexuality is one of the concrete areas to focus on.

Often, the point of a dream is painfully obvious, and there is little to add by way of interpretation. The purpose of the dream is then easily read from the dream text itself. By way of example, we may take a dream from the woman whose dream of the snake crawling under the out-house door we examined in Chapter 3. This dream took place after she had been consulting me for some time:

> *I dream James has come back and am delighted and go and give him a big hug and while he holds me very tightly, he puts his hands over my breasts. I do not feel this is an erotic gesture, but after a while, I feel worried by his intensity and ask him if he has seen his wife yet. He says no and we sit at a table while he looks at a notebook and I tell him I am going to Dr Broadribb and he seems annoyed about this and says, 'I don't know why you needed to do that'. Then he asks me how much Dr Broadribb is charging and when I tell him he says that it is too much and I feel surprised and say that it is the same as he charged and then I realise that he is jealous or feel this is the case and then I feel guilty and that I have betrayed James in some way. Later I ring my friends and tell them James is back. These are friends he has seen as patients and they don't seem very excited about it because they now have Dr Broadribb to see.*

MARILYN Q., #2

James was a psychotherapist who enjoyed a high reputation, but who died shortly before I arrived in Perth. After his death, a number of his former patients came to consult me. These included Marilyn, and various of the other people alluded to in the dream. Marilyn had been particularly fond of James, it would not be stretching things too far to say that she was in love with him.

This is a 'working over' type of dream; that is, a dream that tries to sort out an emotional or other type of muddle. 'Working over' types of dreams are fairly common, and some dreamers report that they form the majority of their dream material.

The dream has cast James' return from the dead is a very erotic context. Marilyn knows, in the dream, that James is in love with her. By the tone of the dream, Marilyn had also fallen in love with me, and during the night, her mind was working over the guilt feelings she had that she was betraying James in loving me. She is, however, at the end of the dream reassured to some extent that this is okay, for her friends are no longer interested in

James now that I am around, and she can assuage her guilt feelings by seeing me as his successor.

This is a slightly more complicated form of transference dream than we
have seen so far. In its narrow sense, transference refers to the emotional
feelings of the patient about the therapist, and it especially refers to the
patient's imaginary ideas about the therapist's feelings about the patient.
There is no evidence that I have been able to find that James was ever in
love with Marilyn, but in her dream, this is the case, and there is the
hidden but assumed continuation that I too will fall in love with her, as she
imagines James to have done.

Essentially, Marilyn's dream goes over the pros and cons of abandoning
her loyalty to the now deceased James or transferring her loyalty to me.
The intensity with which he holds her breasts disturbs her, in part because
he is married and she fears the consequences of sexual contact between
herself and James. Since James is dead, it is easy to imagine that he has a
strong sexual attraction to her, because he is not present to verify the
matter. But James is dead and the dream concerns not the real James but
her memories and fantasies of him. If she loved him, or, more importantly,
if he loved her, then is it not a betrayal of that love to transfer her affection
onto me? She imagines that James would view me as inferior, worth only a
smaller fee than he charged, and the reason behind this would be his
jealousy that she prefers me to his memory. But others have made the
switch, so why not her?

Often, a dream gives reassurance in a situation where there is anxiety or
uncertainty. Here, the anxiety is that she may be fickle to James by wanting me. The dream confirms that she is doing rightly. As we remember
from Marilyn's earlier dream about the snake under the out-house door,
she had on her conscience then a worry that she was doing wrong by carrying on an affair with another man while being married. This dream of
James follows the same type of concern, though it has not resorted to
symbolism, but has stated its message outright.

It is a common experience that the message of a dream is enhanced
when other dreams from the same person are taken into account. A person's dream series makes a point, or several points, concerning her/his life-
style and emotional contact with the world outside and the world inside.
When a long series of dreams is examined, it becomes apparent that the
dreams are trying to set right the attitudes and approaches to life that are
askew. In this way, the dreams help to maintain emotional equilibrium.

Human beings are both blessed and hindered by the fact that their
personalities contain conscious approaches to the inner and outer worlds,
and unconscious approaches. One of the most important discoveries of this
last century has been the extent of the unconscious in each of us. The role
of dreams is to bring out the interplay of conscious and unconscious. What
is a relatively new discovery for most people is that the unconscious con-

tains not merely shitty stuff of which the dreamer would do well to get rid, but, quoting the old alchemists, gold among the shit also.

We are used to the idea that the physical body has its methods and abilities to maintain physical functioning and health under most circumstances, and even that symptoms of an illness may represent the body's attempt to deal with an invading organism, bacterium or a virus. But it is still a new concept to many people that the same applies to the psychosomatic unity that each of us is. Psychological processes take place alongside and are intimately intertwined with physical functioning. Dreams are a very important part of these processes. For this reason, it is important that we listen to our dreams and take to heart what they have to tell us.

Is it likely that dreams that we do not remember also have an important role to play? We all dream during every sleep period, but most of these dreams, for many people even all of the dreams, are forgotten on awakening. It can only be speculated, on the basis of what is known about remembered dreams, that unremembered dreams serve to maintain mental health and emotional stability. There is some laboratory research on the results of dream deprivation that is inconclusive but that adds weight to this suggestion. Experience of working with many dreams from many people leads to the feeling that spontaneously remembered dreams are important because they require some active intervention in the emotional fabric of life, while, on the whole, unremembered dreams would seem to be part of the mechanism of our existence to maintain emotional homoeostasis. This may be to some extent thwarted, however, when a dream is 'intentionally' not remembered because its message is too unpalatable. The mechanism of repression, which means the automatic suppression of a dream because of its unpalatability, may to a greater or smaller extent prevent the process of emotional equilibration from taking place.

As we have seen already, although dreams frequently serve to deal with what is wrong in our life, they can and do often give positive reinforcement to what is happening. When they are remembered spontaneously, it is usually because we need the reassurance. Similarly, when we spontaneously forget a dream, it may be because we do not want to hear what it is saying. I mention unspontaneous memory of dreams because it is easily possible to train yourself to remember dreams that you would otherwise not remember, or not remember for long. If you are in the habit of writing down any dream memories as soon as you awaken, you will likely find that many of the dreams have been so forgotten that only the handwriting shows that it was you who had the dreams and wrote them down.

It is difficult to show in the confines of a book how a series of dreams serves to help make basic emotional readjustments for ongoing personality growth and maturation, though, in Chapter 7, I attempt to present some aspects of this with a series of dreams from a single dreamer. One of the best ways you can prove it for yourself is to read through your dreams of a few years ago and to compare them with a similar number from recent days, to see how changes in emphasis and imagery have taken place and that there is a definite direction in them.

However, to illustrate the statement that dreams over time show a direction and purpose, we can, at this point, pick out from a lengthy series of dreams from one person a selection that deal with a similar issue throughout. The following dreams have come from the man whose dream about being a business man on a train we examined in Chapter 1. I have picked out a series of dreams, in sequential order, dealing with his relationship to women, which was a point strongly stressed in the text and discussion of the dream in Chapter 1. I present the dreams as a whole sequence, and discuss them at the end of the series:

(a) *I am in a vast, high building with many wings. It has many stair-cases, terraces, platforms, and rooms at various levels. It seems to belong to my university department. A group of students, of which I am not a part, is staying there. I talk with some people. Someone mentions that Susan has purchased an apartment in this building, on one of the upper floors. This purchase was considered very sensible.*

Then a sensuous young girl comes, she is about twenty-two years old, is very self-confident and independent. This girl flirts with another man and with me at the same time. I do not like that, but I think she has a right to do this, and if I do not like it, then I can withdraw.

(b) *I am with the secretary, but she is a lot younger than in reality, maybe twenty-three, capricious and feminine. She feels a need for affection, she wants me to caress her. I lie on a bed, she is at my side, in my arms. She somehow wants to justify her behaviour, to explain that she is entitled to my embraces. I like this behaviour of the secretary, I find it pleasant, but I do not feel any deep affection for her. I also remember that at four p.m. I have a date with another girl.*

Since the secretary says that she would like to be with me again, I ponder where we could meet, where we could find a bed. First, I think that we could use my parents' bed, my mother would surely have no objection. Then I remember, though, that my father is still there so that it would be impossible to use my parents' bed. Finally I remember that the secretary has her own room in my parents' apartment.

(c) *I am going to a company where I want to look for a job. I go north on foot, through a small park. By chance, I meet Selma there. I am overjoyed to see her. She beams at me, and seems just as overjoyed to see me. We greet each other warmly and embrace.*

(d) *I am in an unknown, idyllic, sunny country village. I ask a girl, who is about fifteen years old, whether she would like to become my friend. She giggles and says that she is too young still. I am carrying a table covered with numbers. I look up the girl's size in the table, to see whether she is really too young. But I cannot determine this. I leave the place and seem to wait for the girl at a sort of border customs checking post.*

(e) *I am in a barn with a large group of people. They seem to be men and women in equal numbers. Some sort of sex game is going on, with definite rules and procedures. People change partners at a signal. A girl with dark hair, about twenty years old, comes to me and invites me to play, but I am frightened and reluctant. Then partners are changed again, and the girl goes to someone else and I am left alone. I seem to be the odd man out. I feel, sadly, that I cannot participate.*

The following dream came in between dream (e) and dream (g), and is included because of its later discovered importance for the series, although it relates to Jim's parents rather than to a girl-friend.

(f) *My parents live in a house in Italy or southern Switzerland. I live with them. One day, I think I am alone in the house, and I go about doing something. I go up some stairs and down again, I open and close many doors and make quite a lot of noise doing so. As I go through one room in which there is a sofa-bed, my father suddenly yells at me because of all the noise I am making. He is lying on the sofa-bed, and turns towards me. I tell him that I did not know he was in the house.*

Now I am sitting at a table in my parents' house. My father and/or my brothers are also at the table. My mother serves a giant heap of food on a platter. At first, we eat what is on top of the heap. Now the outlines of an animal become visible on the platter. I am asked what sort of animal it is, but I have no idea. I am told it is the 'mousey from . . .' (I forget where.) But it turns out, finally, to be a very fat little dog which is half transparent but is still alive. It jumps down from the platter onto the floor and runs about nervously. I tell the others that this is necessary, the dog needs movement in order to get rid of its fat. I accuse my mother of torturing the dog.

(g) *I am with Selma. We embrace and seem to like each other very*
     much. She is much shorter than I am. She looks up to me and
     smiles and speaks.

(h) *I am with Mary, who is hanging out clothes. She is hanging*
     freshly washed black shirts. A third, unclear person, whose sex is
     uncertain, is also hanging up washing. I do not know if that per-
     son is a friend or enemy. I tell Mary that I think she hangs up the
     black shirts according to a complicated, harmonious mathemati-
     cal formula. She laughs and answers that I am right, and asks
     whether I can tell her what the formula is. I object that I do not
     know the exact formula, and that at the moment I do not have
     any interest in working it out. I am quite content to know that
     there is some formula by which the shirts are hung.

JIM K., #2: (a)-(h)

These dreams, which are from a series of 178 dreams covering a period
of just about a year, have been selected to show how a particular theme —
contact with the feminine world — reappeared over the course of a fairly
lengthy series of dreams. Actually, quite a few more dreams could be
added, because the theme was a consistent one, but to present them all
here would make the series unmanageable because of length.

Contact by a man with the feminine side of the world is what Jung speaks
of as the anima problem. In a young man, this means the task of separating himself from attachment to his mother and the forming of attachments
with women outside the family. In this young man's life, this separation
and reattachment has not taken place, and the theme runs consistently
through his dreams. I have selected dreams that show the mixture of attempts to form an attachment with specific women, and for Jim to have his
own feminine side cultivated and brought into the open through these relationships. All of the women mentioned in (a) to (h) are real persons with
whom Jim comes into contact in daily life. His dream movement from one
to another seemingly at random represents his difficulty in coming to terms
with a relationship with any of them. It would also be possible to select
dreams where separation from Jim's parents is the dominating theme and
the crucial issue. But I have chosen only one, dream (f), for our attention.

Dream (f), which refers us back again to the parental problem of Jim
with both his mother and his father (also indicated in dream (b)), came
about three months after its predecessor, dream (e), and about three and a
half months before dream (g). The content points to a clear struggle between Jim and his father, but beyond that, a mother problem looms large.

The first two dreams, (a) and (b), point to a problem in relationships.
The first is set in the imaginary context of a vast, high building belonging
to the university department where Jim is studying. There is a bit of a feel-

ing of alienation about it. Students, but not Jim, live in the building. Susan, a girl whom he likes and would like to have a relationship with, also lives in the building. Indeed, she has purchased an apartment there. Jim does not feel quite a part of the students' group, and he seems only to hear about Susan, not to actually meet her. Yet another woman, a dream invention, now comes and flirts with Jim and another man at the same time. Jim does not like this, but he feels that the only thing he can do is withdraw. There is as yet no hint that he might have sexual rights and needs as much as anyone else. For him, so far, feminine contact is minimal: he must share any contact he has, with others.

In the second dream, Jim is with another real person, the secretary, who, in an imagined situation, makes sexual advances to him, a veritable daydream. But there are three catches in it: he feels no deep affection for her, he has a date with another girl at four p.m., and he cannot find a bed to use. Mother might agree to his using the parental bed, but Father would make it impossible. These sound strangely like excuses for his sense of isolation: 'I can't have sex with her because I don't love her; anyway, even if I wanted to, there isn't time because I have a date with someone else; and even if we did decide to go to bed together, there isn't any bed to use, and if we used my parents' bed, Father would object'. Finally the dream removes even the last objection; the woman has a room of her own in his parents' apartment.

In this second dream, there is a strong tone of the remains of an oedipus complex, i.e. a sexual attachment of Jim to his mother, which is vetoed by his father. This comes out when considering beds: there is only one bed available, but though his mother would be willing for him to use it, his father would not. The fear of moving outside the family proper is answered by the dream: 'There is room in your family to accommodate the secretary too'.

Dream (c) indicates that some of the emotional blockage has been removed. Another highly attractive young woman is available, if not for sex, then at least for embracing. Selma reappears in dream (g) in a very similar fashion. This dream and dream (g) could as easily be day-dreams. Perhaps they were. In the overall context, it does not seem to matter very much. They represent an activation of Jim's need and desire for affection.

In dream (d), the scenery is reminiscent of the train dream of Chapter 1, which was dreamed rather earlier than this series. Jim still does not trust his judgment when it comes to relationships. In this dream, and perhaps also in dream (h), there is a mechanical element: in the one instance, looking up the girl's age in a table to find whether she is too young for him; in the other instance, pondering about a mathematical formula by which his girl-friend hangs up shirts. In dream (d) the scene ends with a customs post, an authority that can approve or disapprove of what Jim is carrying with him. This is reminiscent of the assumed role of his father, as discussed, and of his doubts about his right to have a relationship with a woman at all.

The same doubt carries over into the following dream, (e), where the rules and procedures relating to sex befuddle him to the extent that he rejects the advances of an attractive young woman, then feels isolated and lonely. The dream is saying, 'Because you are frightened and reluctant to play the sex game, you are going to feel left out and lonely'. There has been progress in this regard in the dreams. It is no longer Jim's father or mother who holds him back, but his own fears and reluctance.

In the later dream (g), reassurance reappears. Jim can be liked, even loved, by a woman. Even more, there has been a progression. In the first dream, it was he who was looking up to the girl, Susan; she occupied a place far above him. Now it is the girl, Selma, who looks up to him. The dream may have picked Selma specifically because she is rather shorter than Jim, and the dream accentuates the shortness.

The reason for the dramatic change traces back to events connected with the intervening dream, dream (f). Here, the discussion is entirely of Jim's father and mother. We have already seen that a dream-house can represent the dreamer's personality; more exactly, the framework in which the dreamer's thoughts and emotions take place. The house in this dream is a dream invention, it bears no similarity with the real house where Jim's parents live. From the dream, we might assume that Jim lives with his parents. This is true, in the sense that, although living physically separate from his parents, he still lives with them emotionally. We saw the role of the Italian-looking fellow in Jim's train dream. Italy features quite a lot in Jim's dreams overall. It has for him the feeling of vacationing, enjoyment and unrestrained expression of emotion. So we are in the realm of emotion in this dream, and at first, Jim thinks that he is free to move about as he wills. But then, belatedly, he discovers the presence of his father, and his father's voice vehemently tells him to quiet down. The place where we learn the basic emotions and how to express them, the parental home, has become engrained in Jim's mind as a part of himself. The convenient term 'superego' is handy for representing the restraining voice, which has become internalised and is in conflict with Jim's wish to be free.

Now attention shifts to Jim's mother. She has cooked and served up something rather gruesome. She calls it a 'mousey', a childish way of saying 'mouse', and that would be bad enough, but it turns out really to be a small dog that is still alive, despite the roasting.

Jim had quite a number of dreams in which dogs featured. He was very puzzled by them, and attempts to understand their role in his dreams had been pretty unsuccessful. But shortly before this dream, he attended an exhibition of art done by mental patients, and afterwards, he said to me, 'I know what dogs mean now, sex'. This conclusion, which Jim had drawn by observing dogs in patients' paintings, stayed with him, and whatever they may have represented in earlier dreams, now they came to mean sex, to him. The final phrase in the dream, 'I accuse my mother of torturing the dog', he said, means 'I accuse my mother of torturing my sexuality'.

The oedipus complex, in which a son's love ties are with his mother, with fear and hatred of his father, had, as I have mentioned, been particularly strong in Jim's life. It appears that his mother was intentionally strengthening these ties. The dream now told him that she had come close to roasting his love life for him, but, fortunately, life has not been extinguished in that particular 'dog' yet.

The final dream, (h), came when a radical change had taken place in Jim's life. A true romance had grown up between himself and a girl-friend, Mary. She was fond of his black shirts, which turn up in the dream. The scene could almost be real, which may be an indication of something important that is quite near the surface of his mind. Jim had had absolutely no experience of the female sex. Mary was the first woman with whom he had had anything but casual conversations. The woman's 'world' was completely new to him. He frequently remarked to me on new discoveries he had made about women, and, in particular, women's clothes and approaches to daily chores. In reality, laundry usually is hung out in some sort of order. But since he is unfamiliar with hanging out laundry (he uses a laundromat), he is curious to see the way a woman does it. His dream exaggerates the pattern of clothes-hanging that Mary actually has into a mathematical formula. He is unable to figure out the formula, though he is sure there is one: he is used to ordering his own life according to definite, unvarying patterns, and assumes Mary would do the same. (He once said, before he became closely acquainted with Mary, that to invite her to have a cup of coffee after a class would be like trying to make an appointment with her, she would take out her diary and work out a date and time two months hence. Fortunately, this fantasy proved to be untrue.)

There is a fairly clear movement in these dreams: at first, (a), the most he can hope for is to share a girl's flirtation; then, (b), the secretary makes herself available, but he finds excuses to prevent a sexual encounter; (c), he is joyously embraced by a woman; (d), he has adolescent sexual fantasies, but wonders if he can get past the check point; (e) he would like to join a sex game, but through fear, misses his chance; (f), he realises the part his parents have played in 'roasting' his sex life; (g), he finds a girl who looks up to and embraces him; finally, (h), he forms a close relationship and rejoices in discovering the feminine world.

The general progression in these dreams is clear. Slowly but surely, the dreams are steering Jim in the direction of establishing a firm relationship with a woman, and freeing him from the emotional bonds imposed on him by his father and mother.

We must not overlook the fact that the course of the dreams was influenced by the act of examining and discussing them as they came along.

When one dream's import has been basically understood, another dream picks up from the discussion and carries it along. It is virtually impossible to disentangle the dream sequence from the simultaneous discussion and reaction to the dream contents; each influences the other. This is true whether the dreamer conducts the discussion internally, or with another person.

In this way, a dialogue with the unconscious can be set up. Often, very little interpretation is required for the dialogue, and sometimes, intensive working over of dreams can lead to a daily dialogue. More commonly, the dialogue is slower. When a particular theme, or image, or person is selected out from the dreams and those dreams are examined, they regularly make a meaningful series. Individual dreams can have a great impact and deliver a strong message also, but this is relatively infrequent, whereas series of dreams point to a meaningful message that is usually more obvious, if not so dramatic.

The background of an individual dream is often multi-determined. We can see this clearly in a fairly impressive dream of a man in his late thirties:

> *The group of us crawled on our bellies the rest of the way up. I had my camera ready. At the top, the light started to grow intense and we got onto our feet and looked down over the railing or cliff. Below us, we saw a compact castle, which was the Emerald City. Now we were down on the level with it. I and a companion stayed back to take a picture. At first, the sun was against us, but we moved into a better position. I adjusted the camera and wound the film to the next picture. Then I tried the winder a second time and wound a bit more. I managed, I thought, to get a full picture of the castle. The other companions had gone off . . . that was to be a diversionary action to attract attention while we two reconnoitred. We saw an elderly man, a gardener perhaps, and a small cat on the grounds beside the castle. I went up to them and spoke to them. The man said that the cat was usually not friendly to strangers, and, indeed, it growled when I touched it. But I thought the cat and I would soon be friends. The man invited us in for tea. He said that since court etiquette had returned under Princess . . . tea now consisted of . . . We entered.*
>
> JOHN W., #5

John said that, in the dream, the Princess's name was mentioned, but he forgot it on waking. This was also true of the foods for afternoon tea.

The Emerald City is a feature in *The Wizard of Oz*. In that story, the Emerald City is at the exact centre of the country of Oz, the remainder of Oz being divided into four parts, each of which borders on the territory of the Emerald City. In the second book of the Oz series, *The Land of Oz*, the plot centres on the discovery and restoration to power of the rightful princess, Ozma, who had been bewitched and turned into a little boy.

Two other influences on the dream are less obvious. One is P. G. Wodehouse's novel *Something Fresh*, which John was reading just before the dream. In Wodehouse's novel, Lord Emsworth, owner of the castle, potters around the garden and is often mistaken for a gardener. This seems to be reflected in the dream, where the gardener invites John and friend in for tea in the castle.

Another direct influence comes from the biblical *Book of Revelation*. John had also been reading this the day of the dream, and was struck by the description of the New Jerusalem near the end of the text. It resembles a castle fortified with a wall, and John made a colour sketch from the description to see what it looked like. This has influenced the dream imagery, which has turned the Emerald City of Oz into a castle, contrary to the story, similar to the way in which the city of New Jerusalem is shaped as a castle in the Bible.

There are, then, three major influences on the imagery in the dream, yet the story of the dream is quite distinct. The dream has picked up images fresh in John's mind, but blended them in a way to suit its own purpose. The result is quite unexpected.

There is one other event that figures less directly in the dream. Apart from making a colour sketch of New Jerusalem, John also painted a picture showing temple ruins on top of a mandala (squared circle) design. The two attempts John made to take a picture of the Emerald City-cum-castle in his dream seem to link up with these two artistic attempts. There is a distinct symbolic equation between the Emerald City, the Castle, the New Jerusalem, the temple ruins and the mandala. The Emerald City is at the centre of Oz, and its rightful ruler, Princess Ozma, occupies the castle in the exact centre of the City. Allegorically, Princess Ozma represents the reader's true but hitherto hidden potential, her/his soul, as it were. She must be restored to her central position. The Castle in Wodehouse's much more light-hearted novel is a sanctuary where the most unlikely things can happen. It is Lord Emsworth's home where he can dress and act as he pleases and just be himself. The New Jerusalem is envisaged as an idealised city where God reigns supreme for ever. Our dreamer, a Quaker, understood it as an allegory of the soul. We have already seen the mandala motif in dreams. As a Tibetan meditational image (which is how John knew it), it, again, represents the innermost soul of the mediator. Temple ruins imply an old, covered-up centre of introspection and meditation.

Now let us look back to the story of the dream: John and unnamed companions crawl up a hill, ready to take a picture. There is some trouble in getting the photo taken. The position, the top of a hill or cliff, apparently is not right, but a new location is found. The sun is against them, so they must move yet again. The film winder is a bit uncertain. But the photo is, nevertheless, taken. Now John, with only one companion, sees an elderly man and his cat. The cat dislikes strangers, but John thinks it will become friendly. He and his companion are invited into the castle for tea, which, under the Princess's new court etiquette, seems to have been enlarged.

The timing of the dream is important for its understanding. It was dreamed on the night of January 2, so it is a New Year's dream. As such, it holds out very bright prospects for John: he manages to get an image of his centre, and is even invited in. This is better than having a mere photo. The dream is saying to him: 'You do not have to be content with a sketch or a painting, you can experience your own centredness directly'. That is where the dream leaves us, with the invitation for a cup of tea being accepted.

This dream had a great impact on John, and he remembered it years later. It held out a promise to him that life is not meaningless and his searching not in vain.

Major festivities like New Year's, Christmas, Easter, a birthday, frequently elicit major dreams, for the symbolism of the festivities evokes a response deep inside us. It is not at all unusual that the response takes on a form quite distinct from the dreamer's usual mode of thinking. Sometimes, this is because we are so used to traditional imagery that something rather spectacular and fresh is necessary to convey the message. Sometimes, it is because something really deep within us is touched off by the festivities.

As an illustration of how far-ranging dreams can be on such occasions, let us look at one of Robert M.'s dreams, whose two dreams of his son in a soup-spoon and the woman who was a little queer we examined in Chapter 3. For the significance of this dream, we must know that Robert is a Protestant minister:

> *I was at Inari (Ivalo?) in Finnish Lapland. I was talking to a lady up there. I met a Swedish doctor who knew many languages.*
>
> ROBERT M., #3

This dream came on Christmas Eve.

The impact of the dream is realised only when we investigate the geography involved. Inari and Ivalo are, respectively, a lake and a locality in northern Finland, of interest to tourists because of the lake's islands. Robert had once visited there with his family, and was impressed by one island where the ancients, i.e. the pre-Christian ancestors, brought their sacrificial gifts.

Robert had little to offer in regard to the rest of the dream. He characterised Lapland as wild, open country and forest, sparsely inhabited, primitive and rustic. He characterised Sweden as free, especially in regard to sex. We need to note also that Robert is of Swedish ancestry. The doctor was unclear, he did not know whether it meant a medical doctor, or a Ph.D. It could be a reference to me, since I once specialised in ancient languages.

As a Christmas dream for a Protestant minister, this dream is rather startling. In waking life, he is caught up in the hustle and bustle of Christmas preparations. In his dream life, he visits a pre-Christian centre far, far away. His 'Lady Soul' is there, not here.

In effect, the dream is saying: 'Tonight is a special occasion, but for you, it has become too institutionalised to hold its meaning. What I will show you is the religion inherent in nature, long before your Church came along. That is where your soul is and your heart belongs'. And there, in the setting of nature, following the dictates of his heart, he can meet the 'doctor' for his soul. The doctor might be patterned on me, but is really the ancestral potential within Robert himself, who can play a great role in resolving Robert's sexual problems. This 'doctor' knows many languages, can speak to him in many different ways: dreams, art (Robert is a good artist), active imagination, meditation — in short, all the ways in which a person can commune with what is deep inside.

Sometimes, dreams may have a special import for the dreamer, but not strike the observer as having so much impact. Two dreams, three nights apart, can illustrate this. They are from Margaret J., whose tea-house dream we examined in Chapter 2. The first of these two dreams, we already examined in part in the last chapter.

> *I was again at the temple in Memphis [Egypt]. There was a beautiful mosque with a key-shaped door. I was told to enter. Inside was a finely decorated black box partially buried in sand. A beautiful woman was sitting by it with a jar.*
>
> MARGARET J., #2

> *I was at the Marsh's, and brought Roberta a big black wooden box. We were disappointed to find it full of hairpins.*
>
> MARGARET J., #3

A brief review of the details already mentioned in Chapter 3 is in order. Margaret had visited Egypt, but this mosque is quite imaginary. She took the black box to be the Ka'aba, which is actually a large stone, to which Muslims make pilgrimage in Mecca. As with Robert's dream just discussed, these dreams have chosen as their focus a powerful, yet alien, religious symbol. This is not at all uncommon. The symbolism of foreign religions often holds more power than the all-too-familiar jaded symbolism of one's own religious tradition.

After the lead-up in the first dream, which promises something really special, the second dream looks like an anticlimax. Inside the sacred box are hairpins, which comes as a disappointment in the dream itself. Yet, if we keep to our premise that dreams are meaningful and have something to impart to the dreamer, we must look again at the hairpins.

The tea-house dream emphasised the need to understand and accept death as a part of the natural rhythm of the world. Accepting one's own body is also an important lesson from nature. Hairpins mean an attempt to accept and beautify the body. To some, this comes easily and naturally. To others, it means re-evaluating one's view of oneself. Very frequently, dreams have just that purpose, to see and understand oneself differently. Sometimes, this means lowering one's estimation of oneself, but, perhaps more often, it may mean raising it.

The first dream has particularly beautiful imagery. Memphis is the place of long-lost culture, some of the most beautiful works of ancient Egypt. To it has been joined, in this dream, a remarkably beautiful mosque. The key-shaped door means entering a hitherto closed-off sacred precinct. Margaret herself is the key to this door. Inside the Mosque is the sacred Ka'aba, but it is partially buried in sand. It must be uncovered, Margaret must discover something that is both beautiful and sacred within the temple of her soul. The emphasis throughout the dream is on beauty, culminating with the beautiful woman who, like the woman in little Anne's ship's curtains dream in Chapter 2, represents the potential within the dreamer.

The second dream specifies in very prosaic terms what this means in practice for the dreamer. She is at her place of employment, and discovers exactly what is in the box. Hairpins, to her, meant dressing up, in order to participate in social settings, a contrast to more mundane jeans and T-shirt. For her, the dream says: 'Sacred beauty rests in this, the opportunity to commune with equals in a social setting'.

Usually, a dream of this sort comes when the dreamer is discouraged and needs encouragement. Encouragement that comes from inside oneself is more valuable than what is said by other people. That is why watching dreams and listening to their message are so important.

Such a type of dream has many variations. The basic theme of discovering unexpected treasure is one of the most frequent and most impressive of all. In the light of George Fox's vision, discussed in Chapter 3, and Margaret's dreams, it is helpful to look at two dreams from a patient in a psychiatric hospital, who had had several dreams one night, but she remembered only a couple of fragments. She had described herself, previously, as feeling quite empty inside, with nothing of value to give anyone. The feeling of hopelessness pervaded her, and the psychotherapy that she was undergoing involved examining these feelings. So it was after several months that these two remarkable dreams, remembered one morning, took the limelight:

> *She walks across the floor of her living-room. She discovers that there is an enormous hole under the floor, where mining is being done. She runs on tiptoe across the floor.*

> JUNE T., #1

There is a gas pump. She digs for treasure which is buried beside the pump.

JUNE T., #2

Digging is going on under the surface of daily living, something is being mined. She was not sure what, but she thought of coal. Her framework of living (house) is being under-mined, but what is being mined is an energy-giving source tapped under the surface, within her. She runs across on tip-toe, for fear of falling through. She said she could not believe that any-thing but shit could be found deep inside her. But coal is not shit. Coal may be dirty and look like valueless rock, but it is an enormously valuable resource. The dream portrays June's response to psychotherapy, trying to run lightly over foundations that seem to her insecure. But the dream adds an important note: something valuable is being unearthed.

The theme of energy continues in the second dream fragment. But this dream, as if knowing her doubts, specifies that it is she who is doing the digging, and the goal is real treasure. Psychotherapy is not something done to a person, it is done by the person with the help of psychotherapists. It is very aptly imaged by digging under the surface. But most important, there is something of real value to be found in this digging. She is not as empty as she feels.

As we have been seeing, to understand the meaning of a dream we must do something beyond examining the story-line, the characters and the symbolism. We must place it in the context of daily life and ask ourselves what the dream is saying that is a surprise to the dreamer. When we do this, we discover what a vast treasure-land dreams are.

One final example will close this chapter — a dream that is attempting to bring a very serious message indeed to its dreamer:

I am a marshmallow floating in the middle of the ocean.

MARK L.

This is a dream statement that is best left uninterpreted. Its meaning comes through only when the impact of its imagery is felt. It holds out a feeling of total hopelessness and powerlessness. What does it feel like to be a marshmallow bobbing in the sea? Very wet, and in the process of being dissolved. 'The universe is like a vast ocean, and you are like a small marsh-mallow afloat in that ocean.' Such is the wisdom of this dream. It has a real, existential meaning for the dreamer, and it is screaming for atten-tion. Mark's personality is in the process of total disintegration. The dream puts this message across more vividly and more graphically than any word-description could do: 'You are disintegrating. You must take every possible measure to get out of the ocean of despair you are in.' This suggests a radical reorientation of the life situation in which Mark finds himself.

Such dreams as Mark's indicate that very severe crises may also be portrayed, and that they are a warning to get help while there is still a vestige of life left. In its own way, Mark's dream is a true nightmare, and gives us a good transition into the world of nightmares in the next chapter.

Chapter Five

NIGHTMARES

One thing that makes many people wish they could control their dreams is nightmares. Nightmares, however, are like other dreams in that they convey a message. It is also likely that they play a valuable role in allowing emotional release, in that emotions can be experienced directly and without censorship.

The content of a nightmare is determined by the same factors that determine other sorts of dreams. The unconscious makes use of images familiar from waking life to create a horror story which, like all other dream stories, is meaningful.

There has been a widespread belief that nightmares are caused by certain kinds of food. It is difficult to know if there is any truth in this. It is known that dreaming and nightmares are affected by various drugs. Some medicinal drugs tend to decrease, or even eliminate, the REM (rapid eye movement) phases of dreaming sleep. It is controversial, but not out of the question, that some promote and increase dreams and nightmare production. But a related observation is well verified and important, that some drugs, especially tranquillisers and sleeping pills, allow nightmares to surface that would otherwise have been kept at bay by the traditional defences against nightmares. These include insomnia, where fear of nightmares keeps the person awake; panic anxiety states, where physical reactions seem to convert nightmare content into physical anxiety systems, which include uncontrollable trembling, sweating, jerking of limbs, faint, sense of an urgent need to run, and the sense of severe panic of unknown provenance — many of these physical symptoms are also commonly found during the nightmare phase of sleep; and a defence device that comes quite easily to some people, to wake oneself before the nightmare becomes overpoweringly close to its climax. Drugs that encourage sleep or eliminate the physical manifestations of anxiety can make the dreaming state more easily entered, so that latent nightmares can be activated.

Apart from these considerations, there are other backgrounds to nightmares, also. Physical illness is regularly represented in nightmares. Withdrawal symptoms from discontinuing addictive drugs, medicinal or otherwise, including alcohol and nicotine, also appear in dreams with a nightmarish feel. Some ages are more prone to nightmares than others, and apart from emotional stresses imposed by the individual's social environment, hormones appear to give rise to nightmares, as at puberty, childbearing, menopause, in post-partum depression, and perhaps other occa-

sions. It is also intriguing that there is a decided tendency for the nightmares of one individual to resemble the nightmares of other individuals
than is true of ordinary dreams. When nightmare themes are discussed, it
is the rule rather than the exception for the listener to comment, 'I have
had that nightmare too'.

A nightmare may be defined as a dream that frightens, usually terrifies,
the dreamer both during the dream and on awakening. The emotional
reaction to nightmares is very important. It is usual to feel fright or terror
when awakening from a nightmare; and a common symptom of mental illness not to feel such fright. Because nightmares are dreams, it is important
for us to look at the story and content of each nightmare, despite the feeling of fright, sometimes sheer terror, that adheres to them. But because of
the 'typical' character of many nightmares, that is, their tendency to use
images shared by all of us, the individual story-line may be difficult to pick
out and to correlate with ongoing emotionally toned events of daily life.

Let us begin our examination of nightmares with a relatively simple and
'typical' nightmare from Carl N., the child whose dreams of the marble
trees, the recorders and the clock-house we have already examined in
previous chapters:

> *I was on a school camp near Kalamunda. A lady—who was the horse-
> riding teacher in the real camp—was teaching us something about
> what you can do on railway tracks. I found it very boring and I was
> not listening. On one side of the railway tracks was a barb-wire fence.
> On the other side of the barb-wire fence, there was someone's dead
> crop, I think it was wheat. Suddenly a train came rushing towards me.
> I started running one way off the tracks. The train was on the track I
> was on. I changed my mind and went the other way, I tripped over
> many tracks. I looked at the train. It had a bright orange light at the
> front. I looked at it again. It had a red one instead of an orange one
> now. I looked at it again. Now it was orange. I woke up.*

CARL N., #4

This dream contains one of the most frequent nightmare motifs: railroad
tracks that the dreamer tries to cross while a train is coming towards her/
him on the track she/he is currently on. Typically, there is a multitude of
tracks.

All of the motifs in this nightmare were drawn from life experiences,
though the particular combination and theme is special to nightmares.
Although the image of a lot of tracks side by side is not an everyday sight,
Carl had seen such multiple tracks on at least two occasions during his lifetime, but, interestingly, neither close in time to the nightmare. One of the
most remarkable features of dreams is their ability to bring images from
the very distant past. It seems that there is an unconscious storage of

impressive imagery, often for many years, and the dreams make use of it on appropriate occasions. The meaning of this theme of the railroad tracks and train is that the dreamer must attempt to change direction, to avoid a catastrophe looming ahead.

Most nightmares refer to the feeling of the situation that the dreamer is in at the time of the nightmare. They are not making pronouncements on the whole course of life, but on a situation that feels terrifying at the time. Often, it is the emotion, rather than the specific imagery, that is the purpose of the nightmare. Quite frequently, not enough emotional attention has been consciously paid to the situation, so that the emotion has to find release during sleep. The message of the nightmare is that such attention is needed during waking life, and steps must be taken to correct the situation.

Carl's nightmare came quite some time after returning from a school camp. At the camp, there was some horse-riding instruction. In his dream, he is again at the camp, but this time, the horse-riding teacher is teaching about railroad tracks, and Carl is not interested. The tracks run alongside a wheat field, but the wheat is dead. It is also fenced off with barbed wire. This makes the crossing more difficult, because Carl ultimately can run in only one direction, and it would not be possible to leave the tracks on the side of the wheat field. He is forced in one direction, and the menace of the approaching train is made stronger. He trips on the tracks. The light on the front of the train is ominous: orange, then red, then orange — caution, stop!, caution.

What are the tracks that need to be crossed? In life, including school life, there are set tracks that one is expected to follow. Freedom is restricted, goals are set, curricula dictate what the child is to do, be interested in and follow up during its growth towards adulthood. The sterility of this is represented in the dream by the 'adult' world beyond the barbed-wire fence, the field of dead wheat.

If Carl can cross the tracks to the other side, he can escape. But who knows what he may find there? The dream gives no hint, it is left to our imagination. Free fields in which Carl can play, without being tracked into any specific adult goal, but can be a child, free and in love with life? Perhaps.

Trains are collective vehicles. They hold enormous numbers of people, and they go along predetermined routes. A person using a train may choose one of a finite number of destinations, and thereafter, is limited to getting on and off the train. In this respect, it is not unlike an allegory for the school situation, which offers a limited selection of learning goals, and once embarked, the student has little choice except to stop or to continue.

The onrush of the train means the inevitability of going along with the stream of collective life. Home offers a very limited and sheltered environment for this. School camp means being plunged into quite new communal life-styles.

The dead crop alongside the tracks catches our attention. There is some personal history connected with this. Carl had asked what growing wheat looks like, some time before the dream, after a school visit to a flour mill. He was reminded that, when quite young, about age two, he had lived out in the countryside and seen growing wheat, but of course, he could not remember this. Like a dead crop, it is a part of life closed off to him. As a city child, he cannot hope to be involved in a living encounter with growing wheat.

But Carl had had some contact with nature, if not growing wheat, back during the school camp when he had been taught to ride a horse. But now, that horse seems to have been changed into an onrushing train that cannot be stopped and threatens to destroy him. It glows with the message of caution!, stop!, caution!. (Many people call the amber light between the red and green lights 'orange'.) The flashing of the light draws his attention to the danger. Early in the dream, the horse-riding teacher had been teaching about railroad tracks, but Carl was too bored to listen. The dream has a double message: 'If you do not listen to the petty details about life, the outcome may be quite disastrous', and 'When nature is dead and turned into mechanised living, there is no real life at all'.

The theme of the railroad tracks and the oncoming train that is difficult or impossible to avoid is a typical one. But of course, by no means all nightmares employ typical motifs for their message. Sometimes, typical motifs are turned around, also, and used with a very atypical meaning. For example, the motif of the treasure hidden under the floor or ground, which we examined in Chapters 3 and 4, can have a very threatening aspect to it. A young psychiatric patient had the following dream, which bears extensive enquiry:

> *A man was burnt to death under the floor-boards in a mental hospital. He lived in the room next to me. He had made a hole in the floor-boards, climbed in, sat there with a radio and lit a cigarette. After finding him, he was still moving. I said he should be cremated but Dad said no, he would ring the police later and to be careful not to light any fires in case the evidence was destroyed. The man talked for about half an hour before he died and got up and kissed me.*

> JACKIE W.

The cast of characters in this dream is important. First, there is the man who:

lived in the adjoining room;
made a hole in the floor-boards;
climbed in and sat with a radio and lit a cigarette;

was burned to death there;
talked for about half an hour before dying;
got up and kissed the dreamer.

Next, there is the dreamer, Jackie, who:

found the 'dead' man still moving;
wanted to have the man cremated;
was kissed by the dying man.

Finally, there is Jackie's father, who:

said he would call the police later on;
warned against lighting fires so as not to destroy the evidence.

Jackie thinks of herself as a mental patient. She is deeply depressed and has several times attempted suicide. But the mental hospital in the dream is not the one where she is staying, and the man in the dream does not correspond to any real person. We have seen the feminine counterpart to this in the anima, which we have examined several times in this book. The masculine form is called the animus, and represents Jackie's masculine half of her personality. The masculine aspect of character is usually learned from one's father, and in Jackie's case, where the relationship between her and her father is particularly close, the masculine traits learned from her father are quite pronounced. It is important to note that I make a distinction between 'female' and 'feminine', 'male' and 'masculine'. Every person has a share of feminine and masculine traits, which are socially conditioned personality characteristics and which vary according to time, place, culture, class and personal history, having little to do with biological gender.

Two striking features appear in this dream. First of all, it is not Jackie who dies but the man in the adjoining room. In other words, it is not Jackie's conscious wish to commit suicide, but something in her that is roughly her equal, masculine and mentally ill. Jung spoke of such figures as 'autonomous complexes' or separate sub-personalities. By this is meant that an individual's personality is not a unified whole but split. This particular case of Jackie's is a good illustration. Jackie in her normal state is neither suicidal nor ill. She is capable of accepting heavy responsibilities, planning her future and striving towards the goals she wants. But from time to time, it is as if a feeling comes over her and holds her in its grip, and when this happens, she is highly suicidal and depressed to the point of feeling absolute hopelessness. Such splits exist within us all and do not necessarily suggest mental illness. The dream portrays these two sides of Jackie's personality by speaking of two persons in adjoining rooms: one, Jackie as in normal life; the other, her very sick animus, which is capable of acting on its own as a sort of separate personality. The tragedy, of course, is that, as a portion—even if a split-off portion—of her own personality, this animus, in destroying itself, would destroy all of her.

The other striking feature of the dream is that the problem is not only clearly portrayed, but the dream is attempting to help Jackie find a solution to her problem. It is not only presenting the problem, which she knows well enough, even if not in quite the terms set by the dream, but it is suggesting what to do about it. So this nightmare has a valuable function.

The story of the dream is quite simple. A man, a patient in the same mental hospital, makes a place for himself under the floor-boards and there is burned to death from a fire started by his cigarette while listening to the radio. He is on affectionate terms with Jackie, and takes a considerable time to die. Jackie wants him cremated, but her father says the evidence must be kept intact for the police.

The man, who is a dream invention, goes underground—under the floor, more exactly—to smoke and listen to his radio. What does he hear on the radio? Possibly messages from outside, from the world beyond the walls of the hospital, that is, from the 'normal' world beyond the confines of Jackie's illness. It is equally possible that he is listening to messages from inside, i.e. Jackie's inner voices. We all have inner voices, and though we usually take that statement as a metaphorical description of feelings or thoughts that come to us, dreams do not hesitate to take it literally. In either event, the man with his radio is Jackie's link with the world, probably both the external and the inner worlds. His kiss suggests that he also represents erotic attachments—or, rather, the lack of such attachments, since he dies.

Now Jackie's father turns up at the scene. He is concerned that evidence be conserved for the police. Who are the police? In this instance, very probably me, since it is to me that Jackie reports with her dreams.

Quite near the beginning, where the man makes a hole in the floor-boards and climbs in, a different direction in the dream could have led to a totally different outcome. Suppose the man had simply sat on his bed and smoked while listening to the radio. What would have happened? He would not have been burned up. Jackie, and consequently we too, would have heard what the radio had to say. The radio might have brought unpleasant messages, to be sure; or it might have brought reassurance. In either event, Jackie would be assured that she is not alone, that there are others in the world besides her father who care. Consequently, there is no need for suicide.

Obviously, Jackie is not in control of the storylines of her dreams, and to know what this suggestion would mean, we have to put it into terms that she could understand and implement consciously. The image of the man going under the floorboards to listen to his radio suggests that she is shutting a bit of her personality off from herself, namely the masculine world—this, in turn, probably means that she is covering over any concrete interest in men. Her father's appearance later in the dream suggests that she is still so attached to her father that any other relationship with a man is beyond her grasp and has to be burned up, as it were. The prominent role played by Jackie's father must be given its due. As the first male love, he becomes the model for masculinity in Jackie's mind. But when she remains too attached, if he never loses his divine status in her eyes ('He is always right', Jackie said to me, quite unabashedly and quite seriously, of her father), then he may remain the only male love and no other man may be able to measure up to him and claim her affections.

Nightmares can be sheer terror, without any hint of an alleviating possibility. Here is one from John W., whose dream of the rubber shoe-laces we examined right at the beginning of this book:

> *Juvenile Delinquents are fooling around, slugging each other. I and my co-worker cannot quite keep them under control. Then a girl brings a snake to scare me with. It is an asp. It lunges for my chest and bites hard. The venom enters the wound and I scream in agony as I die.*
>
> JOHN W., #6

John had had a migraine headache several hours before this dream. This probably is represented by the dream image of the Juvenile Delinquents slugging each other, the thump thump thumping feeling in the head during such a headache, and the impossibility of keeping it under control. John also commented that the wound on his chest resembled impetigo sores that his young daughter had come out with that day. As for the asp, he knew of it as a biting snake, but no more.

Juvenile Delinquents also turned up in the shoe-laces dream, where there was nothing to fear. John had, in reality, some years earlier, worked with Juvenile Delinquents, so their appearance as a threat in these dreams is not so odd. There is a reminiscence about the girl with the asp: John remembered a scene from one of the 'Carry On' movies. Someone is talking with Cleopatra about a proposed murder. Cleopatra says, 'That's simple, a bite of this asp will do it'. The fellow proceeds to bite the asp, and Cleopatra cries out, 'No, it bites you!'

Juvenile Delinquents are characterised by anger, rebellion, discrimination, self-centredness; in short, rebellious, angry feelings and conflict. Are the dream's Juvenile Delinquents an image of one side of John's own personality? There is good evidence that they are. John was separated from his wife, and their youngest child had come down with impetigo sores when John visited her that day. Within him was a boiling cauldron of anger and fury directed towards his wife, a wish to enter into violent conflict with her. In his dream, he is attempting to keep all these seething feelings (which probably were at the root of the migraine) under control. With him is a helper, not further identified in the dream. I concluded, when discussing the dream with John, that the fellow worker was John's superego — the dos and don'ts and shoulds and oughts learned from society and incorporated within us as a quasi-separate personality.

So neither John nor his helper can keep the Juvenile Delinquents under control. The angry, rebellious feelings are too powerful. But why keep them under control at all? Convention says calm and politeness are required at all times and particularly when a very powerful emotion is touched. The dream has a rather different view.

Now the girl with the asp appears. She intends to frighten John with it, but, in fact, it kills him. Who is this girl? She is not identified in the dream, nor in the dreamer's memory, as any real person. We might suggest that she represents John's wife, the cause of his not being in close touch with his daughter. As an unidentified woman, she represents the feminine world, felt by John at this point to be murderous, but she is not really his wife, she is his own murderous, aggressive feelings of hatred, personified as a woman because he saw his wife as the threat, which he conflated with other earlier bad experiences of women. The woman in the dream is an anima figure, representing his (then) feeling of being hurt by the feminine world and reflecting his own desire for revenge. In specific terms, this traces back to his childhood experience of being rejected by his mother, at a young enough age to feel the experience as a murderous attack. Consequently, we must take this anima figure, the girl with the asp, as meaningful both on the objective and the subjective sides: objectively, his experience of the feeling of deep rejection by his mother and by his wife; subjectively, as his own internalised murderous feelings which are destroying him from inside.

What is the message of this dream? It uses imagery to express a situation that is not all that easy to untangle. From Juvenile Delinquents to dying from snake-bite, it is not enough simply to label it 'nightmare' and to suppose that we have done with it. The nightmare is telling us something: that John is filled with rage and fury, as imaged by the Juvenile Delinquents and by the girl with the asp, and that he has turned this against himself. Because of the fatal outcome of the dream, it is saying, 'Look! If you don't find some way for that rage to come out and be expressed, you yourself will be its victim!' It is directing him, and me to whom he told the dream, to find a way to get the rage out into the open. Otherwise, if strong enough, it may lead to serious trouble, conceivably even one of those murder plus suicide cases that are far from unknown in situations of family disintegration.

One of the important features in examining a nightmare is to look at its ending, to see to what it leads, and to take this seriously as portraying the dreamer's emotional disposition. Obviously, it is not enough simply to seek out the kernel meaning of the nightmare and say in words, 'You feel like you are being threatened and murdered', or 'Feelings of rage and

murderous actions are seething in you'. This is only an early step in working with the dream. Something has to be done with that rage, and the
dream gives us a clue in which direction to turn. In the dream story, John is
the one who is threatened and murdered; it is with these feelings that we
must work in order to calm the inner turmoil and prevent his externalising,
or 'acting out', the aggression.

Often, a nightmare is a direct appeal to the analyst, me in this instance,
to recognise something that has either been overlooked up to the present or
that has been withheld by the patient. We examined Thomas O.'s dream
of the Acropolis in Hobart back in Chapter 3. Here is a nightmare that
gives further insight into his make-up:

> I am being pursued by two men. Joining crowds, I flee to a holiday
> island. Someone is killed by them with .22 rifles. They postpone
> executing me to look for an analyst, to see if he is really dead. I escape
> by joining a line for rowing-boats back to the mainland, and rowing
> away.
>
> THOMAS O., #2

These assailants, two men, are again anonymous. Such anonymous figures
represent the feeling of threat — both the feeling of being threatened by life
around us, and the feeling of aggression inside the dreamer, directed
towards the outside world, but potentially turned against herself/himself.
Of the assailants in this dream, we know only that they carry rifles and are
willing to kill; indeed, they have already killed one man, and before killing
Thomas, they want an analyst, obviously me to whom Thomas brought the
dream, to determine whether the man they killed is really dead. In other
words, has something in Thomas' personality already been killed off,
which might pose a threat to the rest of his personality? Or is there still life
in that 'man', similar to the life left in the roasted dog in Jim K.'s dream
#2(f), which we examined in the preceding chapter?

Let us look very briefly at the story-line of the dream. Pursued by
murderers, Thomas flees to a holiday island — perhaps Rottnest Island,
which is a frequent holiday resort a short distance from the west coast of
Australia where Thomas lives. They kill one man and want me to determine whether he is really dead before they shoot Thomas himself. Thomas
escapes by rowing to the mainland from the island.

The off-shore island is a very frequent motif in dreams. It represents an
escape from daily life, but it also represents a separation between the
dreamer's emotional desire and everyday life. In Thomas' Hobart dream,
the island of Tasmania was a place where he could feel the freedom that
comes from divorce. In Castaneda's books, the Island of the Tonal
(roughly = ego-consciousness) has an important role as representing the
isolation that we feel from nature and the way in which our conscious life

expectations must be modified. Frequently in dreams, islands represent
the emergence of a discovery about oneself that has not yet been integrated
into the mainland stream of life and thought. In Thomas' dream, it is an
island resort, a holidaying place, a retreat to which he can turn to get away
from the pressures of daily life. The implication in the dream is that I will
be found on that island, so perhaps the island here represents Thomas'
sessions with me, in which we discuss his dreams and link them up with
daily events, a 'secure' island where he can feel relief from the pressures of
daily work, an island amidst the hustle and bustle of work life. There is
another connotation for island, though, which we must not overlook. It
represents placing oneself outside the mainstream of life, an attempt to cut
off from the world:

> No man is an Iland, intire of its self; every man is a piece of the Conti-
> nent, a part of the maine; if a Clod bee washed away by the Sea,
> Europe is the lesse, as well as if a Promontorie were, as well as if a
> Mannor of thy friends or of thine owne were; any mans death dimin-
> ishes me, because I am involved in Mankind; And therefore never
> send to know for whom the bell tolls; It tolls for thee.

> JOHN DONNE
> 'Devotions Upon Emergent Occasions' XVII)

This brief passage from Donne sums up much of the feeling of the dream.
Who are the two men pursuing Thomas? They obviously represent the feeling of the threat of death. What has been killed off in Thomas? Looking at
him and speaking with him, there is a definite feeling that something in
him is dead. He is, in fact, so worried about appearances, that much of his
energy has been invested in maintaining his prestige. He has come to
believe his persona is really his whole being. A persona is the image of oneself carefully built up to present to the outer world. For Thomas, loss of
social standing is felt as catastrophic. But it is disastrous to be convinced
that one is really the image one tries to impress upon others.

   The dream presents conflicting themes. On the one hand, the two men
wish to consult me, the analyst, to see if the killing-off procedure is complete; and on the other hand, Thomas escapes from the island, unwilling
to follow through on the gunmen's concern and unwilling to discover what
these gunmen are about. This is a fairly accurate summary of Thomas'
attitude when he brought the dream: 'Ferret into my life and see what part
of me has been wounded or killed, but don't let that interfere with my daily
life, the mainstream of my existence.' The murderers shoot with rifles. As
the cannons in the dream of 'The Mouse that Cried', discussed in the last
chapter, probably were a sexual image as well as aggressive, there is good
reason to suppose that the rifles in Thomas' dream are both phallic and
aggressive: part of him was wounded, perhaps killed, by a sexual experi-

ence in the past, that is for me, the analyst, to ferret out; and, as in John's dream, there is a lot of pent-up aggression in the sexual sphere. The prognosis in this dream is poor. Thomas escapes by merging with the crowd and rowing back to the mainland, instead of confronting the gunmen or even seeing what the analyst has to say.

Really gruesome nightmares do occur, and represent a deep emotional crisis, or sometimes, a real situation that has a destructive effect on the dreamer. Joan's pregnancy dream, which we discussed in Chapter 2, was but one of a vast number of dreams I discussed with her. One of the most gruesome nightmares in my experience comes from her:

> *My doctor is at the head of a team who have been elected to shoot people. A friend and I were being forced to stay in the room where it was all going to take place.*
>
> *At some time, the scene changed and the crowds had all disappeared. The room was now all white and clinical—whereas before it had been wooden, barn-like. Now the doctor came in, chose three men (I think they're Maltese) and told one to sit in the chair. He was marked for three bullets—one in the head, one in the stomach and one either in the genitals or thighs. There was a supervisor to either see that the man died bravely, or that the doctor did 'the job' properly. At first, the man to be shot was quiet and composed. But they left him for so long he became hysterical. I felt I was going to scream or cry and somehow left the room. My girl-friend wouldn't come with me. When I got outside, it was dark and a group were walking toward me through newly planted lawn. I thought they would try to take me back inside, so I bent down to the ground and pretended to do something. They walked by and I tried to run off.*
>
> *Then I'm at home, and a lot of people are staying there. My doctor has turned into another man—but I feel afraid of him (just the same feeling as in the room). I wanted to get away from the house before this man left because I was afraid he would follow us. We got into my car, and the man was parked in front of us, sitting with his girl-friend. It was as if everything we owned was in our car. The man's girl-friend seemed to be 'pretending' friendliness, and said she knew they were 'vulgar'. Then she asked what had upset me about them most? I pretended they hadn't bothered me at all.*

JOAN L., #2

A specific doctor whom Joan was consulting is mentioned in this dream, but I have deleted his name and put 'my doctor' in its place. A minor surgical operation was planned, which quite frightened Joan. The friend, the three Maltese men, the changed form of the doctor, and that man's girl-friend are all dream inventions. The real doctor seems to set the scene, whereupon her dream fantasy could build this nightmare in which all her fears and anxieties could find a place. In this nightmare, Joan is frightened about consulting her doctor because of the possible consequences, and it is this fear with which the dream is concerned. She feels that she must keep up a pretence of calmness while she is in inner turmoil. She is terrified that something inside her is going to be killed off.

This was Joan's first dream that she brought to me, in her first consultation with me, never having seen me before. We can expect, then, that much of the fear in this dream is doubly determined: fear of what her medical doctor might do, and fear of me. Though I am not named specifically in the dream, I may well be the 'other man' into whom the medical doctor changes in the final paragraph of the dream. Joan was on the edge of a nervous breakdown, which is why she decided to consult me, but as soon as she heard my distinctly American voice on the phone, she got into a bit of a panic, having had bad experiences with Americans before.

First, we see the doctor and his team who have been elected to shoot people. Elected by whom? Ultimately, by the dreamer's terror over the forthcoming surgery. However, it goes a bit deeper than that, because this dream was supplemented by several other dreams, before and after, that expressed mortal terror. In other words, the terror was in Joan and took many forms.

Joan's terror changes surgery into murder. But there is no direct reference to the idea that Joan herself would be murdered. Somewhat further on in the dream, in fact, she simply walks out on the whole thing, and invites her girl-friend to do the same. Joan and her girl-friend are apparently not set up as victims to be executed next, but as witnesses to what is happening. So let us see just what is happening.

First, the crowds disappear. We had not been told there were crowds present. From being part of an anonymous crowd, Joan and her girl-friend are singled out. The feeling moves from 'this happens to some people' to 'this is happening to me!' Who is this girl-friend? She appears to play no significant role in the dream, except that she is an observer. Both Joan and her girl-friend are supposed to stay throughout, and the girl-friend does so. There is no reference to the girl-friend being in terror, and we may take it that she is the calm, observing side in Joan, the side that knows rationally that the treatments, surgical and psychological, are to preserve life, and she therefore stays. We are dealing here again with an inner split, a split that is due to real fear Joan was experiencing. One part of her lived in mortal terror, while another part made all the arrangements, calmly and rationally. There is nothing pathological or unusual about this. We are all of us 'in two minds' about something important, and that is what the dream is portraying.

We next move into a clinical setting. The original setting was more like a barn, everything made of wood. Joan moves from crude speculation to a somewhat more realistic environment, though it still has its peculiarities. The doctor chooses three Maltese (?) men, and has one of them sit in a dentist's chair.

Malta featured in the news about this time, and Maltese in the dream probably means simply 'foreigners'. It is Joan's animus that is to be destroyed. The masculine character within Joan's personality appears in triplicate here. Again, we have the strange but common dream phenomenon of portraying the dreamer and those relating to her as four persons, in a three-plus-one formulation.

The terrible deed then to be performed is to shoot one, or possibly more, of the 'foreigners' within her make-up. Here is where the fear of her doctor and her fear of me before first seeing me coincide. Interestingly, the man is sat in a dentist's chair, and one of the most familiar images for an analyst in dreams is a dentist. The doctor who she fears might kill off a part of Joan's inner masculine character is me.

One man is selected to sit in the chair, and he is marked for three bullets. Despite the detail given to the preparations for shooting, there is no evidence in the dream that it ever takes place. This may indicate that Joan's terror at what might happen with the doctor and with me is greatly overstated.

The man is marked for three bullets, one in the head, one in the stomach, one in the genitals or thighs. This is a very odd arrangement. Head = mind, stomach = ability to digest facts, genitals and thighs = sex. It would seem that the man is to be very thoroughly shot. But what sort of man is he? He is relaxed, ready for the shooting. He only becomes hysterical when the time spent in waiting is so long. He is, therefore, a willing victim. He must represent a part of Joan that is willing to die. There is even a supervisor present, either to ensure that the execution is done properly, or that the man dies bravely.

In short, one part of Joan's personality expects 'the worst', i.e. that her mind will be destroyed, therefore, she comes to me for treatment, bringing this dream as an explanation of her plight; that her sexuality will be destroyed, a reference to her fear of what the surgeon will do; and that her digestive system will be destroyed, perhaps another reference to her doctor. It is, however, not she herself who undergoes these horrors, but a man who apparently is a demonstration that Joan and her girl-friend are to watch. She has split herself up into component parts, as it were: her fears about the forthcoming surgery, represented by her doctor; her fears that part of her will be destroyed, represented by the victim; her calm witnessing of what happens, represented by her girl-friend; her conscious terror, represented by herself in the dream. The sexual fear has two supports: the surgery she was about to undergo, leading to a fear for her physical sexuality; and the fear that her sex life would be minutely examined in analysis. These fears were mostly suppressed and kept out of her conscious thinking, so that in the dream, they appear as figures from the unconscious.

Apparently, there was no force used to ensure that Joan witnessed the scene at all. She left the room, feeling it was all too much for her to stomach. But her girl-friend refused to come with her. One part of Joan wants to know what is going to happen. Outside, in the dark, she heard a group come towards her, and assumed they would take her back inside; she evaded them. She is left, therefore, with a fear that is neither supported nor refuted by events. Throughout the dream, there is no evidence that she would be hurt. When, a bit later, she met the transformed doctor and his girl-friend, they appeared friendly, though she presumed it was only pretence. So we see a great deal of fear and panic, but not much support for it.

The two 'doctors' whom she was going to see in real life were a surgeon for care of a serious physical condition, and me, her analyst. The dream has transformed this by imaging what is to happen as an execution or murder. The body expressed its reaction as murder, because any interference is felt by the body to be hostile. (We are reminded of Helen's pack-rape dream in Chapter 2.)

From the psychological side, we see the intended murder of an animus figure, that is, the death of one form of her inner masculine character and its replacement.

Death is not necessarily a bad thing in a dream. Just as in the Tarot, the Death card is interpreted as positive, so also in a dream death may mean transformation, the death of an old character trait leading to a more highly evolved state. In this particular instance, it was a classical problem: after having been single and on her own for a fair time, she was not prepared for the changes that have to be made in a marital type of situation; in particular, allowing the new husband to act in his own way, and, especially, to react in his own way, though the responses varied a great deal from what she was accustomed to.

The next scene sees her 'at home', by which is meant her parents' house. She does not yet feel the place where she is living with her husband as her real home. Like the first scene, there is a crowd of people there, so personal care is not to be found there; and, in fact, neither parent appears in the dream. Her doctor has turned into another man. This is most likely me, whom she had never seen before this dream, so that the dream's fantasy can run rather wild. If the first doctor had the appearance and name of her real surgeon, then the stress was on the much-feared coming treatment, in the first place, with slivers of me added in. The second part refers to her fears about me. She has fear, in fact terror, that something drastic and unbearable will take place. Her life of terror, not only of her surgeon but of other events as well, apart from the very serious personality problems that I have not mentioned, brought her to me, more out of desperation than of choice.

In the dream, Joan is occupied with how to leave her parents' house without the man discovering and following them. In the earlier parts of the dream, there was just Joan herself attempting to escape. Now she is accompanied. 'We' refers to her husband and herself. They get into her car, appropriate because it is her problems with which the dream is concerned. But the man and his girl-friend are already parked in front of them. It appears that a confrontation has to take place, Joan can no longer run from it. She has committed herself to the psychological doctor out of sheer necessity.

Who is the man's girl-friend? In the context of the situation, this dream was immediately before her first session with me; the man and his girl-friend would be her imagination of me as a man and of my own inner self, my gentle, caring 'feminine' side. Her fear could be fed because, never having seen me, she could naturally make all sorts of assumptions about me, what I am like, how I look, to what extent I could be trusted with my American voice, and the like.

It is as if all their possessions were in her car, that is, all that she and her husband valued were with her. A small amount, obviously, but some chance of salvaging her way of life.

The dream ends with the subject of pretending, both on the part of the man's girl-friend and on the part of Joan herself. Throughout the dream, there is never any verbal protest. And we really do not know what is to happen next. Will she be caught or escape? If caught, will she be shot like the man she saw or not? It is all unresolved, corresponding to the panic state she was suffering from when she brought me this dream. In a state of panic, there is no way to work out a calm plan of approaching a danger; and so it was with her — her panic due to enormous fears of the situation she was in, imaged in the dream as witnessing a murder, with the assumption that she would be, if not the next, then nearly so.

In reality, all Joan can, in fact, do is pretend. She had work to contend with, a husband to care for, an upcoming operation. If she gave way to her fears, she would collapse. It was either that or to adopt an air of pretence, the pretence that 'everything is alright'.

The turning point in this dream came when Joan walked out of the room where the execution was taking place, and successfully left the premises. When she got home, she was on safe territory. Here, she could have asked the doctor and his girl-friend what it was all about. But sheer terror prevented this.

To deal with this nightmare, at least two people are needed, Joan and someone else. It is rare that the terror of a nightmare can be assuaged by just having a rational look at its contents. Emotion is the principal factor in nightmares, and the imagery helps one way or another to find what the emotion is all about. But to become free from that emotion, the help of another person is required, so that emotion and dream imagery can be brought together and the dreamer's experience can be strengthened and

then calmed — and most important, so that the dreamer will not be left
with the feeling that the worries, doubts and fears are left without a sympathetic ear.

This nightmare has a twofold purpose. Firstly, as a dream immediately
before consulting me for the first time, the nightmare is a message to me of
how deep the terror is, and something of the fantasies that plague her
mind. Secondly, it allows the release of the fears and terrors that she has to
hide during waking hours, giving vent to feelings that are tearing her
apart. In this respect, it should be noted that nightmares lose much of
their power when they are written down immediately upon waking from
the nightmare. There is a natural tendency to want to forget the whole
thing as quickly as possible. But if this is thwarted, and the entire nightmare is written down post-haste, not only is the emotion given an outlet,
but the conscious mind also has a chance to intervene by judging the
reality value of the nightmare. Once it is understood that the dream is
portraying emotion-packed feelings and fears, usually the nightmare loses
its power and you can go back to sleep peacefully. Sometimes, this does not
work and the attempt to sketch or even paint one or more of the disturbing
parts of the dream will be needed in order to give adequate voice to what
has to find release. Attempting to interpret the nightmare immediately
usually does not bring much success — although it can be tried if all else
fails — because the nightmare is not an intellectual enterprise, and the
heart rather than the head needs to be dominant.

Nightmares are not always such action-packed melodramas. Their
symbolism often speaks out loud and clear. To judge the importance of a
dream by its size is to miss out; often the most important dreams are quite
short, while a long text may be largely waffle. As an illustration of the
power that may be packed inside a short dream, let us look at the following
dream from Maria X, a woman in her early fifties:

> *A very fragile wooden box supported by spindly legs was burning
> fiercely inside: the females were starting to emerge. I was standing
> pushing against the drop-down lid trying to prevent the fire from
> engulfing the box.*
>
> MARIA X.

This is a small nightmare. Like many dreams, it is open-ended. We see one
scene of what promises to be a full-length feature film, and can only speculate about the outcome.

The interpretation of this nightmare has to rely rather heavily on
symbolism. But before turning to that, let us see what we can make of it in
its own terms:

1. There is a box.
2. The support for the box is weak.

3. A fire burns in the box, flames flare up.
4. Maria attempts to put out the fire by keeping the lid tightly closed, but we get the impression that this method is destined to failure.

There are several points of entry into this dream, but we may as well start with the first. The word 'chest' has a double meaning, i.e. a wooden box and the region of the heart. The poetic image of a fire burning in one's chest or breast is well known. It means great passion, usually love. This threatens to engulf Maria. She attempts to put it out by clamping down the lid and refusing to allow any of this passion to show.

The legs of the box are indeed very fragile, for she had been badly hurt in love before. Of course, no amount of forcefully trying to close the lid on this passion can succeed, and it was only a few days until she found herself openly declaring her love.

What is the dream doing, in this case? It is saying, through symbols, that Maria is ardently in love, so much so that she could not keep it down — being married, she felt guilt at the idea of letting the love flourish. She prepares herself, knowing of my interest in dreams, to voice her love without voicing it, through symbolism. Only afterwards comes the courage to say it openly.

Maria's dream is a nightmare only from one point of view. It is felt as a nightmare because the conscious intention and the burning passion inside are opposed to one another. It ceases to be a nightmare once they are brought together.

This principle, that nightmares may come from the conflict of conscious intent and inner emotion, holds in a great many instances, though by no means always. A fairly typical nightmare is the following, which uses familiar dream motifs:

> I am waiting to go to work, me and another workmate. We are on different sides of a T-junction. I see a rocket go up that resembles an F-111 camouflaged jet fighter. I notice the sky is cloudy, so I yell across the road at the T-junction to my workmate (this guy has got the same job as myself) and I say to him, 'There won't be any work today because of the cloud cover'. Because the job we have is to watch these rockets go around the sun, or something. We are just observers, and that is a full-time job. Then a rocket turns side-ways, roars across a paddock, hits an embankment, and then I realise that it is a nuclear rocket. It bores into the embankment and I run and hide behind the walls of the pig-stall on my parents' farm. I think that is stupid, because the wall is not going to be of any help if the rocket comes in my direction, and by this stage, the rocket is going in all directions around the paddock.

Jɪᴍ Y.

This is a fairly common nightmare motif, in which either an aeroplane or a rocket is following the dreamer with the threat of exploding or crashing on her/him. It is interesting to note that, before the advent of aeroplanes, the same dream motif used meteorites. It is such a widespread dream motif, that we are justified in wondering if it is archetypal. Ancient tales of things falling from the sky are common; and not so ancient, too: remember Chicken Little! Unfortunately, the theme of rockets falling from the sky is not only a dream motif. Fortunately, the theme of the rocket chasing the dreamer still remains a dream motif.

But let us look more closely at this nightmare. Jim and a work-mate are waiting for their work to begin. Their work is to track rockets as they circle the sun. Because of the clouds, they doubt that will be possible. But the rocket turns out to be a nuclear rocket and flies all around the paddock, there is no secure hiding place. We are left with this panic-stricken situation, for the dream comes to an abrupt end.

Jim is back 'home' at his parents' farm. In this story, he is not yet the independently living fellow with a life of his own, as in waking life, but still an appendage of his parents. That particular point, of independence vs parental ties, is by no means unique to this dreamer. One's real parents may or may not be alive, but in dreams, they continue to live and rule no matter what the age or accomplishments of the dreamer. In this way, the dream is saying, 'If you persist in living life as if you were emotionally still back "home", a real explosion is bound to come. There is no refuge to be found in retreat to outworn attachments. You can't go home again.'

By asking Jim to watch and keep track of his dreams, he is made into a watcher, as in the dream. Much has happened in his world, and he and his friends must watch the results at a T-junction.

A T-junction is one where a road ends at a cross-roads, so that the traveller must go either left or right but not straight ahead. Jim and his workmate are stationed one on each side of the road that has come to an end. But after this point, we hear no more of the workmate. The workmate is, presumably, a personification of Jim's everyday life. It should be mentioned that the workmate in the dream was not identified as a real person by Jim.

The dominating motif in this nightmare is terror, the realisation that there is no safe place to hide. There is really only one means of safety, and that is to leave the influences of home altogether. Something more requires to be done, not merely observing the process, imaged by tracking the rockets as they circle the sun. The danger is one of total annihilation: a nuclear explosion. By using such strong imagery, the nightmare is trying to make its emphasis on how serious the situation is in which Jim finds himself.

Which way should Jim take at the cross-roads? The dream gives no hint of an answer to that. He is, in real life, stymied as to which way to go, bewildered and confused. But he feels a threat, terror, as what he had been watching suddenly starts to threaten him. Up to now, he has been an observer, a person who observed rockets at, so to speak, arm's length. But what does the rocket represent? There are various possibilities, but it is well to ask ourselves initially to what extent the rocket need symbolise anything at all, or whether it should be taken as is. This is easier to do if we look at the dream as a brief drama, and seeing what it says as a whole instead of bit by bit.

The dream uses imagery from contemporary life: we are in the nuclear age, rockets and other objects are put in orbit around the earth, or are sent off to other planets, or into outer space. The dream is only very slightly ahead of its time in speaking of rockets orbiting the sun.

The two workmates have a job, which is to observe the rockets that have been launched, apparently to track their orbit or their trajectory around the sun. Sky visibility is poor, there is heavy cloud cover. Jim calls off work, because of the bad visibility. Then a rocket, which they saw rise earlier, comes to pursue him.

The rocket is a camouflaged F-111, an American-built military plane, very expensive and, at least in its early production, not very reliable. The F-111 was topical during Jim's adolescence. Then the anxiety-filled conclusion comes, as we leave the theatre: there is no hope. This is what makes the dream into a nightmare.

What would the explosion of the rocket mean, if the dream had continued? It would be the demolition of Jim's parents' property and probably his own death. The symbolism of a rocket comes in here. Rockets, like cannons, are increasingly popular phallic images in dream language. This type of rocket is not a manned space probe, but a nuclear-armed military rocket. One of Jim's most serious problems was to form a relationship, no matter how tenuous, with a woman. Sexually, he felt extremely frustrated — the number of times he had had sexual intercourse, apart from with a prostitute, could be amply counted on the fingers of one hand. The source of this problem was very clearly his family relationships. The sexual problem was, he felt, threatening to destroy him. The nightmare lays the reason for this squarely with Jim's parents.

Anticipating the next chapter, 'Sex in Dreams', we may ask why Jim's dream chose a phallic image, a nuclear rocket, instead of an overtly sexual image. There are several good reasons for this. To begin with, by choosing a rocket, the dream is emphasising the mechanical and impersonal nature of Jim's male sexuality, as it was formed by his parents' influence. This was one of his chief problems, the inability to form a personal, close relationship with any woman, and the reason he turned to prostitutes to satisfy his sexual needs — a very impersonal, mechanical way of approaching sex. As a rocket, the sexual image is represented as lethal and explosive, a reference to the feeling that a real sexual relationship would annihilate him because, at heart, he was his parents' child, and though long independent of home, Jim felt internally that he still lived back on the farm. That the rocket was camouflaged as an F-111 could be a reference to me: I epitomised the whole sexual issue for Jim, and one part of him felt, rightly, that he would have to blow up the domination of his parents over him, and the side of him that was still his parents' child would be destroyed along with it, if my influence prevailed.

SUMMARY

Enough has been said to provide entry into the world of nightmares. In understanding them, the same principles apply as for ordinary dreams, but perhaps with the slight difference that nightmares are almost pure emotion, and the threat posed in the nightmare is a result of conflict between inner emotion and waking attempts to thwart the emotion. More than any other type of dream, nightmares require to be felt and not merely observed. The interpretation of a nightmare relies very heavily on this emotion. But also, more than any other dream, a nightmare requires linking up with events of the day's life, and the conflict of emotions brought out into the open. Our inclination to forget nightmares as soon as possible actually thwarts both the healing process and the attempt to sleep peacefully. A nightmare needs to be confronted head on, not through interpretation but through recognition of its emotion. They are best written down while still fresh, that is, during the time of panic on awakening. Later, preferably with another person's help, they should be investigated the same way as other dreams, though with perhaps more emphasis on the dramatic story-line and less on the details. But nightmares also must be integrated into life, and this is done firstly, by discovering which persons and situations in waking life the nightmare is linked with; and secondly, by facing the conflict of emotions that has produced the need for the nightmare, squarely and honestly.

Chapter Six

SEX IN DREAMS

Of all the types of symbolism that occur in dreams, sexual symbolism is the best known. Sigmund Freud is usually credited with having introduced the sexual interpretation of dreams, so that the term 'Freudian symbols' has become popularly applied to sexual symbolism. Freud himself did not automatically turn to sexual symbolism for dream interpretation, although sexual imagery was certainly emphasised by him. In popular usage, 'sexual symbolism' has become so widespread that virtually everything in a dream can be converted to sexual imagery. When this is done, dreams come to mean little more than sexual analogies, and the unique message of each dream is in danger of being lost.

The reaction to 'Freudian symbolism' has, however, swung the pendulum almost to the opposite extreme, so that even overt sexual references in dreams may be denied. We see some examples of that later in this chapter. Both extremes seem equally improbable. We should expect to see sex turning up in dreams certainly as frequently as any other theme, and because sexual problems are still very prevalent in our society, rather more frequently than other possible themes. We should expect sexual themes and imagery to turn up quite often in present-day dreams, but not exclusively or necessarily as the dominating motif. Overt sexual imagery is actually fairly common in contemporary dreams; so is sexual symbolism. When sexual themes are represented not openly but through symbolism, we need to ask ourselves why the specific symbols were chosen. We have touched on this question several times already. We need to examine it more systematically in this chapter.

Gerald D., whose dream of taking lectures under me we examined in Chapter 1, has contributed the following dream, in which sexual symbolism plays an important role:

> *With Jane in a service station. We go to put gas in the car. We find an old van on a crane or tow-truck at the pump. We decide we should fill this first. We find we have not put the nozzle in the tank, gas leaks onto the ground. We fix this. When the tank fills up, the front of the van tips and smashes into the ground, damaging the roof. This sets up a harmonic motion causing the van to smash into the building and two motor cycles owned by the garage owner and his friend, who are very angry over the damage, especially to the bikes. They demand*

that we pay for all damage to the bikes even though it is slight. I go for
a closer look and see slight damage, yet feel guilty over the incident, so
obliged to pay. The men demand an excessive amount so I say we had
better get the police. I have trouble contacting them. The men won't
let us leave until we pay or the police arrive. I try to reason with them
but it is useless. I fear they will come round to my house and beat me
up if we leave without settlement.

GERALD D., #2

Jane is Gerald's current girl-friend, with whom he is living. Gerald, a
student, pours much of his time each day into study, to the neglect, Jane
feels, of herself. This had reached the proportions of a serious conflict by
the time of this dream. The relationship had degenerated to the point that
little was left, even in the sexual sphere.

Inserting the hose of a fuel pump into the fuel tank of a car in order to
fill it can be seen as an analogy of sexual intercourse. A tendency to premature ejaculation may be alluded to by the leakage onto the ground. When
Gerald told the dream (instead of reading his written text), he recalled it as
repeatedly attempting to insert the fuel hose, rather than just once, which
might point to impotence on his part, another problem when the relationship had deteriorated to the point that sexual excitation had largely disappeared.

But what is this dream saying about the sexual relationship of this
couple? First, it is not their own car that they are trying to fill, but a van
they find at the gas station. And the pouring of energy into this threatens a
total collapse. What does the van represent for this couple? There are three
plausible candidates: the analytical sessions with me, Gerald's studies and
the relationship between Gerald and Jane. Jane sees the unbalanced aspect
of their lives to be Gerald's obsessive studying — that Gerald is pouring all
of his energy into study, instead of into their relationship (which would be
imaged as their own car). Gerald was willing to agree with this (I had the
good fortune to be able to discuss the dream with them both in a conjoint
session). That his energies were going into the relationship with me, in the
analytical sessions, Gerald denied, and I rather agree with him on that.

Looking at the story-line of the dream, if the van represents Gerald's
attempt to contain all of his life's concerns in one load, then the pouring of
energies into one aspect only causes the whole to collapse, the roof caves in,
and there are other damages, the cost of which is a matter of dispute. In
reality, Gerald did under-value the damage he was doing to his relationship and, ultimately, to his own life. In the dream image, the fuel is put
into the tank at the front of the car, implying that the engine is at the rear,
as in a Volkswagon Beetle, i.e. the actual mechanics of Gerald's life movements are hidden behind, where he is unaware of them.

While Gerald estimates the damage to be minor, the garage owner and his friend take it to be quite major. So there is a conflict in Gerald's mind as to how much damage the collapsing of his relationships to life causes. If we take the garage owner and his friend to represent the aspect of Gerald's psyche that attempts to keep emotional life in good repair, their estimate of the damage done is very much in conflict with Gerald's conscious estimate.

Gerald attempts to get in touch with the police. Who are they? Since they are the ones to whom mistakes are to be reported and who will adjudicate on responsibilities, they probably are me. Gerald told me the dream after a lengthy break, and he also commented that he felt I was trying to cut down on his intellectualism in favour of developing relationships, a matter about which he felt very uneasy. But I was not immediately available after the dream, only several days later. In the meantime, the coldness between the couple continued to grow. Sexual symbolism, then, refers in this dream to the entire sphere of relationships, and not merely the act of sexual intercourse itself. And reporting to the police means discussion of the situation with a person felt to be an authority figure, and probably a biased one at that.

There are other possible ways of looking at the imagery in the dream. Gasoline is energy; pumping energy into the van causes it to tip over and collapse. But in Gerald's life, we need to ask just what it is that is collapsing. What is it that requires examination? The answer is, specifically, his relationship with Jane; and, more generally, his overall relationship with life.

Freudian dream theory has popularised the viewpoint that a hose is an image for a penis, particularly such a hose as this through which a liquid flows when it is inserted into a receptacle. An objection to this is that there are many objects that would be equally suitable images. The gas hose is special in that it is used for transferring energy from storage into a vehicle, which is the means by which the road of life is travelled. In this dream, rather than being poured into the relationship with Jane, Gerald's energy is going into something else, which causes his vehicle to overbalance and collapse, a vivid image of the state of his relationships in general at the moment.

Without resorting to symbolism, dreams are quite capable of representing sexual organs as such, and they frequently do so. Take, for example, this dream of a middle-aged woman:

I was with a man who was a paraplegic or something and he was sitting down. It appeared we were both undressed, the lower halves of our bodies were undressed. He had a very small penis like a little boy and I was very surprised when he had an erection. So I sat over his lap in order to have sex with him, which was a bit difficult because of his small penis and because other people were present, and it made me urinate instead. And he said to me, 'I don't mind if you piss on me or tell me how much you hate your parents. I will still love you.'

GLADYS J.

The man was, Gladys said, a combination image of a number of men she had known. The difference was that these men had not loved her, while the man in the dream concluded the dream by his declaration of love. The dream came on a night when Gladys was not, in fact, sleeping with anyone and had not had sex. This was, in part, an assertion of independence, of her right to self-determination, particularly in respect to her husband, from whom she was separated.

The attitude to the man in this dream is derogatory in several ways. He is paraplegic, unable to walk, reminiscent of a real man Gladys once knew and was fond of, but whose only interest in her was sexual. Her dream image of the dream-man, then, is that he is crippled, and childish. Small boys do have erections, so it is a bit surprising that this should surprise her. The important thing is that the penis is so small. The scene is public, which embarrasses her. They are both exposed sexually. Involuntarily, she urinates on him. But to our surprise, he declares his continuing love for her, even though she pisses on him and tells him how much she hates her parents. There is a reference here to a real conflict with her parents, and especially her father.

Normally, a child's conception of what an adult male is like comes from its father. If there is hatred for the father, the image of the male is likely to be negative, and relationships difficult to establish. Also, and very importantly, the child's evaluation of its own masculinity is likely to be negative. A woman's masculinity is — as we have seen — expressed in dreams through animus figures, usually imaginary men who turn out to represent traits in the dreamer herself. Because we have been socially conditioned to ignore, or deprecate, a woman's masculine traits, she finds herself attracted to men who mirror her undeveloped masculine traits. As a woman may bring out in a man feminine qualities he was not aware of or accepting of, so a man may act for a woman. A girl's animus largely derives from her father, and, to some extent, also her mother's masculine traits. So a dream that deals with a woman's animus has two levels. It deals with the men in her life, but ultimately, it deals with her own masculine traits and her relationship with her own soul, that is, her inner personality.

This dream deals with a man who is sexually still like a child, which means that Gladys will tend to pick men that she will want to mother, who will evoke mothering in her, instead of being her equals. They will need assistance, be incapable in one way or other of totally caring for themselves. For this reason, she will disdain them, as well as love them. They, in turn, will be able to accept the disdain, according to the dream, if they truly love her.

At the same time, the dream is saying, 'You pick that sort of man because your own masculinity is undeveloped, it is adult and childish at the same time, and you despise it. You, like all people, are both feminine and masculine, but you look down on your own masculinity.' Children often confuse urination and sex, and this is alluded to in the dream. But a stronger influence may have been the popular slang usage, 'piss on you!', which means to degrade someone. She degrades her own masculine traits. She does this by being apologetic about herself and what she is doing, her work, her qualifications, her interests, her skills. And she has a way of talking in a degrading manner about the men she loves. But, the dream tells her, this does not prevent a man from loving her, and it does not prevent there being a real love relationship with her inner self. What this means is finding a man who loves her and also encourages her development of her natural masculine traits.

It is doubtful whether there really are such things as 'feminine' or 'masculine' talents or traits; but society has traditionally ascribed some to the woman and some to the man, a matter over which the feminist movement has rightly been protesting in recent years. When natural roles that society deems to be masculine are suppressed or pushed into the background by a woman, they remain undeveloped, suitably imaged as being unable to walk, having a tiny penis. Incidentally, this dream came during menstruation, a time when Gladys' mind was on her female body and her masculinity tended to recede still further into the background. Exactly the same situation occurs in a man in regard to feminine qualities. His undeveloped feminine qualities appear in dreams in the form of a woman, and we call these female dream figures anima images.

Things are not as simple and straightforward as this in reality, what I have written is over-schematised. A woman may be conditioned to suppress feminine traits too, to a greater or lesser degree, and a man masculine traits, so that feminine dream figures in a woman's dreams may represent under-developed or undeveloped feminine traits; and male figures in a man's dreams may represent under-developed or undeveloped masculine qualities, too.

It is rather more helpful to examine the role individual men or women play in a given dream than to classify the characters, though sometimes, when the figures are dream inventions or there is little to be learned about them, it is necessary to fall back upon a kind of type analysis, and say that so-and-so is an anima figure and represents such-and-such traits in the dreamer, or an animus figure may be treated likewise.

While dreams are perfectly capable of giving clear outright sexual messages, a sexual interpretation is not always called for when anima or animus figures appear. Take, for example, the following:

Susan, Marjorie and I have been assigned bunks in a tiny cottage by

*the railroad tracks. Susan has been there already for a time, Marjorie
and I are newly arrived. We make an arbitrary allocation of bunks
(both upper ones) and Marjorie has me help her try to close the windows in this old, disused cottage. Some feeling that we are assigned
there to finish writing theses.*

This is a dream of my own, that I had shortly after I started writing this
chapter. It refers to two former students of mine, both specially known to
me for their writing of theses—one very successful and one a failure. In
both instances, length of time in writing featured prominently, as it has
with this book.

The ambition to write a book is not really authentically mine. It came
from my mother's long-standing ambition, which she eventually achieved,
to write a book of her own. For a long time, she impressed upon me that I
must write a book so that I would, thus, fulfil her ambition vicariously.
Book-writing became associated, then, with her. This association of book-
writing with women, in the hinterlands of my mind, seems to be the reason
that my two women students were singled out as my companions in the cottage. Both Susan and Marjorie had to force themselves to withdraw from
society in order to write their works. As I write this chapter, my own external work is at a minimum while I pound the typewriter keys.

In the dream, I find myself assigned a room with these two women: we
are all three shut off from the world, which thunders by us in our isolation.
I must take a personal part in this isolating process by helping shut the
windows. Susan has already been in the cottage for some unknown length
of time, representing the fact that part of me has been in this withdrawn
writing state for a long time now, but still not finished. Now something
drastic occurs: Marjorie, who found such self-isolation very difficult
indeed, must shut herself up there as well; and I, as a conscious waking
person, must do likewise, an extreme of shutting myself up in order to
finish what I have begun.

I have had no relationship with Susan and Marjorie in years. Neither
figures in my life at present. I have not heard of Susan for years. The
dream takes me back to the days when I taught in university, and research
and publishing were expected of me.

The dream content suggests a sexual connotation. What stops us from
taking that at face value, and reading the dream as one of sexual wishing?
The answer is that the sexual aspect of the dream is not all that clear cut.
Unlike the first dream of this chapter, in which the couple were in a relationship, and sexuality was a major issue, this dream is more like Gladys'
where the partners seem to be represented for their symbolic value. If we
hold to the contention that dreams are concerned with what is happening
now, then the enforced isolation necessary for writing a book is relevant.
The dream is necessary, because my initial response to the isolation is to

say, 'I want more time with other people and less time on my own', while
the dream is saying, 'You must shut yourself off from the rest of the world
and set your hand to the task that has been waiting for you for some years
now'.

If, sometimes, the sexual nuances in a dream are symbolic rather than
literal, nevertheless, dreams may probe very deeply into sexual concerns.
In Chapter 3, we examined a dream of Ronald P.'s concerning his feelings
of inferiority and self-doubt. The following is a dream from the same man,
at a rather different period:

> *I was living in a house with my father, brother and Robert. It seems
> that Robert and I had a separate unit (self-contained) from the rest of
> the house. Behind the refrigerator, I found a trap door which led into
> another room. When I discovered this, I took Robert into the other
> room and we made love there. I was enjoying it more than what he
> was. In fact, I was getting into a very erotic state. The next morning,
> my father came looking for me and could not find me. When his back
> was turned, I sneaked out of the secret closet and went to him. He
> looked around my unit to try and see where I had hidden from him
> but with relief he did not find it. My brother also came in and I
> showed him my secret cabinet. Then I discovered another room where
> a woman lived. When she wasn't there, I masturbated myself. After-
> wards, I opened the door and saw her running from the house. I
> chased her in the hope of getting her to come back but she just caught
> a bus and disappeared.*
>
> RONALD P., #2

The 'unit' is a self-contained apartment. Robert is a young man with
whom Ronald lived several years ago, and with whom he had a homosexual relationship. One of Ronald's fears is that he is predominantly
homosexual, and he came to me for treatment in part to resolve this fear.

As before, it is helpful to dissect the skeleton of this dream to see just
what it is saying:

1. Ronald lives with his father and brother and Robert, in the same
   house, but Ronald and Robert have their own self-contained apartment in that house.
2. Ronald discovers a secret room and makes love to Robert there.
3. Ronald does not want to disclose the room to his father, so he sneaks
   out and his father cannot find the hiding place.
4. Ronald is willing to let his brother in on the secret.
5. There is another room where a woman lives.
6. Ronald masturbates in her room.
7. She goes to get a bus so Ronald is unable to catch up with her.

The symbolism in the dream is fairly common, and we have seen it before: that of an unknown or secret room that is discovered, and that turns out to represent a hitherto unknown or concealed part of the dreamer's personality. As with Ronald's dream of the critical client, discussed in Chapter 3, the theme of secrecy plays a big role here. So does his family, though it is noteworthy that his mother is missing from this dream. Only the male parts of the family are mentioned.

The brother is a real person. In the dream, he is allowed to know about the secret room that must be kept concealed from his father. This is an initial dream, that is, the first one brought to me when Ronald decided to undergo analysis. So much emphasis is placed on secrecy, in the dream, and the need to keep the secret room totally hidden from his father, that we may take it that Ronald felt a great deal of guilt over his homosexuality, and quite possibly, his father stands in my place, since his real father is dead. Does he think of me as a new edition of his father? And does the great to-do about keeping the room secret reveal a lot of ambivalence about letting me know of his homosexuality?

There is also a feminine component in the dream: still another room is discovered in Ronald's house where a woman lives, but there is no sexual relationship with her. Rather, in her absence, he uses her room as a place to masturbate. When he glimpses her, he tries to reach her, but she runs and disappears on a bus.

We may take this woman as both subjective and objective. On the objective side, she may represent the difficulty Ronald has in coming to terms with the world of women, his failure to relate satisfactorily with women — and we remember that it was a woman ex-client who featured in the dream discussed in Chapter 3, a woman who accused him of having absolutely no interest or concern. This is a very one-sided view of Ronald, and the third of his dreams that we examine will do much to right the balance. But for now, we will concentrate on the present dream.

On the subjective side, the woman who has a room in Ronald's house but who leaves to catch the bus represents Ronald's failure to come into contact with the feminine side of himself, so that he searches for it in other men. Ronald has a great fear of women, stemming from his own very disturbed mother, and to find the feminine qualities he craves in a woman would mean coming to terms with this fear. The woman in the dream is imaginary, while the male partner Robert is a real person.

We again see the tendency of dreams to image the whole personality of the dreamer as a group of four. The combination of three masculine and one feminine is very common, as is the reverse. Here, the three male figures are real persons, and the female is imaginary. This seems to imply that Ronald finds relationships with males an important part of his real life, but relationships with females are more fantasy than real. The woman lives only in his imagination. And, significantly, in the dream, he masturbates in her room. She is a masturbation fantasy rather than a real person.

This does not mean that Ronald has had no contact with women. On the contrary, he has an illegitimate child by one of his school teachers, and has had a string of short-lived affairs with other women. His immaturity is shown by his total lack of interest in his child, and the total lack of further contact with the child's mother. These things are merely events of the past to him, of no current importance. He has been unable to establish a relationship with any woman. As an initial dream, this dream sets out Ronald's problems in a fairly clear and direct manner. He wants to become heterosexual in mood as well as in deed, but his heart is in homosexuality, a fact that he wants to hide not only from others, but from himself as well.

Although Ronald's brother is a real person, he is not someone with whom Ronald has much actual contact. Ronald does not, despite the dream, live at home with the rest of his family. But in the dream, he does; he has not really grown up, he lives with his brother in a separate world, a self-contained apartment separate from the rest of his personality. This apartment seems to be separate also from the secret room in which he has sexual relations with Robert, and separate also from the room in which the mysterious woman lives.

But to leave the matter there would be to seriously misrepresent Ronald and his inner personality. Dreams have a tendency to be one-sided, and in order to make a point, they often exaggerate the details, largely as a reaction to a one-sided waking viewpoint. The picture that has been drawn of Ronald is very grim indeed, if it is not balanced by another voice. So let us turn to a third dream of Ronald's, which was dreamed the same night as the dream we have just examined and rights the picture quite considerably:

> *I was a social worker and I was showing a deserted wife a house (State Housing Commission) I had spent much time getting for her. Both of us were visiting the house for the first time before she moved in. When I saw it, I decided that she couldn't live in this house. It was so very old—ancient, full of cobwebs and decaying furniture. It was uninhabitable. I went to the State Housing Commission and spoke to a man there. He said it was the only thing they had at the moment and he had thought that, since the situation was so desperate, it would do, even though the house had not been inhabited for the last ten years. I told him that it just would not do and that she would just have to move in with me if nothing else was available.*

> RONALD P., #3

The deserted wife is his heterosexual function that he must get together with again. We remember that, some years earlier, he had blithely deserted the woman who bore his child. But unlike the situation in dream #2, where the woman leaves his house, a reunion with the feminine world is envisaged here. The house available is in ruins. The State Housing Commission is a government department charged with providing housing for people on very low incomes, at a nominal rent. As a social worker, in the dream, Ronald would have made the initial arrangements for the house to be made available to the deserted wife, but the condition of the house — unlike real life — is such as to make it uninhabitable.

Just as the house in dream #2 represents Ronald's personality, a feature we have seen before, so the house in ruins represents his personality now. We may take it that this represents his current state, that he feels his life to be in ruins. But in the dream, Ronald is appalled by the state of the house proposed for the woman, and determines to do better than that. In the dream, the solution seems to be to have the deserted wife move in with him in his own house. In dream symbolism, this means opening himself to feminine possibilities, both in the sense of developing his own natural feminine characteristics, and of coming to a real relationship with a real woman. At first thought, we tend to suppose that male homosexuals are already too feminine, because their sexual preference is for other males. But in fact, the 'feminine' affectation of many homosexuals is precisely that, an affectation, not a natural expression of authentic personality features. Ronald needs to come to terms with the problem of relating to the feminine world, and in consulting an analyst, he is proposing just that.

With a flight of imagination, we can see in the deserted wife the woman who ran from Ronald in dream #2. There he was trying to catch up with her, now this dream says he must house her, make her a part of his 'inner' family. There is no suggestion of homosexuality in this dream, unlike the preceding. For this reason, the two dreams need to be considered together, because, being dreamed on the same night, they give two views of Ronald's sexual problem.

Bisexuality, in the sense of sexual relations with both women and men, is probably a latent part of all of us, though usually one predominates over the other. Most people have had a homosexual experience at some time in their lives, but only a minority of them continue to be actively bisexual, as this young man is. In practical terms, the task is not to eradicate the homosexual element, but to make it non-pathological; that is, to free it from neurotic contamination and along with heterosexuality, to encourage Ronald to gain empathy, compassion and meaningful relationships with other people, both women and men. Taken together, the two dreams indicate that the problem is a very serious, deep-seated one, but also indicate a willingness on Ronald's part to work on the problem and come to a better relationship with life.

The sexual elements in Ronald's two dreams need to be taken literally, as representing actual sexual problems in relating, but also symbolically as concerning his own relationship with his latent femininity and his way of relating to himself.

As is obvious from the dream examples presented so far, 'sexual' dreams are not merely a case of substituting a symbol for a sexual organ or sexual activity, as is commonly assumed by many people, but a working over of sexual problems in all their many forms and features. Are there 'sexual' dreams that do not fall into this category? In the sense that there may be dreams that are nothing more than a simple substitution of image for sexual phenomenon, the answer is probably no. Dreams are, by their very nature, a compensating force for an unbalanced waking emotional attitude or experience. But in the sense that dreams may present an overt or covert expression of sexual desire that is frustrated in daily life, the answer must be 'yes'.

To investigate further the role of sexual imagery in dreaming, let us turn now to the initial dream of another man of very different background and emotional state:

I've washed my hands in a large enamel sink in a corner and have water running and it looks a bit yellowish in the basin, like urine. I then see that there is a stopper in the sink and the sink will soon overflow as the water is pouring out of the left-hand tap at a great force, so I frantically shut it off, but the water keeps running and then I see, using a flashlight, that the right-hand tap is also running water and shut it off, and keep looking into the basin to see if the water is running out—it is, very slowly, and I want to put my hand in and remove the plug but am afraid the water may be too hot.

Just then, I hear a noise and look through a door on my left through to a dark hall—it seems there's a gawky-shaped, thinnish female figure there, and my thoughts are something like 'Get on with it, look after yourself, look after yourself'. I awoke, and as usual had resistance to writing. I'd not been asleep long, having awakened before, aware I'd no dreams to record 'for Donald', and on going to sleep, hoping I might produce something.

Later the same night, I've returned to work, I think unobserved. It's tea-break time. June and I are in a fairly large room, and she makes sex indications towards me, and I lay on my back on a couch and she prepares for fellatio—then it's not June, but a somewhat younger and cuter girl—a brunette. Then I'm aware of a lot of noise in the room—stove gas-jets burning, water running, etc., and I say to her, 'Wait 'til I shut these things off or we won't be able to hear if anyone's coming, and we might get caught', I got up and started turning off the gas.

Then we're moving around the building, see Jim, the foreman—I wonder if he's seen me—don't think so—then decide they'd not know I'd been in as I'd not reported for duty, and decided to spend the rest of the day with June.

Vague bits about us walking along passages, down flights of stairs, etc. —I'm alone, but others vaguely around—in sort of a square arena-like area and on one side is a large concrete wall with a round-shaped gate and bars, in the right side—looking through the gate showed a number of walls with similar gates behind one another, making the doors or gate-way look like a tunnel.

I've the feeling there may have been another such structure at right angles so that when facing the first, the other was on the right. I think I was seated on a small buggy and moving back and forth, looking up these tunnels alternately trying to see a message printed behind them, which maybe also was a voice reading aloud. It was something like 'It requires a lot of strength to bear with, or cope with, the Shadow, but the balance is on our side', or 'We have the balance', and I felt encouraged.

RUPERT M.

'The Shadow' is a term much used by Jung to indicate the repressed parts of our personality, generally—though by no means always—the unsavoury parts that we attempt to keep hidden from ourselves and are very quick to discover in other people. Rupert had been interested in reading Jung for many years, and he had been recording his dreams for quite a few years. The dream(s) given above were, as the text says, dreamed 'for Donald', that is, for me, following Rupert's first consultation with me.

There are two sexual references in the dreams. The first dream relates to a disastrous event of the distant past. In the interests of discretion, I cannot go into the details here. We must be content that Rupert was indeed very much in 'hot water', and the whole thing had a most unsavoury smell. The later dreams relate to the present time, specifically to June, the woman Rupert is living with. The very unsavoury Shadow with which Rupert had to struggle had to do with the unsavoury event of the distant past, and we did indeed have to go through very many gates, along a lengthy tunnel, to sort it out. Its after-effects lasted for many years. But the present relationship with June is fully as important, and though the secret past plagues Rupert still, the present situation presents an equal or even stronger problem.

The first dream, relating to the basin with the water taps that won't turn off, and with urine-like water that Rupert fears may be too hot to touch, proves to be a very good image for the progress of analysis over several years. There was an enormous amount of 'piss' to get out, a never-ending stream, it seemed. Most of it related to sexual matters. Rupert did not find it pleasant to talk about these things, and his resistance to recording his dreams was well justified in the sense that they brought up much that he would like to forget if he could.

Twice in the dreams, there is water running, and the feeling that the taps must be turned off. In practice, Rupert flooded me with dreams and other material to interpret. There was far more than could be handled adequately, no matter how many sessions a week Rupert had. But let us go back to the beginning of the dreams and look at them systematically.

Rupert has washed his hands in a sink. He has 'washed his hands of' the affair in the distant past; there is, he feels, or should be, no more to concern himself with in this regard. Past events are past. But it is not so. Once having turned the taps on, he cannot turn them off again. Once the flow of dreams has started, it continues unhindered. And once the old matters have been raised, as raised they had to be, they will continue to haunt him in one way or another until he learns how to deal with these memories and the emotions that go with them. They won't turn off, and only slowly do they drain away.

He sees a female figure and thinks, 'Look after yourself, look after yourself'. Like the woman who was a 'bit queer' in Robert M.'s dream #2 discussed in Chapter 3, this female figure represents Rupert's own feminine relationships. At the time, Rupert did not realise how problematical his feminine relationships were. This dawned upon him only gradually over many years. He had come to consult me because of problems associated with his work, but the initial dream points out to me that the fundamental problems lie in the area of the feminine. There is the spectre of the past, unsavoury events; there is the problem of relating with June. Rupert catches a glimpse of this in the dark, and is reluctant to write it down when he wakens, except that he is aware of a new factor, that he needs to 'dream for Donald'. And so the spectre is saved for us.

When are we to take these anima and animus figures as referring to actual relationships, and when are we to take them as referring to our own masculine or feminine qualities buried deep inside us? This sounds like a very difficult theoretical problem, and posed in that fashion, it is very difficult to answer. But the matter becomes clear if we approach it from a slightly different angle. Under normal circumstances, we do not recognise the existence of unconscious personality characteristics in ourselves, though they may sometimes be obvious to others. We become aware of these characteristics only when we find a man or woman who manifests those same characteristics, and we feel mysteriously drawn to that person. When a relationship grows up between ourselves and these men and women, there is a sort of magnetic attraction emanating from those persons that encourages and draws out the same characteristics in ourselves, so that they are no longer unconscious but out in the open. In therapeutic work, it is very important to examine our choices of partners and close friends in order to learn just what it is that is hidden within ourselves. Dreams can be a very valuable asset in assisting us to do so. If the anima and animus figures that feature in our dreams are understood to be figurations of our own internal, unrecognised personality that we live out vicariously through other people, we can emerge from the study much the better for it.

However, when real persons are represented in the dream, it is, at least at first, the most profitable course for us to use the dream as a means of understanding these other persons and our relationship with them. It is usually only in retrospect, when we see what the effect of these persons has had on us, that it is helpful to see the 'real people' in the dreams as symbolic of something within us. Both approaches are valid; circumstances decide which approach is most helpful in any given instance.

To illustrate this: in the case of Rupert's dreams, June exhibits a lot of qualities and interests that Rupert has *in potentia* within himself. June has active art interests, and Rupert inherited but has not put to use a genuine art talent of his own. Through her influence, he has been encouraged to paint. June is immensely interested in the occult, and Rupert had a secret interest in the occult that only emerged into the open at a later date. June drives a car, while Rupert for many years had no licence, and only after years of trepidation, became mobile on his own behalf. In short, June lives out openly life interests and talents that were latent in Rupert but, for one reason or another, had not been developed previously.

The oral sex in the dream takes on a symbolic meaning, as a mating of Rupert with June and, due to her influence, with his own inner qualities, which she represents. Discussion of June's attributes as actually being undeveloped attributes of his own would be on the cards, and, in fact, was attempted several times, but it was impossible for Rupert to recognise and accept this situation. That is normal. As long as there is a real-life person to exemplify the qualities, it is difficult to see them in yourself. June, after all, 'really is like that', while because they are only latent and undeveloped, Rupert feels a natural resistance towards discovering the attributes in himself.

If we recognise that dreams have a message, then we may ask why it is that the dream should choose to use June when, earlier on, an invented female figure was used. Also, at first it is not unequivocably June who is referred to, though Rupert chooses to identify her as June as the dream progresses. We can answer that the dream chose to use June as herself at a point when the relationship between Rupert and the real June was the central issue to be dealt with, while it used other female figures when Rupert's own inner 'femininity' and his tendency to find it in women instead of himself were intended to be the central focus. I have put 'femininity' in quotes, because what Rupert regarded as feminine was specific to him, and not objective qualities that could be applied generally to women.

As said, Rupert's work held no interest for him; he came to me originally because of work problems. His attitude towards his work comes out clearly in his dream. His heart was turned towards June and what she represents for him.

Eventually, a scene of multiple tunnels appears in the dream, indicating that there is a long underground pathway ahead; that is, there is much that is still unconscious to Rupert that must be explored. Because Rupert was so well read in Jung, and had chosen a Jungian analyst, his dream ends with a very Jungian-couched message: 'It requires a lot of strength to bear with, or cope with, the Shadow, but the balance is on our side'. The 'Shadow' is part of Jung's terminology and represents all those qualities that have been repressed or suppressed because they are unpalatable, but that nevertheless remain alive and active. What the dream is trying to express through this application of Jung's terminology is that to examine himself thoroughly and all of his personality, without holding back when unpleasant things are discovered, takes a lot of inner strength, but it can be done.

Sex in dreams by no means always plumbs such depths of the soul. Often, it represents precisely what it portrays, the sexual drive. A simple example:

> I was in a group sex party of some kind. I had sex with a girl that seemed very tender towards me.
>
> ROBERT M., #4

Robert is a strictly monogamous man in his waking life, but his dreams portray a strong yearning for other sex partners. His own marriage is on the rocks, it was rushed into following the break-up of a previous engagement, and it causes him great distress. In such a situation, while high standards of morality keep him faithful to his wife, his dream life portrays, both in this dream and many others, the desire for other women.

Sexual symbolism is, of course, a frequent aspect of dreams. I would like to return now to two dreams discussed in earlier chapters. The first is the little boy Carl's dream in Chapter 2, which I will repeat here to refresh your memory:

> Daddy had found his treble recorder and had started playing some tunes he knew. I wanted to play too, so I found my plastic treble but I wanted to play the tenor. I found the bottom to the tenor. I searched for hours for the top part, and then I lost the bottom part and found the top part.
>
> CARL N., #2

The middle part of the tenor recorder, the barrel, is not mentioned in this dream. The dream is one of rivalry, in that Carl wants to play a different instrument from the one his father is playing. The instrument he prefers is not the small descant recorder, such as is commonly taught in schools, but the large tenor recorder which, like the treble, comes in three pieces and which is much thicker and longer than the treble. The holes on the tenor are widely spaced, so that it is impractical for small children. Carl was just able to cover the holes with his fingers, a difficult feat but one he just managed.

The question I raised in Chapter 2 was whether this dream should be given a sexual connotation. Various possibilities were suggested, of which this was one. The oedipal complex would still be active at age eight, though driven underground and, thus, ripe for symbolic representation. By this, I mean that the oedipal complex, which at heart is a desire to supplant the father in the family constellation, is most obvious in a direct sexual form at an earlier age. By age eight, the child has learned that he must wait until he is grown up before he can begin to rival his father sexually, and sexual jealousy is usually subdued, to reawaken at puberty. It does not, however, completely disappear. It turns up in rivalry and competition between father and son, and observation of the child at play shows that phallic-like objects are frequently the choice playthings, and positioning them anatomically in the appropriate spot is a frequent source of fun.

Because of its shape, the recorder is an excellent phallic image. The fingering of the holes on the treble is different from that of the tenor, but identical with that of the small descant. Thus, for Carl to switch from the treble to the tenor would also require a different fingering technique and, incidentally, the tone of the tenor is, of course, considerably lower than that of the treble. It should be mentioned that both father and son were proficient at all three instruments, with the proviso already mentioned that the holes on the tenor were only just within the child's reach. Sexually, the dream would seem to be saying, 'I can get an erection like you, but I cannot get a penis the size of yours, no matter how hard I try'. This interpretation is supported by the dream's description that Carl can find one piece or another of the tenor, but he cannot find all the pieces at one time so as to put them together.

That an eight-year-old child is a very sexual being is obvious to anyone who knows an eight-year-old well. That an eight-year-old boy is jealous of his father is also fairly obvious. But what, then, is this dream saying to Carl? That, in this one area, he cannot outdo or equal his father — the area of sexuality. But, at the same time, it leaves hope that the situation can change in the future: he may never outdo his father, but he is well able to become his equal eventually.

It is a frustration dream, and yet it also tells the child not to lose hope but to keep looking, eventually his quest will be fulfilled.

I also wish at this point to return to Roger H.'s dream #1, which was also discussed at length in Chapter 2. To summarise the dream, Roger is getting married to his daughter Sonya, but they occupy separate beds. Sonya has brought presents of bottles of whisky. They decide to visit Roger's parents to celebrate the wedding. But Roger feels uncomfortable and hears an argument going on next door.

This is the other side of the oedipal situation, in which the girl wishes to supplant her mother and become her father's mate. We see it in this dream, though, not from the child's perspective but from the father's. Sonya, a pre-pubertal child, was like her father in many ways, not least in temperament, although she expressed her rage openly, while Roger kept his feelings under wraps, so that they came out in the form of severe migraine headaches that totally incapacitated him from time to time. They both had serious gripes about Sonya's mother, Roger's wife, and although rebellion was expressed in different manners, both rebelled against her authority.

In Chapter 2, I mentioned that, sometimes, overt sexual imagery is deleted from dream recall because of its taboo nature. This would tend to be the case with Roger, who was of a very conventional nature, and who was not always willing to look facts in the face. In this particular instance, sexual relations between Roger and his wife were missing and had been so for a long time. Roger attempted to sublimate his sexual desires by strenuous exercise, and he believed this to be successful. But the sexual desire must go somewhere, and this dream implies it went towards his children. He could not admit this to himself, so that his dream had to hint at it.

We need not, however, assume that the original dream did include copulation between father and daughter, which was then censored out. The same taboo that prevented the acting out of sexual desires in waking life was equally active in Roger's dream life. This leads us to ask why it is that some dreams seem quite explicit sexually, and others not. Why, for example, was Robert's dream, discussed earlier, quite explicit about the group sex party? Another father dreamed:

> I was fondling Emma's genitals (she is naked). I get a sexual thrill from it.
>
> HAROLD U.

Emma was Harold's teen-aged daughter.

The answer to why some dreams are quite explicit sexually, while for other dreamers, they speak in hints, symbolism or disavowals, may be a simple one. Robert had once been told, or had read, that sex in a dream is always symbolic, and never to be taken literally. He could, therefore, dream copiously of sex, at ease because he was convinced that the dreams did not mean what they said. Roger, on the other hand, had had no such indoctrination, and consequently, never reported a dream in which sex figured. Harold, as a medical person, was well aware of parents' sexual desires for their children, so that, although deeply disturbed by his dream, he was not as shocked or suprised as he might otherwise have been.

Jim K., who contributed a number of dreams to our discussion in Chapter 4, was able — just barely — to report overt sexual dreams, but more frequently, his dreams used symbols. First, let us look at an overtly sexual dream, which he was most unwilling to discuss:

I was living with my brothers Frank and Edward in an apartment.
There seemed to be some sort of erotic relationship between Edward
and myself. I remember that (though he was physically a tiny child,
consciously he was an adult) he was lying, naked, on my lap. I too was
naked. We were fondling each other. (It may be at the start of the
dream that Edward was a girl. I also think I remember that he took
the initiative.) Frank sat in the same room but took no part in the
activities.

JIM K., #3

It may be mentioned that, in at least one other instance, Jim had an overtly homosexual dream that he also refused to discuss. The dream above was perceived as a nightmare.

Edward is Jim's seven-years-younger brother; at the time of this dream, he was a teenager about to enter university. He was living with a girl-friend, at the time when Jim was still celibate.

The dream portrays a homosexual relationship between the two brothers. As far as I was able to ascertain, there never had been such a relationship between them in real life, and the sexual fondling is purely a dream motif. We cannot exclude a sexual attraction between the two brothers, only note that Jim disclaimed such a relationship as ever having evolved in real life, and he reported no other dreams of this type involving his brother. It seems more likely that the sexual fondling, rather than being a reminiscence of a real relationship between Jim and his brother, represents the sexual awakening of Jim, who turned, in his unconscious fantasy, to the closest sexual love object, his younger brother. We cannot discount the possibility of mutual masturbation and sex play between the youngsters when Jim was, say, ten and Edward three, nor do we have any evidence for it. What interests us at this point, however, is why the dream came up at the time it did.

It probably rests upon a foundation of burgeoning sexual feelings when Jim was coming to puberty and Edward still a small child to be fondled. Presumably, the dream arose when it did because Jim was undergoing a delayed psychological puberty, when sexual feelings were making themselves heard more and more strongly, as we saw in the series of Jim's dreams in Chapter 4, but were repudiated very violently in favour of celibacy. These sexual feelings had not differentiated themselves into homo- and hetero- forms, but were still an amorphous sexual feeling such as is common in adolescence.

It was very rare in Jim's dreams to find explicit sexual references, though they did occur. This may be because he was psychologically still in a rather pre-genital state, where the capacity to make relationships at all was very undeveloped. His sexuality was still in a, so to speak, undeveloped form; that is, although the sexual drive existed in him and was felt, it had not yet matured enough to be related to other persons, and was primarily auto-erotic (i.e. confined to fantasies, with or without actual masturbation). Animals are often used in dreams in a way that suggests a very 'primitive' form of relating, just as in real life, it is not uncommon to find persons who treat pets with a passion that seems quite sexual, even if not genitally so. One of Jim's dreams featuring animals is this:

> *I was in a room with a cat on my lap. On my right, a second, black, cat sat on a shelf staring at me as if it wanted something from me, to come to me. I wanted to prevent that.*
>
> *I took the cat on my lap in my hands and tried to throw it at the black cat. But it (the cat in my hands) did not seem to care for that. It tried to hold on to me and scratched me. It made a turn in the air and jumped back down onto the floor, away from the black cat and towards me.*
>
> JIM K., #4

The cat as a representation for sexuality, in particular, female relationships, is very common. This dream came about a week after the dream of fondling his brother, with some dreams intervening. In this dream, Jim repudiates the female sex (represented by the cat) in a very violent fashion. He will have nothing to do with it. Nevertheless, it persists, and it appears that it is going to take hold anyway. Instinctual sexuality cannot be got rid of so easily, by a single act of repudiation. The cat that he throws is on his lap, where his brother was in the previous dream. 'Threatening' him is a black cat on a shelf, staring at him. On his shelf, Jim really kept books for study. It is the cat that wants to be studied now. It wants something from him, it wants to come to him. And it is a black cat, which, by tradition, is an ominous sign, associated with witches and evil, generally. If we take the cat on his lap as representing sexual desire directed towards his brother (because of the earlier dream), he is trying to throw the one sexual impulse against the other, hoping to be rid of both.

In life terms, the black cat represents for Jim a sexual attraction towards a particular woman, who, he believes has a cat. But the attraction is still on a purely instinctual, non-conscious level, and is, therefore, represented by an animal rather than by a woman. The first dream of Jim's that we discussed, in Chapter 1, had an anonymous girl waiting anxiously to use his typewriter. That dream preceded this by almost precisely one month. That dream was an initial dream, outlining the basic problems and pro-grammes set before us. The dreams that followed it then proceeded to backtrack and deal with individual issues.

Just in passing, we may look at one last dream from Jim, a dream that came considerably later, and before the roasted dog dream discussed in Chapter 4 (dream #2(f)), following Jim's discovery from patients' paintings that dogs may represent sex. He dreamed:

I go down a street in a city. Two fire-red dogs begin to sniff about me. I think it is in bad taste to paint dogs red, and besides, it is very unpleasant to have the dogs sniff at me so. I jump high into the air in order to escape the dogs. I look down at the dogs and wonder what they will do now.

JIM K., #5

Jim was able to interpret this dream himself, as his own sexual instincts from which he tries to flee by intellectualism. He understood the jumping into the air to escape the dogs as intellectualising. This dream was, in fact, a major breakthrough in working with Jim and his dreams.

The dogs are fire-red, burning passion. Dogs are notorious for sniffing at people's genitals, and in the dream, Jim finds this very unpleasant. Thus, the leap into the air to escape the dogs. They are interested in his own masculinity.

Chapter Seven

Dreams Can Heal the Soul

Soul, heart, breast, bosom, the inner man, inmost
heart, heart's core, heart-strings, heart's-blood, heart
of hearts . . .

Everyman's Thesaurus of
English Words and Phrases,
by D. C. Browning, London, 1972, p. 257.

While individual dreams have a function in helping set right the balance of
life, over a period of time, they disclose a wider purpose — that of promot-
ing emotional health and leading through time to a better quality of life all
round. Their message is not limited to individual situations, but is part of a
wider message, which is unique to every person, aimed at directing the
dreamer's life and life goals. This can only be seen when a very large
number of dreams is viewed, taken from an extensive period of time.

I have chosen the case of Peter R., whose dream of the winged serpent
we examined in detail in Chapter 3, to illustrate the way in which dreams
may progress along a definite, observable route towards a goal. The serpent dream came immediately before phoning me to arrange his first
appointment. In that dream, the American Revolution featured, and
Peter went into the back room of an inn to get weapons. While there, he
aroused a winged serpent, capable of shrinking to invisible size, that pursued him thereafter and against which he must continually be on guard.

In discussing this dream, I made special note of the fact that the war for
independence was his own struggle to get free from his family, and that
concerns of relationship and sexuality feature prominently.

In all, I saw Peter for thirty-five sessions, to which he brought 193 con-
secutive dreams. Since time was limited, a great deal of interest and concern was shown in the dreams by Peter, who wanted to get all he could
from them. The dream of the winged serpent was brought to our first
session. Among the dreams brought to the second was the following, which
very dramatically indicates the direction the therapy needed to follow.

*This dream begins in some European city. I'm riding (and perhaps
Julie) on a kind of ski lift, which travels at high speed from just one
point to another—in other words, no stops in between. First along a
city street and then one is seemingly projected out into the air, the
ground falls away so quickly. There is a large cathedral or such-like*

165

structure on a large plateau-hill to which the lift proceeds through air. The ride ending on the steps of the large structure leaving one with many steps still to climb. There was some interaction with an old woman on the steps of the church— or perhaps her little girl—perhaps she has a fruit or vegetable stand. I became anxious to get a better view of the cathedral and thought I might do so from the lift—and almost immediately, I was projected high up into the air on the lift and saw the moon very bright and full in the sky above the church, the church being almost transparent. The lift was moving again above the city street when there was some difficulty—perhaps one of the cords from which it hung snapped and I found myself hanging in the air. I was unharmed and jumped into the street. I was walking on the street when I met my old friend-enemy Richard. I then found myself trapped in his cellar. It's hard to explain, in one corner, there was a large walled structure much like a miniature walled castle; in an adjoining corner, there was a large furnace cone shaped as high as the ceiling and rather opening towards the floor into a ball-sphere inside of which there was a stew boiling. Everything in the cellar was very old, dirty and dark. The whole basement was filled with rick rack and odd things but these were all I noticed. I believe there was food in the castle as well as the furnace but I didn't feel I could take it as it was my capturer's. I felt I was being held prisoner and needed to be discreet. I considered holding myself up in the castle but felt he had superior force and could remove me.*

I next found myself bobbing in the sea—near a shore—but the waves were huge—there were others bobbing in the sea also. I was bobbing just like a cork, and though the waves were high, they didn't put me under. I experienced groups of waves that would come at me from different directions or that I would swim over to meet, as personified faces. Water spirits I was sparring with. At one point, a mask floated by which I knew to be the personified image of one of the faces I was sparring with. Later, I noticed Julie also in the water.

Then we are both this time again in the cellar. I show her the furnace and the castle and there was a change of feeling about the place there. I either no longer felt myself prisoner—or no longer felt intimidated or afraid of Richard, or both. Richard from the beginning of the episode in the cellar, though not directly seen but felt, had taken on the auspices of a very dark and powerful figure, perhaps a pirate.

PETER R., #2

It is easy to get lost in this very long, complicated dream, so it may be as well to outline it here:

1. High on a ski lift, ending at a cathedral

2. Fruit and vegetable stand
3. Again on ski lift, cord breaks
4. Walks and meets Richard
5. Trapped in Richard's cellar
6. Miniature castle and furnace with stew in it
7. Bobbing in sea, sparring with water spirits
8. Julie also in water
9. Back in the cellar, with Julie
10. No longer feels afraid of Richard.

Peter was very well versed in reading psychological literature, particularly on symbolism, and his dream has picked up some images from literature to express itself. This does not invalidate the images. The dream has picked up and made use of imagery familiar to Peter in order to make its points. Had Peter been versed in some other area of study, the dream would have taken imagery from that area to express itself.

We see in the dream the familiar division of the world into three parts: up, on the surface and below the surface. Tradition has made the upper realms spiritual and unrealistic ('to have your feet off the ground'), to be on the ground is to 'be well grounded', i.e. oriented towards reality. To be beneath the surface is to see what is hidden, a point very graphically made in Fox's vision discussed in Chapter 3, and several other dreams we have looked at.

At first, Peter is way off the ground, in the air, looking down at the world below, and ending up on the steps of a semi-transparent cathedral. This points to a religious concern, but Peter is not willing to stop and examine it yet, though he did so later on. Fruit and vegetables are very mundane things, they are staples of food, indicating that Peter should stop and see what nourishment the area of religion has for him, but he is not yet interested. He goes up in the air again, but cannot keep his position there for long. Instead, a cable snaps and he finds himself again on the ground. This corresponds to the need to examine the problems of everyday life. The production of dreams such as these has two faces. On the one side, they satisfy Peter's need to produce impressive imagery to capture the attention of his analyst (me). On the other side, they point out to me, by the way they use the imagery, where the problems really lie.

On the ground, Peter finds Richard, a one-time friend now turned enemy, symbolic of the past and the chains the past puts on us, making us prisoners of our own past. Richard is an example of the type of figure introduced in Chapter 6 as a 'Shadow' figure, representing what has been pushed aside and rejected because we do not like to look at it in ourselves. In this instance, as very often, it is unsavoury events from the past that haunt Peter under the guise of Richard. In terms of character, Richard was a school drop-out, and had an intense tie to his mother. He was also involved in the drug scene, in which Peter had once been active. One of the reasons Peter consulted me was the fact that he suffered what appeared to be permanent damage from the abuse of drugs, and was prone now to spontaneous hallucinations.

In the dream, Richard captures Peter and imprisons him in his cellar. Peter has, thus, moved from his position up in the air, down to ground level and now to underground. The underground cellar looks very much like having been influenced by Jung's writings on alchemy, some of Peter's favourite reading. The queer-shaped furnace is reminiscent of the alchemical vessels in which the attempt was made to create gold or some other treasure. But the furnace is being used for something far more prosaic in this dream, namely stew. The miniature walled castle may also have come out of alchemical illustrations reproduced in some of Jung's books. In this particular instance, it represents the desire to hide. What would hiding in an underground miniature castle mean in practical terms? Probably a retreat into himself, which could mean withdrawing from the world, a kind of schizophrenic state to which he was prone because of his intensive misuse of drugs earlier on.

The stew cooking in the furnace is a good sign. Plain, home-like food is being prepared for him, nothing exotic, an image of what his unconscious mind has planned for him: not exotic and occult studies of the Mysteries, but plain, everyday preoccupation with the problems of practical living and relationships. Perhaps because the stew is such plain fare, Peter pays it no further attention in his dream. (At a later stage, when Peter's dreams had come to using ordinary, mundane imagery, he lamented the loss of the 'archetypal' imagery his dreams once had; a sense of sadness that the great Mysterium of life is not the unravelling of occult teachings but the task of living and relating.)

Next, Peter finds himself bobbing in the sea, where there are huge waves. He is tossed about like a cork. We have seen a similar image before, with a much less favourable outcome, in Mark L.'s dream of being a marshmallow in the ocean; and in John W.'s dream of floating on the ocean in a spoon, discussed in Chapters 4 and 1, respectively. In Peter's dream, we must remember, the sea is under the ground. The turbulent emotions raging under the surface of every-day life are meant. The groups of waves were experienced in the dream as water spirits with which he was sparring. These nixies probably want to drown him. Unconscious emotions are personified regularly in dreams as figures with which the dreamer must relate in one manner or another. In the earlier dream of the American Revolution, the far reaches of the hinterland of the mind were represented as the back room of an inn, and there, the danger was a winged serpent. Here, the same area is imaged as the sea, and the danger is the water spirits.

Water spirits have been portrayed for thousands of of years as dangerous creatures that lure a man to his death. In the case of normal people, this motif usually turns up only in art or poetry and in dreams, where death not of the body but of the personality is meant, i.e. insanity. In the case of the insane, these experiences may extend into daily life. They may hear the internal voices speaking to them, what we are used to calling hallucinations. However, Peter was not insane but what is called a borderline personality, a person on the verge of insanity, who could be given a shove in either direction—over the edge into insanity or back over the edge into reasonably solid sanity. His dreams are working towards health and sanity, if they are listened to attentively and given a sympathetic understanding.

Julie, Peter's girl-friend, is in the water with him. It was unclear whether she was with him earlier on in the dream. Now Julie was undergoing analysis by another analyst for some time before Peter contacted me, and it was because of the very positive effects on her that he was willing to undergo the process. She, too, was floundering in the sea with him, i.e. having to contend with her own emotional problems.

Finally, they are both back in the cellar, and Richard is no longer a threat. In other words, Peter's unconscious can be examined for what it is, without danger. This is a happy ending for the dream and augurs well for Peter.

The fact that the water spirits were replaced by Julie in the dream was a good omen. There is an Australian Aboriginal myth of a man who has to seize hold of one of the water spirits, drag her onto land, hold her over the fire and roast her in order to make her human. This means that internal fantasies have to be dragged out into the open, examined carefully and made into food for thought, so that they can turn into genuine human relationships. Julie replaces the water spirits in the dream: a real-life relationship can be examined and Peter's problems observed and dealt with.

The long bizarre dreams gradually dried up and were increasingly replaced by more mundane, common type dreams. This went along with Peter's progress towards a healthier personality able to grasp and cope with the everyday realities of living. But the transition was not abrupt. It took place over a lengthy period of time. Rather than anticipate, let us look at the third dream in our series, which was dreamed about four nights after the cellar and the water spirits:

> *Julie and I go to a house where there are students living. However, we were alone most of the time we were there and I was doing 'active imagination' and I believe Julie was reading. When we first came into the apartment, we took some note cards and I noticed that the make-shift cardboard shelf that they were on was very precariously balanced. One had to very carefully draw out a card or the whole shelf would fall down. We were sitting on the couch and I began doing what in the dream was understood as active imagination—and I*

*found myself in a very long pedestrian tunnel. I was first walking
towards the light at the end of the tunnel and then changed my mind
and turned back walking towards a bend in the tunnel. A man walked
past me toward the light and, at this point, we were the only two in
the tunnel, whereas previously there were many people. Suddenly, a
black and white dog came charging around the corner and past me
after the man. The man responded by transforming into an even
larger black and white dog, and quickly put down the other dog and
came racing after me. I believe I was then back in the apartment and
I think I told Julie I was having very vivid fantasies (there were other
images that I was fantasying in the dream that I don't remember).*

*We got up to leave and we noticed that one of the residents of the
apartment was there. He took no particular note of us as there were
often visitors. I was still having extremely vivid fantasy images wake
over my consciousness, and as I was returning my card in the box on
the shelf, the shelf fell over. As I examined it, thinking of its flimsy
construction and how I might balance it, I noticed the man who lived
there standing behind me. I turned to him and expecting sympathy
for it was so apparent that the construction was weak. I was instead
met by an angry, menacing glare. I tried to explain to him that I was
experiencing fantasies that were absolutely vivid when one came over
me and I felt like I was sinking and I cried out for help and turned
over in bed and reached over to Julie (she wasn't actually in bed at this
time). She embraced me and put her breasts to my face and they were
like white waves and I was in a sea of light. I began to suffocate, however, and thought I might lose my life and became frantic when I saw
her arm, which was long, thin and elastic bend over to my heart
region and rub, excitedly in a circular motion. Over my heart, there
was a white disk she was rubbing. The combination of the rapid beat-
ing of my heart and my suffocation quite terrified me and I awoke.*

PETER R., #3

This was one of a number of dreams dreamed during the four nights
after the cellar dream. Peter said that the students were university students
and the note cards looked like course enrolment cards.

I have already discussed Active Imagination in the beginning of Chapter
4. It has very little similarity with the 'active imagination' mentioned in
this dream. Actually, Peter had never succeeded in doing active imagination, and since his dream life was so rich, there would be little point in
teaching him the procedure.

Again, with such a long dream, it is helpful to seek out the skeleton of
the dream story:

1. Julie and Peter are in a students' house.

2. Julie is reading, Peter is doing Active Imagination.
3. On entering, they draw cards from a precarious cardboard shelf.
4. Peter has a terror fantasy of a man who changes into a dog and attacks him.
5. Peter tries to return his card and knocks down the shelf.
6. Peter turns to Julie, in bed, for help.
7. Her breasts begin to suffocate him.
8. She begins to rub his heart vigorously.
9. He awakes in terror.

This nightmare is instructive. It reminds us yet again of how precarious Peter's emotional balance was at the time. The whole framework of his life then — study, relationship with Julie — could turn into disaster. The shelf of course cards was itself flimsy cardboard, which soon collapsed. And Julie, in her attempt to comfort him, suffocates him and makes him fear for his heart. The fantasy within the dream is interesting. It concerns dogs, which, as we saw in the last chapter, often represent the sexual instinct. It is this instinct that ties him to Julie. She is otherwise more of a mother figure for him, as the dream suggests by her suffocating him with her breasts. In reality, Julie often said that Peter confused her with his mother.

The fantasy in the dream was like a hallucination from Peter's drug days. Such hallucinations were more important to deal with than courses of study, the dream is saying, for the entire edifice of study courses, represented by the shelf of course cards, was so fragile that it came tumbling down at a touch.

The point of the dream is that, while studying and fantasising, Peter's relationship was destroying him. His way of relating to Julie as to his mother results in his being suffocated. This does not mean that his relationship with Julie should be given up. It would merely be replaced by a similar one with some other woman. It means, rather, that the relationship needs to be examined closely, and altered so that the couple support one another, instead of destroying one another. (We must remember that there are two sides to any relationship, and Julie had her own problems to work out too.) The ending of the dream suggests that Peter needed, first of all, to stop seeing Julie as a substitute mother.

Looking back over the dream as a whole and the outline of it that I presented, what do we find? First, that Peter and Julie are in a students' situation, which is correct — both were studying. Julie is reading and Peter is doing Active Imagination. This pretty likely has to do with me, since the dream came so close to starting analysis. Peter had read about Active Imagination in books, though I do not think that much had been said in them about the technique or use of it. Many people, especially those attracted by some of Jung's ideas but who have never read any of his work directly, assume that Active Imagination is a sort of meditation in which heroic deeds are visualised and that this in some way enriches the spirit.

Active Imagination is actually a kind of semi-dream state, in which a waking person meets unconscious imagery and the two interact. It is, in its essence, a fairly dangerous type of procedure, and should be undertaken only under the direction of an experienced analyst. Its principal value is to bring out unconscious fantasy material if dreams are lacking. This was not the case with Peter. But what his dream called 'active imagination' was a terrifying image, a man who changes into a black and white dog that kills a smaller dog and then runs after Peter. This would seem to mean that Peter sees danger threatening him, and, as said previously, probably of a sexual nature. We can only speculate at the present moment on what that danger might be.

Since dogs tend to represent male sexuality, which is seen as both evil (black) and good (white), who would the man be who changes into that image? Given the situation, and some hindsight from what came out later on, I would suggest that the man is me, and that Peter's latent homosexuality was being awakened, which felt like a threat to him. It is frequently the case that a patient's erotic interest turns towards the analyst, even very early on, especially having undertones of a fantasised, idealised father or mother who will give her/him love in all its forms, both emotional and physical. Such a fantasy has little or nothing to do with the analyst's real qualities, but those that are the product of fantasy. As a fantasised homosexual love-object, I would both attract and repel: attract him because of his latent homosexuality, and repel him because of his fear of being homosexual. At the same time as being analysed, Peter is a student, but his studies seem no more substantial than a cardboard castle, in the context of what he has to confront emotionally.

An example of the two-sidedness of the problem of the relationship between Peter and Julie comes out in a brief dream that Peter had not long after the active imagination dream:

Dream of Spanish or Italian waiter who was working hard towards a goal and who was cheated or robbed. He was working very long, hard hours; he was also a very good worker. He started again right from the beginning working and saving. He struck me as very courageous.

PETER R., #4

Julie was of Latin origin. The waiter in the dream sounds like her animus, the masculine aspect of herself that she tended to neglect within herself by passing the buck to Peter, who had to personify her masculine ideal. Julie's problem was to be helped to develop this inner part of herself, which, in turn, would bring Peter emotional food. In Peter's dream, the Spanish or Italian waiter, who evidently represents Julie's animus, has been cheated or robbed. What might this mean in every-day terms? There had been a quarrel between Julie and Peter just before the dream, when Julie asked a question that Peter took as probing into his analysis session with me, and that he wished to keep private. He answered her that the hour with me is confidential and that he could not talk about it with her. She took this as a rebuff, and turned cold and silent. Later in the day, she asked her question again, in a different form, and he realised that she had had something very different in mind than he had supposed. She, too, was in analysis, trying to start over from the beginning. His task in relation to her was to help her robbed and cheated animus, who, after all, does bring him food. He had to serve to develop her animus positively, just as she had to help him to develop his anima. Put in other terms, Peter's task in the relationship was, in part, to help Julie bring to the surface and develop those qualities within herself that had hitherto been neglected in favour of passing the load onto men. Just as Peter tended, to Julie's dismay, to see her as a substitute mother, so Julie, to Peter's dismay, tended to see Peter as a substitute father. She expected him to provide for her as a father to his child, while he expected her to care for him as a mother for her child. Peter's dream of the waiter is a compliment to Julie's willingness to work on herself.

A few days later, Peter brought in a dream that opened up a new area of discussion for us:

> *Three very muscular men wearing only loin cloths, and brandishing large hammers are in opposition to each other and strike each other on the head whenever they meet. At first, they are all equally opposed. Eventually, I am one of them and opposed to the other two. After a while, I discover that one of them is my brother, and the third is revealed as the father of both of us, who says he was waiting for the two of us to recognise each other, before we could cease to pound each other's heads.*

PETER R., #5

This dream features persons who are dream inventions alongside Peter. We have Peter himself, his brother and their father, all represented as cavemen and at odds with each other. The key point to the dream is the father's statement that he was waiting for the two brothers to recognise each other, so that the mayhem could stop.

Who is Peter's brother in the dream? The dream figures bear no resemblance to real family members. I think we can say that Peter's caveman brother is what I earlier described as a 'Shadow' figure, the features of Peter's personality that he would prefer to disown, and does not accept as an image of what he is really like, but which are very noticeable to other people and which sometimes over-rule Peter's better judgment and take control. To be more exact, it is violence that is featured in this dream. We may take it that Peter's brother represents those aspects of him which tend towards violence, quarrelling, desire to impose his own will. As is usually the case, Peter does not recognise these traits as being genuine aspects of his personality, he sees them as something he wants to stamp out, and, typically, stamping them out means cônsciously trying to keep them suppressed, which works for a time until they build up so strongly that they cause an explosion and Peter erupts like a volcano, thus bringing friction and threatening his relationship with Julie. The recognition of each other as brothers, having the same father, means Peter's coming to accept that these facets of his personality really exist and cannot be extinguished. But they can be kept in check by the simple device of not suppressing such feelings when they first occur, but expressing them in a manner agreeable to both himself and Julie before they build up to explosion force.

Who is Peter's dream father? In the first instance, it probably is an internalisation of me, since I was trying to get Peter to recognise that his personality included much more than he assumed, and that the various parts must co-operate to make life a harmonious whole. But I would serve only as a transitional father in such an instance until Peter's own genuine inner 'father' is recognised. Put briefly, the father of the conscious and unconscious aspects of Peter's personality is his own self. It is the core of his own personality that gives rise to such inner conflicts, with one set of values battling another set. This inner 'father' has two origins: first, in the social pressures and experiences that teach Peter that he must subordinate his personal interests to a wider, social context; second, in the innate drive towards emotional wholeness that attempts to reconcile inner conflicts and bring them to peaceful co-existence.

That Peter was coming more and more to see me as a kind of spiritual director for his life is shown by his dream that followed immediately upon our discussion of the caveman dream. It is inevitable that the therapist takes on the feeling of a guru, or guide, to life for a time, until the patient realises that the real guide is something within herself/himself.

A frustration lunch counter. Escalator stairs going down past coin machines with food and other items. I'm very hungry and want something to eat. But as I go down the stairs, which I try several times, and there are several escalators going past such machines; the machines either cannot be reached as one moves past them, or understood as to what they contain, or they require a different amount or kind of money than that which I have. There is a counter at the bottom of the stair where sold are such items as magazines. At first, I notice a young woman there, later I see a middle-aged man who strikes me as very hardened and cynical. He is very slow about selling me a cold sandwich after I explained to him my difficulties with the machines, as a matter of fact, I'm not sure I got one at all. He has currency from exotic places in the world and shows me two examples. I feel each bill

has a memory attached to it for him. The one bill I remember was
from the Caribbean area and had a large triangular tree on it, very
colourful.

PETER R., #6

There is, of course, here, a reminiscence of the fall down the rabbit hole
near the start of *Alice in Wonderland*. But Peter's dream has used the
motif in its own way. Here, we have a mechanised fall, escalators going
down. Instead of shelves, there are coin machines. But for one reason or
another, it is impossible to use the coin machines as Peter descends, though
he tries repeatedly. The journey downwards represents a movement down
into his own inner depths. It takes him to a counter where a woman briefly
appears, but is replaced by a cynical middle-aged man who may or may
not sell Peter a sandwich, but who has exotic currency with memories attached to the bills. When I asked Peter to draw the tree, he produced what
looked like a conventionalised picture of a Christmas tree.

Was I the hardened, cynical middle-aged man? Probably so. Peter
regarded me as lacking in Christian charity, when I discussed with him a
disagreement he had had with Julie about housing visitors in their apartment. Coming from another part of the world, my values seemed strange,
or exotic, to Peter. The dream points out that I deal in memories, and in
the rebirth of the soul (represented by the Christmas tree image on the one
bill he remembers). By this, I mean a new birth such as I discussed in
Chapter 3 in regard to Margaret's mosque dream. Christmas, which celebrates the birth of the divine child, appears regularly in dreams to represent such inner rebirth.

Spiritual nourishment cannot be had mechanically — that is the message
of the coin machines. You cannot merely put in a coin and automatically
receive nourishment without any involvement of your own; similarly, you
cannot just consult an analyst and pay a fee and expect everything to fall
into place. Peter's earlier dream of the ski lift also represented the necessity
of going down under the surface and doing battle with the water spirits,
who, in this dream, are replaced by the middle-aged man with exotic
currencies. Much of what I stand for was still exotic to Peter, who had had
only nine sessions with me before this escalator dream.

Rather than obtaining food mechanically, in his dream, Peter must deal
with human beings. The real source of spiritual nourishment would of
course be a source within himself, but he is not yet ready to experience this,
so I serve as a model for the dream image.

This is the rule, rather than the exception, that outer events and persons
serve to represent what is going on inside oneself, because we are not used
to recognising such processes in ourselves. Instead, we turn to someone outside, failing to realise that it is a leader within the depths of our soul that
we really must turn to. This 'leader' within us sends us dreams every night,

which serve as a guide for change, albeit usually very slow and gradual.

The same night produced another dream, which enlarges our view of the situation within Peter:

> *I'm in a large church and I go near an altar where I see a nun. I immediately know she has a conflict and what it is about. I ask her, 'Wouldn't you prefer the sacred objects on the altar to be of the same period and style?' The altar has two groups of two-three objects each of sculptors and objects of distinct styles and casts of mind, both of which are interesting in themselves but incongruous with each other. I especially remember an angelic-cupid sculpture representing one group and an indistinct pyramid mass representing the other. She is the only one of her nunnery (she may be the Mother Superior) to have the aesthetic sense to feel conflict, and she feels guilty since it is her desire that new altar pieces be purchased. She does not respond to my question but looks troubled. I offer the information that I've recently been in Europe and that there they are very particular about such things. This encourages her and gives her the determination to go ahead and do what she can about purchasing suitable altar pieces.*

PETER R., #7

The nun represents Peter's religious bent, which was very strong. He is of Roman Catholic persuasion, and the nun well represents his inner religious attitude. It is almost as if Peter has now stopped in the cathedral (in the ski lift dream) to see what is there. The icons on the altar do not match, they come from differing styles and 'casts of mind', i.e. attitudes. In religious history, different icons represent different viewpoints and conceptions of God.

The altar pieces fall into two distinct groups: one represented by an angelic-cupid sculpture, and another representing a pyramid mass. The angelic-cupid sculpture follows traditional European lines. The pyramid mass is Near-Eastern and pre-Christian. With only a little stretch of the imagination, we can see here a conflict between Peter's religious upbringing, which was orthodox Roman Catholic, and his religious studies at university, which stressed the ancient world and the Near-East. There is not necessarily a conflict between the two, though traditionally, Christianity has tended to separate itself from the other Near-Eastern religions ideologically. The pyramid mass suggests Egypt, where the identity of the individual soul with the universal divine soul was stressed. This contrasts with the traditional Christian teaching that posits a sharp dividing line between human beings and God. There is, however, a link between them in that the divine Spirit indwells the human soul in Catholic Christian doctrine.

The pyramid shape appeared in the earlier dream of the same night, where a stylised triangular tree was found on one of the bills of exotic money that the middle-aged man possessed. In that respect, I suggest a Christmas tree, as a symbol of being born again. The Egyptian pyramids were for the same purpose. Not only did they hold mummified bodies for the resurrection day, but the wall paintings make it clear that rebirth takes place immediately, not merely at death but even before, when the human soul recognises its immortality. Something of this is found in the recent pyramid fad, according to which pyramid shapes bring about revitalisation; the dream takes this a step further, suggesting that pyramids represent a change taking place during life itself.

Peter's religious devotion, represented by the nun, found itself in conflict, and this conflict was a profound one because of me, I think. The subject came to a head a little over a month later, at Christmas time, when Peter and Julie took a trip to Italy. On their return, Peter brought me a number of dreams, one of which was dreamed the night before our first consultation since the trip. As we shall see, it probably was intended, albeit unconsciously, as a communication to me about his religious problem. The dream goes as follows:

> *Julie and myself and another are visiting a black girl in her home. Her family is sitting in the living-room also, but just our small group is socialising. The girl leaves the room and comes back with some crucifixes, which she is showing off. Julie especially is aware that the family is not Christian and that the father would disapprove and punish the girl if he knew she had brought such trinkets for display.*

> PETER R., #8

Peter may not have been aware that I hold a post-graduate degree in theology, and have had a number of years of experience in teaching the history and concepts of religions. But it inevitably became obvious that I am much more attuned to Plato and the eastern religions, especially Buddhism. Peter may have been aware of this from my lectures, published articles on various aspects of the concepts of religion and familiarity with the thought world of the subjects he had been studying at university. But even without that, my involuntary reactions when religious topics arise give away my personal bias. I try to respect my patients' religious beliefs, and to work within their framework, but there is no way in which my tone of voice or choice of expressions can help but make obvious my bias — even such a comment as speaking of the altar pieces, in the dream, as icons portrays something of my leanings. With some persons, like Peter, this brings out into the open their own religious questionings, and an internal crisis can take place, as the dreams show.

Peter has, in a sense, two fathers — his personal father and me — and they come into head-on collision at the point of religion: his father, a devout Catholic, and me, a rather devout disciple of Plato. This precipitated a crisis in Peter precisely because he had a deep split within his own emotions. There is the traditional, pious Catholic, who brings back cruci-fixes from the visit to Italy, despite the feeling that he is defying his 'father' = me in doing so. But there is his 'famīly', many other parts of his deep-felt emotions, which is also not Christian, for Peter had studied very exten-sively in eastern religious faiths as well as ancient mythology and religions. Even if he had not chanced upon me, he would have had to confront a similar internal religious conflict eventually. His Catholicism is repre-sented in the dream as a black girl. A girl, because his conscious 'mascu-line' mind has been taught to be questioning, so that his deeply emotional religious feelings are relegated to the 'feminine', e.g. Julie. (This cannot be generalised; for another person, it might be the masculine aspect that is devout and the feminine that is questioning.) Black, perhaps, because in his American background, it is the Blacks who are most renowned for deep, active devotion.

Our discussion of this dream centred on the conflict within him, and it had a powerful effect. The result was a terrifying nightmare that brought about a realisation in me that I was, in part, responsible for Peter's inner conflict, but also portrayed the culture shock Peter had gone through in moving from a pious Catholic background to the irreverent atmosphere of university courses in religious concepts and symbolism:

Walking through a kind of store. I sit down for a moment in a kind of lobby. A man walks into this sitting-room, who is very mysterious, dark hair, eyes, distinguished bearing, he is wearing a head gear, like that of an Egyptian pharaoh, and a long dark cape over a black suit. He has an enormous jewel in the front of his headgear which is ornately designed with a cross. I think to myself, 'How can this man walk about so aristocratically, who is he?' He sits for a moment and then gets up and leaves.

Later, I meet two women, one of whom has seen this same man and was absolutely fascinated with him.

Later, I see these women again in an empty part of a city, there are city streets laid out in blocks, but no buildings, just trees and wild grass and the wind begins picking up. There are also children with us, two or three boys, one of whom was very disagreeable and designated 'sinister' in the dream, and a little girl. The woman who was fascin-ated by the man is now possessed, 'crazy', and very pregnant—she has been impregnated by the 'devil'. I speak to her and she tells me that on New Year's (?), her girl-friend made rice and green beans and she ate some, 'and then this man (from before) stood over me while I was lying and started rubbing me all over'. The wind is blowing very hard and either the little girl or one of the boys speaks to me and gives the instructions: 'You have the strength, the Antichrist is in the vicinity—

with your left hand, take the sinister boy's left hand, and with your right hand, the hand of the right one's (a well beloved boy) they will both struggle. Under no circumstances let them go.' I take their hands and hold them by the wrists and they struggle and pull but I do not let go. The wind is howling, and I say I AM I AM I AM in increasing volume as I wake up.

PETER B., #9

Yet again, a very long, complicated dream, which we will need to sketch out before discussion:

1. Peter sits in the lobby of a store.
2. A pharaoh-like figure enters.
3. Peter meets two women.
4. In an empty part of a city with no buildings, Peter sees the women again.
5. The wind picks up.
6. There are children, one 'sinister'.
7. The fascinated woman is pregnant by the 'devil'.
8. The wind blows very hard.
9. Peter is told the Antichrist is near.
10. He must hold the two boys firmly by the hand.
11. The wind howls.
12. Peter shouts out I AM I AM I AM.
13. Peter wakens.

So the basic story-line is relatively simple: a pharaoh-like man, who is in fact the Devil or Antichrist, appears. A woman claims to have been impregnated by him. The wind picks up in increasing force. Peter must hold two little boys by the hand, a 'sinister' one to the left and a 'well beloved' one to the right. Peter shouts in ever-increasing volume, 'I AM, I AM, I AM'.

The pharaoh-like man is likened to the Devil, to the Antichrist, so that Peter's very being is threatened with extinction. He must hold fast to both boys' hands and yell out 'I AM' repeatedly. The two boys are regarded as opposites, one as sinister and one as divine. (Peter was familiar with the New Testament quotations in which God says of Jesus, 'This is my well beloved son'.)

The feeling of imminent danger is similar to that in the American Revolution dream. Who is the danger, actually? Who is this pharaoh-like Antichrist? We must remember that this is a dream, a nightmare, and ultimately the characters in it personify sub-personalities within the dreamer himself, even though he may recognise their existence only by his emotional reactions to other people. Thus, for example, I, with my background in Egyptology and religious history, upholding attitudes foreign to Peter's Catholic faith, might well serve as the model for the Antichrist in the dream. The emphasis on 'I AM' at the end indicates that Peter feels the threat of extinction. This would mean the extinction of his personality by becoming possessed by insanity. That is what the 'Antichrist' means for Peter, the threat of insanity. In historical Christian tradition, the insane were for many centuries regarded as possessed by demons, the Devil or the Antichrist.

The two little boys are presented as opposites in character: one is sinister and is held by the left hand. The word 'sinister' meant in Latin 'left', and in biblical tradition, the evil-doers are to stand at God's left at the Judgement. The other boy is 'well beloved' and, as an image of Jesus, is on the right, for Jesus is to sit at the right of God at the Judgement, and the innocent are to be with him. Peter is told to hold both firmly and not let go of either one. He must hold firmly to both aspects of life: those aspects that his upbringing has held to be 'sinister' (unacceptable), and those that are 'well beloved' (conforming to the Christian tradition). He must acknowledge, accept and hold firmly to the realisation that both aspects exist in him, if he is to be able to say 'I AM' with honesty.

The howling wind is another biblical image with which Peter was well acquainted, for the Spirit of God. 'Spirit' and 'Wind' are the same word in Greek, as in Hebrew, so that, in several references, the blowing of a strong wind is used as an image for the presence of the divine Spirit. Peter was very well familiar with this symbolism.

The dream takes Peter out into the realm of nature: trees, wild grass and wind, but no buildings. Buildings can be understood as the conscious work of man, while nature is the creation of God. This dream is a very important religious statement for Peter: the Spirit is blowing but the Antichrist is near. To survive as a whole human personality, Peter must accept the fact of both qualities within himself. This is, of course, also the teaching of the Christian tradition. The function of the nightmare is to bring this to Peter's attention as a fact of existence for him. We are reminded that his emotional balance was very precarious. Nevertheless, there has been considerable advance over the dream of the American Revolution. At the close of that dream, Peter had to be constantly on the alert against disaster that may sneak up on him unexpectedly. In this nightmare, he has ample warning, and instructions on how to protect himself from being destroyed.

The message of this nightmare is something very different from what Peter's education had taught him. It is an ages-old religious truth, held closely by all the major religious traditions of the world.

On that same night, which was fraught with dreams, there was another dream with a religious theme that expands on the matter:

In a colosseum, like the one in Rome, but in one whole piece, or a

*large circular arena, in Greek or Roman style. A priest is standing on
the outer wall alone, against the sky, addressing the crowd. I approach him and he gives me a kind of newspaper page with coupons
that can be exchanged for cash. Later, it is all the money I have
except for ten American dollars.*

*I am with two others strong, physical, burly men, worker types.
One is rather slow mentally and bald, the other is clever in his own
way. We experience some things together and then we are back at the
colosseum on the outside. We are all nearly broke and wish to return
from our travels. At the money exchange window, I learn my coupons
are not worth anything. We enter the colosseum where there are many
people, we hear an announcement which says that for those who want
it, there is work available if one reaches a certain gate in time. The
gate is an opening in the upper outer wall of the colosseum. The three
of us as well as other men run, race up the benches as the colosseum
and outer wall spin at different rates, making it very difficult. We are
approaching, when next we are on a train moving through the
countryside and we are let off. There is a man lying under a lamp post
(it is night, about dawn) he tells us there is some work we might do,
some outside physical work, but first he wants to see some identification, especially something about previous jobs. He just glances at what
we put on the ground next to him (passports, social security cards,
check stubs, etc.). I am hard pressed to find in my billfold anything
concerning work. I have the sense we were all hired though.*

PETER R., #10

Yet again, it is helpful to outline this dream, in order not to get lost in the
complexities of the narrative:

1. A priest in a colosseum gives Peter some coupons.
2. Peter is nearly broke, has only $10.
3. With two companions, Peter learns the coupons are worthless.
4. He hears work is available, but hard to get to.
5. A man under a lamp post offers physical work but requires identification.
6. Peter finds it hard to find any credentials about work.
7. He thinks they are all hired.

The main gist, in summary, is, then, that Peter receives worthless
coupons from a priest, and he is nearly broke. He is offered work providing
he can give identification, but fails in this.

The priest's coupons turn out to be worthless, and hard physical labour
is required to earn money. In real life, Peter is no stranger to this fact, he
worked very strenuously to raise needed money. The important point, in

view of the other dreams, is that, for him, the traditional religious world, as found in Italy, had nothing of value to offer in practical terms. All he had was $10 American, which happened in reality to be a gift from a friend. The dream ends yet again with the question of identity. But there is major progress at this point. Instead of the panic crescendo of the nightmare I AM I AM I AM, there is the offer of hard work and the feeling that he succeeds in getting it. This work is something that identification from the past does not relate to. Peter is used to hard physical labour in real life. But the dream says there is productive and remunerative work that will lead to discovering the values that will be valid for him. The priest's coupons are valueless for him; what he has had given to him in the past will not guarantee his soul food for the future.

A real religious crisis is obviously under way, a crisis that is not merely intellectual but one that affects his whole being.

Credentials seem unimportant. So is academic education. Peter's companions make this point clear. One is dim-witted, the other 'is clever in his own way', which we must take to be an unusual sort of wisdom. I asked Peter to draw me a picture of the man under the lamp post, and he drew me what looked like a hobo.

How can one be a hobo, yet offer hard physical labour? The 'hobo' represents the paradoxical figure of the one who seems to have nothing to give, but in reality, has all of life to offer — like the Beatles' 'Fool on the Hill'. The hard labour that is meant is not conventional, external labour, but the extremely wearisome task of working on himself, finding what life is all about. It appears that Peter lands the job, he is ready for work.

These two dreams of the same night — that of the pharaoh-Antichrist and the colosseum — make an intriguing combination. The one is an existential nightmare, with Peter struggling desperately to keep two opposites, good and evil, in his grip and a vehement affirmation of his own being; the other, a disillusioned look at religion and the realisation that a lot more work is required on himself. But while the nightmare has overtones of the absolute despair associated with the first, American Revolution dream, the colosseum dream promises security and the possibility of gaining new values.

The theme of work did not end there. A few nights later, a short dream picked up the theme:

> *Margie and I are working with a bulldozer. She is in the cabin with the driver and I am shovelling dirt with another person. We're digging half circles into a hillside. Later, we are at a farmhouse. There Margie is given a job, food or money.*
>
> PETER R., #11

Margie was a girl Peter had once known. She had been brutally raped and had narrowly escaped with her life. This so disturbed her that, Peter said, her character was quite changed, and she had to enter psychoanalysis in an attempt to recover.

Margie is an anima image in this dream. That is, she was not a person in Peter's actual environment, nor did he have any contact with her, but the dream utilised her image for symbolic purposes. In some respects, Peter said, Margie resembled his mother. So she helps to portray his mother's influence as personified by a contemporary whom he knew. To use a poetic image, Margie represents his soul. How can a man's anima be raped? By being forced into oblivion and not allowed to develop naturally.

The anima is seen in other people, while it contains features that are hidden within the dreamer. In order to establish a relationship with a woman, the young man must see these qualities in the woman, otherwise there would be no attraction. But ultimately, he must discover that they are in himself. With a young man so close to the unconscious as Peter, it is important that he become able to see these facts earlier than usually is the case, in order to prevent himself from being swamped by the unconscious emotions and fantasies.

In the dream, then, Peter and his anima are working with a bulldozer. He, as a conscious and conscientious young man, together with his raped soul which is undergoing analysis, are at work with a bulldozer. How had his soul been raped? By the misuse of hallucinogenic drugs, and the cultivation of experiences of his unconscious against nature. Also by his failure to see his girl-friend as she really was, but placing her in the position of a pseudo-mother role.

Now we, in the analysis sessions, are at work examining what has happened and is happening, and he in communion with himself is clearing the site for a new personality to be built. For this, a lot of dirt has to be shovelled, i.e. many 'dirty' things have to be cleared up, negative features of his personality have to be examined and shovelled away so that the new personality can be erected. These features include many trivia of daily life, guilt, fears and demands that are unreasonable. In particular, the relationship with his girl-friend needs to be cleaned up. They are digging half circles into a hillside, a hill of remnants from the past has to be cleared away. Later, at a farm-house, the raped girl is given food, work or money. A farm represents working with nature, and this is what Peter is doing with me in the analysis. He is working with his own nature, enabling it to come forth instead of being buried beneath the rubble of accumulated experiences of childhood, young adulthood, drug abuse and retarded emotional development.

The girl receives what she needs, in the course of all this; i.e. by careful consideration of his dreams and relating them to specific events of daily life, we are feeding his soul, restructuring his personality.

There had been several days of coldness between Peter and his girl-friend, relating to a visit by some friends. It had ended, after an analysis session, with a pillow fight and renewed closeness of Peter with his girl-friend.

How does a person get rid of the feeling of soul-destruction portrayed in the dream as a girl who had been brutally raped? By finding a way to express it, instead of hiding it and pretending it does not exist. A pillow fight is a controlled form of aggression, and aggressive feelings were heaped up within Peter. I suggested that he try finger-painting, which would leave a lasting record of his feelings that his girl-friend could see and understand, and so could I. This shocked Peter at first, for he had been brought up to believe that negative feelings should not be allowed to exist, and certainly not be expressed in the open and set out for those close to him to see. Thus, my suggestion and his conscious ideal were at odds with each other; he had felt that he ought to suppress all anger, not express it, let alone have his girl-friend know about it! I commented that this work at simply expressing his feelings in visible form is the sort of spade work that he can do in order to let his soul get on with its own work of becoming healed after its rape.

I would like to present one, final, dream of the series, to indicate the direction Peter's unconscious was taking. It came at the end of the analyti-cal sessions, and like the first dream of the series, it gives an inkling of what lay in store for him:

> *I am working with a group of men. We are in a dug out area. There are gold figurines lying about in the dirt. The figurines are of differ-ent types. There is a woman we are working under, and she has us each take up a figurine of the same kind and break or share it in a certain way. I go about doing this a bit more energetically than some of the others.*
>
> *Apparently, Bill and I had worked on a team doing this and after-wards we interview each other, but especially Bill is interviewing me. At first, we were at a desk and later standing and swinging on a long rope swing, the other standing on the ground asking questions. After-wards, Bill tells me he thought my interview went very well and he thinks it might be printed in the newspaper. Five of the interviews were going to be printed and mine might be one of them. I see a photograph that might accompany the article, first it is seen in black and white and then in colour, but not in focus.*

PETER R., #12

This is a kind of goodbye dream: Peter has been digging, he has been unearthing golden treasures from within himself, a theme we have seen several times before in this book. Peter said that the woman in the dream was like a woman who was his superior in a restaurant where he worked to help support himself in college, a very dominating, dictatorial woman. She is not a positive figure in the dream. She has the diggers break or reshape the figurines that they find, in contrast to the archaeologist's way of carefully cleaning and preserving what is found. She is a mother figure that still dominates from time to time, in Peter's mind, and causes him to destroy the treasures he finds as he examines himself and his relationships.

Bill is a very positive figure. He was a friend who once lived with Peter and an earlier girl-friend in a communal living arrangement, during the drug days, but who did not like the set-up and moved out, giving up drugs as well. He became interested in a girl with whom he established a permanent relationship. He studied agriculture, and saved his money from working in order to be able to buy an apple orchard.

The 'interview' is a record of what Peter had got out of analysis with me so far. To publish the interview means making the results visible to the world, at first dimly and then with the full colour of emotion. The picture is still out of focus. Peter does not yet fully understand the implications of it all, but the broad outlines are clear to him.

Analysis had to come to an end at this point. The series of dreams is, therefore, limited in length. It has been possible only to present a sampling here. Yet from this sampling, we get a view of how dreams work to bring about healing in our innermost being. They make a meaningful series, as we already saw in Chapter 4, when viewed from a distance and as a whole rather than as separate, isolated little dramas. The unconscious in each one of us is at work, maintaining the equilibrium we need emotionally, and it expresses itself in a meaningful way that we can profitably examine and take to heart.

Chapter Eight

DREAM GROUPS AND CONCLUSION

As we have seen in the preceding chapters, dreams have a great deal to offer us. They are a communication from our unconscious to ourselves, with a message that can both enrich and reorient our lives. Many of the dreams discussed in this book came from patients, and such dreams are especially instructive because they show how even major emotional problems can be helped by an examination of dreams. But the majority of dreams in this book have come from people who are not clinically ill in any way, and their dreams show how daily life can be enriched and reoriented to make life more meaningful, to give a sense of goal and to serve as a guide on our way through life. I do not mean this in a theological sense, but in the experiential sense of perceiving, of feeling the movement of a guide within, which can give meaning and direction to life.

Not all of this book has been concerned with interpretation. One of my major themes has been that dreams, even uninterpreted, can still serve their function. There is evidence that the dreaming process itself plays an important role in keeping the balance within our emotional personality. Fortunately, each of us dreams every time we sleep, whether or not we remember doing so. Dreaming is a natural function of our brains just as much as is the regulation of the functioning of our bodily organs.

But when a dream is remembered, there is a value in the remembering itself. Quite without any attempt to interpret them, the simple act of recording remembered dreams in a book, in order and without omission or alteration, has a great deal of value for us. So my first practical suggestion in working with dreams is simply this: buy a notebook and write or type up your remembered dreams as they occur, in a neat, legible form that does justice to the importance that dreams have in our lives. Date each dream, too, so that it is possible to review the dreams from time to time and know when they took place. If this is all you do with your dreams, it already is an important contribution to your life. Something in you understands what each dream is about, even if you are not consciously aware of the meaning. That is why dreams are remembered, because they communicate directly, with no special interpretation.

We are already familiar with this in the arts, where the viewing of a painting or the hearing of a piece of music, or the following of a play or movie, communicates something to us that we do not need to put into words. Our lives are subtly changed each time we look at a painting, or hear a piece of music, even though we are hardly aware of it and would find it difficult to explain why. That is why the arts exist. Dreams are the art of the human soul. Simply to watch them is to enrich our lives.

But something within us wants us to know the meaning of our remembered dreams. We are drawn inevitably into trying to understand them. The first step in achieving this is to understand the story they are telling. It is most helpful to read them in sequence when a dozen or so have been collected. Unexpectedly, patterns emerge in the dreams, from which we can read the themes that our unconscious is emphasising. Again, no interpretation is yet necessary. We need only read through the dreams and listen to the stories they have to tell us. It is important that we do not try to interpret too early. We must first give the dreams a chance to express themselves in their own language and in their own way. The little dreams are vignettes describing how we unconsciously see life as we are living it. Sometimes, these little dramas involve people and events that we recognise; sometimes, they are more original in presenting scenes involving people and situations we do not recognise. Usually, we ourselves play a role in our own dreams, and it is useful to read the dream from our own standpoint, seeing how we react and inter-relate with the situations in which we find ourselves.

There has been a lot of discussion as to whether the dreams we have refer to our relationship with the environment in which we find ourselves — that is, refer to real persons and events — or whether they refer exclusively to the make-up of our personality, expressed by the view that 'everything in a dream is a part of ourselves'. To ask this question is to indicate that we are looking at dreams the wrong way. But the fact that the question is asked so often shows that there is a great deal of confusion not only in the minds of the general public, but also in the minds of analysts whose job it is to work with dreams. The easiest answer is a rule of thumb that Jung gave, and this answer may be the most practical viewpoint to use: take a dream as referring to our relationships with real people and real events whenever possible, if those people and events are portrayed directly in the dream. For instance, if your mother-in-law appears in your dream, first try to understand the dream as having to do with your relationship with your mother-in-law. Generally speaking, this does not work so easily with 'substitute persons'. For instance, if an older woman, otherwise unidentified, appears in your dream, it is unlikely to relate directly to your mother or mother-in-law, for the dream is quite capable of identifying the people it means. But the figure might well represent your way of relating to mother-type people in general, and it might be helpful to take specific examples, such as your mother or mother-in-law, as case specimens to examine in the light of that more general relationship problem. Jung went on to suggest that if the people or events in the dream do not correspond to real persons or events, then it is useful to look at the dream as talking about our relationship to life both outside and inside us.

The basic answer to the question of to what do dreams refer — 'objective' facts 'outside' us, or 'subjective' facts 'inside' us — is that dreams do both. A dream represents the situation we are in in regard to life at the moment, and it may be most profitable to look at it as indicating how we feel reality to weigh upon us, and how we relate to the rest of the world and the environment or the inner world. If your mother turns up in a dream, it basically represents the influence of your mother upon you, both in the past and, if she is still alive, in the present. It includes the amount you have absorbed from her and made your own. Thus, a dream represents the psychosocial situation in which the dreamer is enmeshed, and which must be related to in some way.

Very often, the function of a dream is to point out a situation to the dreamer. As I have been indicating, a dream reflects our relationship with life. It expresses how we unconsciously perceive life and relate to it. Other people and events are a part of life, but we never see them 'objectively', only through coloured spectacles — in other words, from our own personal way of experiencing them. As an example, let us look at an intriguing dream:

> I am a reporter in Russia. But I have to accept the assignments I get. I must choose only about 50% of them. My wife is looking for some cloth she has been given so as to make something of it.

UNATTRIBUTED, #1

This dream mentions real names: Russia, the dreamer's wife, and, in part, a real event. To understand it, we must first learn what the dreamer's feelings about these are.

To the dreamer, Russia had the connotation of being a totalitarian state. But more important than that, his view of reporters in Russia was very explicit: reporters in Russia are told what events they may cover and what ones they may not. And they have strict guidelines on how reports are to be made.

Having learned that this is how Russia was understood by the dreamer, I then asked whether he did not feel himself to be a free agent in what he talked about. If he had been a patient of mine, we might also be justified in wondering whether the dream referred to me, that he did not feel allowed to talk freely with me. But he was not a patient of mine. However, he did reply that he did not feel free in talking with another therapist whom he was consulting. He and his family were consulting a psychiatrist for family therapy, that is, as a group. He felt extremely upset that the therapist prescribed the topics to be discussed, and cut him off short whenever he tried to mention something not on her agenda. Does the 50% make sense in this light? It seemed so. He felt that the therapist not only chose the agenda for each session, but decided which of the 'permitted' topics would be discussed each time. What was his wife's reaction to all this, I wondered. She was even more disappointed than he was. He still had hopes that something good might come out of it all. She had given up hope. In this light, the 'cloth' she was looking for seems to be an attempt to salvage some of the situation and make something out of it.

The purpose of this dream is to alert the dreamer about his innermost feelings about the family therapy sessions: as if he were a reporter in Russia, forbidden to report on what was important to him. The dream is bringing this view of the situation to his conscious attention, saying that he must deal with it and make something out of what had been got, but also implying that he should change the situation. This story has a happy ending. He eventually got the courage to demand, and get, a different family therapist.

It is by no means unusual for a dream to spell out a reality situation for a person who, willingly or unwillingly, is faced with a real-life situation that is disturbing, or worse. Unfortunately, dreams do not always take into account the fact that some situations cannot be changed by the dreamer, such as being racially discriminated against, but they can at least clarify where an external situation is compounding inner turmoil.

How can we tell when we are on the right track in working with such a dream? There is a touchstone for this. If, when reviewing the dream, we feel, 'Hmmm, that does not tell me anything I did not already know', then we have missed the point. The dream is always a communication of our unconscious bringing to our attention something we have missed up to now. Another part of the touchstone is: quite honestly, does the new perspective indicated by the dream find something in us that agrees with it?

Probably this is about as far as we can go by ourselves in working with our dreams. There are countless books around that claim that you can work on your own dreams by interpreting symbols, which the books then list. These books are quite worthless.

The only authority about the meaning of a dream symbol is the dreamer. No one else knows what that particular image has meant in the life and experience of the dreamer. A dream interpreter is only a sort of midwife, drawing out of the dreamer what is inside waiting to emerge. Anyone who attempts to interpret a dream in the abstract, without knowing the details of the dream and of the dreamer, is a charlatan.

The help of another person or persons is necessary to understand our dreams further, because someone removed from the situation is able to feel the atmosphere of the dream and see the inter-relationship of the dreamer with the dream personnel and situations more clearly. The outsider must know the dreamer fairly well, so as to know where the most promising links are to be found. Thus, the outsider is able to ask the right questions, to draw out from the dreamer details of what had been obscure.

A great deal of help can be provided by a dream group; that is, a group

of people who meet together in order to discuss their dreams among themselves. In my own experience, I have found that a dream group can function quite effectively without a trained leader. All that is required is that
members of the group agree to speak openly and without reservation on
any matter that is mentioned in or linked up with the dreams; and that the
group agrees to keep all that comes out during the dream groups confidential. A group may be any size, but between four and a dozen people is best.
One person relates a dream, and the group, including the dreamer, proceeds to discuss it. It is best that the members of the group proceed without
any theory about the meaning of dreams. Dreams do not follow theories,
and it is very easy to read into a dream a preconceived notion if some
theory is followed. It is best to discuss the dream in terms of itself, as I have
been doing in this book. It is just as if a group of friends gathered together
to discuss their impressions of a play they have all just seen.

Many approaches to group work with dreams have been suggested by
various writers. In my own experience, it is most helpful for the group to
take the dream as an event that has really happened, and to discuss it from
that standpoint. It is best to take the dream images as meaning what they
say, rather than supposing that they stand for someone else. It is important
that the dreamer realise and accept that the meaning of a dream may be
very disagreeable, and be willing to accept the discussion without feeling
threatened.

I stress that it is best that members of a dream group concentrate on
what the dream says, without attempting to give symbolic interpretations.
They should define the story-line, and see it as a drama of real life. To use
the same example discussed previously, if an old woman appears in someone's dream, it is best to talk about the dreamer's way of relating to old
women, rather than assume that the dream image is a disguise for the
dreamer's mother. To be sure, after talking with the dreamer about
relating to older women, and after members of the group give their impressions of how they see the dreamer's real-life relationship with older
women, they may conclude that the dreamer has a tendency to act as if
older women were her/his mother. The dream would not be talking about
a mother problem, however, but the problem the dreamer has in relating
to older women in their own right. Her/his tendency to see older women as
if they were like her/his mother might emerge, and possibly, though not
necessarily, the dream might be about that problem.

Of course, it is sometimes impossible to take the dream as meaning
exactly what it says, because what it says is a realistic impossibility (though
that it is the dreamer's wishful fantasy may not be ruled out). An example
might be a dream in which the dreamer is flying, rather like Superman.
This is, in fact, one of the most frequent dream images, probably shared
by everyone. There can be many interpretations of this motif, depending
on the details of the dream. Perhaps the dreamer has a hidden feeling that

she/he is superhuman, able to fly away from all difficulties, where others must walk or confront the problems. But perhaps it is the reverse: she/he feels unable to confront even the simplest of difficulties successfully, and needs the reassurance of being able to rise above these problems. Or, since flying has been a longing of mankind for all of history, and this longing has eventuated in the development of aviation, the motif might reflect the dreamer's attempts and capacity to bring ideals to fruition. It is important to consider how well the dreamer flies in the dream; is it free and easy, or beclouded with problems? Which of these, or whether some other interpretation, holds true for the individual dream must depend on the details of the dream and the attributes of the dreamer. These points need to be talked out by the group, with each person sharing her/his impressions. The dreamer's own impressions and feelings must not be overlooked. After all, it is the dreamer who had the dream and knew how it felt, and who knows whether a suggestion strikes home or not.

Very often, the summary of a dream discussion might begin with some such comment as 'You feel as if . . .' For example, a young man dreamed:

He, his mother, and his younger brother were standing next to a room filled with explosives. Circling about were nuclear-armed airplanes firing missiles at each other. One plane was hit, and crashed near the dreamer, who made his mother and brother fall to the ground while he crouched over them to protect them from radioactive debris. But he feared that the explosive would be set off and they would all be killed.

UNATTRIBUTED, #2

Such a dream needs very little interpretation: 'You feel as if you are in a very explosive situation, where the fallout is already being felt and there may be more disaster to come.' The group might discuss with him why his mother and younger brother are associated with him in this disaster. His father, older brother and his sister are absent from the dream. What is the explosive situation that threatens himself, his mother and his younger brother, but not his older brother, his father and his sister? In what way does he associate himself with his mother and with his younger brother in opposition to the attitudes of his father, older brother and sister?

Often, the group members can help the dreamer by suggesting how they would be feeling in the situation portrayed by the dream drama. It is important to be constructive, and to look to see how the dream is trying to help the dreamer. This is the function of dreams. An example: A manic-depressive man dreamed that:

. . . he was walking towards home, when he saw a manic man performing all sorts of grotesque actions in the yard. The dreamer

stopped and said to the man, 'You are able to perform some excellent
ballet steps, if you submit yourself to training and exercise.' He then
proceeded over the months to make the man into a ballet star, by
stringent training, making use of the manic man's ability to perform
all sorts of leaps and bounds.

UNATTRIBUTED, #3

This means that the dreamer has much potential in his mania, if he can
discipline himself to use that potential responsibly and constructively. One
function of the dream group would be to point out where this potential
lies, and how it can be disciplined so as to turn apparent mad antics into
positive activity.

I do not mean that such a dream group should attempt psychiatric
therapy. In this particular instance, the manic-depressive man was under
psychiatric treatment, lithium therapy, for his illness. But a dream group
can do something that the psychiatric lithium therapy could not do, that
is: to help connect the patient with his dreams and thus aid him towards a
fulfilling life. I am saying that 'lay' dream groups can be valuable for all
sorts of people, no matter what their problems or reasons for participating.
Dream groups under the direction of a professionally qualified psychiatrist
or analyst can be of tremendous therapeutic value for the mentally or emotionally disturbed. But such a professional person's direction is not necessary for a dream group to be of great help and benefit to its members. But
it should ensure that members with psychiatric problems are receiving professional help as well.

To be of the greatest benefit, a dream group needs to meet regularly,
once or twice a week, for at least two hours each time. There must be time
enough to go deeply into some of the dreams brought up. Members of the
group should attend regularly, not merely when they have dreams they
want to discuss. There needs to be trust between the members of the
group, so that each member feels safe in bringing out details not only of
the dreams, but of the events of life that lie behind the dream. If something is held back, it cannot be expected that discussion of the dream will
produce anything valuable.

The value of participating in a dream group does not lie only in having
your own dreams discussed. There is much to be gained from discussion of
other people's dreams. The more you immerse yourself in the world of
dreams, the more familiar you become with their language and their way
of viewing the world, and the more you benefit from an intuitive understanding of the nightly dramas that fill your life, sharpening your appreciation of them as familiarity with art sharpens your appreciation of each art
work.

Telling a dream is not, of course, the only way of bringing a dream to
the attention of the group. Dreams are just as much visual as auditory; that

is, we see as much as we hear and speak in dreams. Some people with a talent for drawing can paint one or more scenes of their dreams, and the line and colour communicate far better than words can do. Often in such instances, much more is conveyed than if words were used, because a painting requires that much of the detail be included that would tend to be deleted in telling the dream. The painting of dreams need not be reserved for groups, naturally. It can be very helpful for individuals looking at their own dreams.

Sometimes, a dream that has a lot of action can be dramatised, and either read out loud or performed by members of the group. It may come as something of a revelation for the dreamer to sit in the audience, as it were, and see her/his dream as performed by others! How very effective this can be is illustrated by a television documentary shown on Australian television a few years ago. People were asked to send in their dreams and a Jungian analyst selected from the dreams that were sent in a half dozen that seemed to have the most 'meat'. Each dream was then dramatised, using all the effects developed over the years for making television drama penetrating and incisive. In the case of a nightmare, for example, it was possible to feel the tension, share the fear as an unknown someone stalked the dreamer or threatened her/him, see the action set in context of buildings, rooms, streets and people. This is about as near as it is possible to get to reproducing a dream of one person so that it can be experienced by others, as well as re-experienced by the dreamer. Such elaborate presentations are not possible for dream discussion groups, but for variety and examination in depth, a short dramatisation may well be in order.

Virtually everyone has some gift for artistic expression, whether visually or in sound. Sometimes, the only hint of this is in dreams, which are not inhibited as we so often are in the waking state, as in dreaming, our imaginative faculty can run free and clear. Many of us have experienced the fact that we can express much of what we feel in poems, free verse usually, when simple prose fails us. A striking dream can often be set in the form of a poem, where the basic feeling can appear, unshackled from the chains of too concrete an imagery — for those of us who tend to get lost in the detail of a dream.

Finally, for dream group discussion, it is sometimes helpful to write up an impressive dream — that is, one that has very deep feeling associated with it — as a short story. The story can be duplicated and read by the members of the dream discussion group before it meets, and then discussed as to plot, characters and the salient points it makes. This needs to be a fairly meaningful dream — whether frightening, as a nightmare, supportive, as a dream of consolation, or working through a problem. Often, dreams feel very powerful, but we are not quite able to put our finger on what it is that makes the dream so powerful. It is then that a poem, a picture or a short story may come to our aid in expressing the inexpres-

sible. These are not techniques to follow through religiously, but suggestions of ways I personally have found helpful from time to time in expressing my dream more clearly, to myself or others. Sometimes, the content of
a dream even asks that some such presentation be made by directly asking
the dreamer to 'take a picture' or write a story.

There are limits to what a dream group can do. Generally speaking, it
cannot interpret symbols. Again, I must emphasise that there are no
universal symbols. The most that group members can do is to suggest possibilities, on the basis of their own experience and reading. But these suggestions should not be taken too seriously. What an image has meant to someone else does not necessarily apply to any individual dreamer. Dream
dictionaries do more harm than good. They lay emphasis on individual
images to the disregard of the context and the total story of the dream, and
they give quite arbitrary meanings. Some of the modern dream dictionaries have tried to give themselves an air of respectability by culling
material from the writings of Freud and Jung. But Freud, and more particularly Jung, discussed symbols in specific contexts, either dream contexts or literary contexts. An exception to this is some of the sexual symbolism discussed by Freud, and some of the archetypal symbolism discussed by
Jung. But it must be emphasised that you should turn to such approaches
only after all the personal associations to the symbols have been exhausted
and no meaningful thread has been found.

In group discussion, the aim should be to understand the dream story as
a story in its own right, and then to apply that story to the life of the
dreamer. Ideally, there should be no need for interpretation because the
dream story will have been understood by everyone in its own terms. The
more group members know each other, and the more familiar they become
with each other's dreams, the more they will be able to suggest ways in
which the dream story can be applied to the dreamer's life.

Dream groups can also be a valuable format for group psychotherapy,
but for this, the presence of a professional leader is essential. Such a leader
needs to be an analyst who is trained in the language and interpretation of
dreams, as well as in mental and emotional malfunctioning. The analyst
will be able to apply the dream to the specific mental or emotional problems of the dreamer, much as in individual analytical therapy.

For a complete understanding of a dream, individual discussion is
required between the dreamer and a qualified analyst. Here, discussion of
symbolism can enter in, as the final stage of dream interpretation. The
discussion of symbolism has two stages, which are not always distinct. The
first is association, in which the analyst draws forth from the dreamer the
dreamer's own thoughts, experiences and ideas about the symbol. In most
instances, this is enough to enable interpretation of the dream. The analyst
is trained to listen to dreams, to gather the gist of the dream story, to guide
the dreamer into giving associations to the dream, and then reflect back to

the dreamer the essentials of what has emerged. There can then ensue a discussion of the application of the interpreted dream to the dreamer's life.

The Jungian analyst is also trained in folklore, comparative religion, literature and the arts, so as to be able to amplify the dreamer's personal associations with a statement of how the various motifs have been used in the cultural context in which the dreamer grew up. In today's cosmopolitan world, where movement between cultures is more and more frequent, and where the ideas and teachings of other cultures have become widespread within our own, such knowledge has become indispensable for work with dreams. The analyst must be familiar with the cultural contexts of her/his patients, and know the ways in which images have been used. One very useful source for this is the folklore of the culture in which the dreamer grew up, especially the folk-tales and the religious teachings.

An abridged example of a discussion of a dream by an analyst and the dreamer may help to clarify the practical approach needed:

DREAMER:

> *I dreamed that I was riding a bicycle which had a car body on it, in the centre of the city. I had stopped to the far right, by the curb, then I wanted to pull into traffic again. Visibility through the car window was poor. There were buses ahead of me, and there was a policeman behind me. I pulled out into the road; there was a red light behind me, so that there was no traffic to worry about, and I was on my way.*

UNATTRIBUTED, #4

ANALYST: So though at first it seemed like a dangerous situation, it turned out to be quite safe.

DREAMER: Yes. I was parked on the wrong side of the road.

[This was dreamed in Australia, where, as in Britain, you drive on the left side of the road and consequently also park on the left.]

ANALYST: It wasn't a one way road?

DREAMER: That's queer. Logically, it must have been, but I didn't think of it that way in the dream. There was no traffic coming towards me, and there were buses going the same direction as me right ahead of me, so it must have been one way.

ANALYST: But you didn't think of it like that in the dream?

DREAMER: No. In the dream I was anxious about pulling into the road from the curb; I thought there would be traffic coming up behind me, and I was afraid the policeman would find something wrong with my driving and book me.

ANALYST: But he didn't?

DREAMER: No. To my surprise, everything went smoothly. The buses pulled away from me, giving me plenty of room. There was no traffic behind me to worry about, because it had a red light so the road was clear where I was. And the policeman seemed uninterested in me.

ANALYST: So you anticipated all sorts of things that might go wrong, but they didn't. You tend to do that a lot, I think: worry over what might go wrong.

DREAMER: Yes, I do. Actually, I have been having a lot of trouble with my car tyres recently; I have had three blow-outs in less than a week. So now I worry, every time I drive the car, that I will have another flat tyre. Or two flat tyres, so that, even with using my spare, I will be in a pickle.

ANALYST: In the dream, though, it is not exactly a car but a combination bicycle-car.

DREAMER: It was a bicycle that became a car more and more as the dream went on, so it was a simple car in the end. But in the beginning, it was definitely a bicycle. I remember the exertion of pedalling uphill; that was hard.

ANALYST: And you were in the centre of the city?

DREAMER: That's right. Which is strange, because I dreamed this while I was on vacation in a little country village. But in the dream, I was back in the city. That reminds me of a curious fragment of a dream I had along with that one:

> I was searching all over behind the buildings, back home, trying to find a service station.
>
> UNATTRIBUTED, #5

It seems a most unlikely place to find one.

ANALYST: You don't ride a bicycle, do you?

DREAMER: No, I don't. I tried, about a year ago, but it was a disaster and I gave it up. When I was a child, I rode a bicycle everywhere, all over the city, for hours at a time. But when I tried to ride a bicycle to work, recently, I found my balance was not good. I kept falling off and injured myself, and with all the traffic, it seemed quite dangerous.

ANALYST: There's that theme of danger again. But in this dream, did you feel any danger riding the bicycle?

DREAMER: No. Danger was only implied later on when it was a car parked on the wrong side of the street. All I can remember about the bicycle is how hard it was to pedal.

ANALYST: Were you all alone in the car?

DREAMER: Yes. Of course, I was alone on the bike, and then the bike gradually became a car. For a time, it was the two bicycle wheels with a car body instead of a bicycle frame, then a regular car. In real life, I was carting my family around in the car on the vacation, but in the dream, I was alone.

ANALYST: And did you have to provide the momentum on your vacation?

DREAMER: It felt like that, that I had to organise everything. It rather got me down. I had been hoping to be able to relax and loaf, with the rest of the family taking care of itself, more or less.

ANALYST: Is this a wider issue, though? That you feel, in general, that you are having a hard go in life — an uphill climb, to change the image a bit?

DREAMER: That's exactly how I feel. I just see endless demands being made on me, and no easy going. It looks very hopeless.

ANALYST: So one thing this dream is doing is reassuring you. The bicycle turns into a car, which goes by itself, you don't have to pedal it.

DREAMER: But my car has been giving me trouble of late.

ANALYST: In real life, yes. But in the dream, there is no hint of that. Quite the contrary, you expect your entry into the stream of life to be difficult and dangerous, and criticised, too — there's the policeman in your dream, who you expect to find something wrong, but he doesn't.

DREAMER: I suppose my car is my way of going through life.

ANALYST: And interacting with other people. You have to fit your car in with the traffic, in your dream: find a place for yourself among the others without colliding with them. A car is a very apt symbol for that.

DREAMER: I always think of Buddhism. The two main branches of Buddhism are called the 'Greater Vehicle' and the 'Lesser Vehicle', your way of approaching life.

ANALYST: Cars are prestige items, too.

DREAMER: Not mine. Not the shape it is in.

ANALYST: Was it your actual car that was in the dream?

DREAMER: I don't know. I don't think so, I think it was just a car. Visibility was bad, it didn't have very large windows. Or they weren't well placed.

ANALYST: So you find it hard to see how you fit in with life. But what impresses me is that, despite all the things that could go wrong, you manage all right.

DREAMER: To my surprise, yes.

ANALYST: There is encouragement, in that, although you start with the uphill pedalling, which is strenuous, it eventually becomes a matter of manoeuvring, after you are parked.

DREAMER: Maybe the parking was my vacation.

ANALYST: Probably. But why on the wrong side of the road? If it was the wrong side.

DREAMER: The policeman didn't seem to notice.

ANALYST: A policeman is a sort of superego, the authority watching out for what is wrong, ready to pounce on you.

DREAMER: But this time, he doesn't.

ANALYST: Because you haven't done anything wrong, really.

DREAMER: I did feel guilty about taking the vacation.

ANALYST: But if that is what the parking means, the dream is saying that it's all right.

This is enough of the analysis of the dream for our purposes. As can be seen from this example, there is an attempt to stick as much as possible with the imagery of the dream, while relating it to events in the dreamer's life, and with a minimum of interpretation. The interpretation of the car and of the policeman were not strictly necessary, though they helped spell out the implied meaning of the dream.

This is not a spectacular dream, but it is a typical one. The message it has for the dreamer is a little message, which gains in importance by being placed alongside the messages of that person's other dreams. This is the stuff of which life is made. It is by little messages such as this dream, which have far reaching implications, that life gradually becomes reoriented. The path of dreams is slow and gradual, but steady in moving towards a goal. The unconscious is not merely a reservoir of experiences and perceptions, but has a meaningful, directed function that, when heeded, enriches and completes life. The discovery of the unconscious opened up vast new vistas of existence for us, and the exploration of dreams lets us enlarge our world by adding to it dimensions of which we were hitherto unaware.

One of Jung's major discoveries, several decades ago, was that dreams do not only serve to 'fill in the gaps' of our day's emotional life (he called this *compensation*, that is, the dream compensates for an emotional attitude or experience that is too strongly one-sided). Dreams over a period of years serve to keep our emotional balance. We now know that each person has around 100,000 dream periods during the average life span, and it appears that no two dreams are exactly alike. Laboratory experiments have given some reason to think that, when a person is deprived of the dreaming experience for a prolonged period of time, serious psychological disorders result. This implies that the nervous system is, during the dreaming periods, readjusting the still unknown methods whereby emotions, memory and thinking take place. To the extent that we remain psychologically healthy, this dreaming process proceeds automatically, without our necessarily remembering that we have dreamed. The same experiments indicate that only a tiny fraction of dreams is remembered even by a person who attempts to remember and record dreams systematically.

When dreams are remembered, recorded and carefully examined, their compensatory nature becomes clear, as I hope I have shown in the previous chapters. In the Appendix, I present sample dreams, with the dreamers' comments and associations, and with my interpretations presented separately, which should illustrate this theme of dreams compensating for an emotional or psychological one-sidedness by filling in those aspects of our day-life's experiences that we have neglected to give their full due. I hope, too, that it has become clear that the interpretation of dreams is not purely an intellectual enterprise, but a highly emotional one. I would like to stress the point that the message of a dream has not really been taken seriously until both mind and heart have come to grips with it.

Generally speaking, an individual dream does not give a solution to life's problems, not even an outline for solving one particular problem. There are rare exceptions to this, but they are far too rare to justify looking at dreams from that viewpoint. Dreams are not the communication of an all-knowing intelligence within us. They are, rather, the voice of a psychological function in us that is attempting to rebalance our emotional attitudes, and occasionally to bring to our attention facts that we have studiously ignored. Jung used the colourful phrase 'the two-million-year-old person inside us', which is a helpful way of expressing the point that our emotional and mental patterns are the result of millions of years of evolution. Insofar as we are still children of nature, attempting to cope with an environment that requires delicate emotional and mental responses in order for us to survive, this 'two-million-year-old person's' voice still speaks — silently, when we do not remember the dreams; or aloud, as when we do remember them.

But, on a wider scale, just as each cell in our body is part of an overall framework determined by the DNA that constitutes our genetic make-up, so each dream produced is part of an overall psychological pattern, undoubtedly also determined by this same DNA. And as the genetic pattern incorporates a pattern of growth and development of the body throughout life, so does it incorporate a pattern of growth and development of the personality throughout life. The pattern is at work from the moment of conception and continues to the moment of death.

Bodies do become diseased, deformed and suffer accidents, and some bodies are defective when born. For these, the art and science of medicine has developed. In the same way, the human personality becomes diseased, deformed and suffers traumas, and sometimes, is defective at birth. For these, the arts and sciences of psychology have developed. Exploration of dreams is one of those 'arts and sciences'.

APPENDIX

Sample Dreams with Interpretation

Test your skills and understanding of the principles of dream interpretation with the following series of dreams. Each dream comes from a different person, and most of the dreamers have not been represented in this book so far. Accompanying each dream is basic information about the dreamer, and the dreamer's own comments about the dream. Each dream has been numbered. Following the series of dreams, I have given my own interpretations, so that you can match my interpretations with your own.

The best way to proceed is to read through dream #1 with its accompanying notes, and try your hand at working out an interpretation. Then, and only then, read my interpretation of the same dream. Think about both interpretations, your own and mine. Do they match? If they do not, as may well be the case, can you work out why? It may not necessarily be that your interpretation or mine is 'wrong'. We may have been looking at different aspects of the dream. Go through the subsequent dreams the same way. As you go, you will probably find that your interpretations gradually come closer to mine, as you become used to looking at the dreams.

My own approach with a dream in practice is, usually, to look at it from various angles, rather than leap directly to an interpretation. I discuss the dream with the dreamer, and generally tend to start not with the first bit of the dream, but with whatever aspect of it strikes me most. Quite often, I find that I have taken the dream quite differently from the dreamer, because she/he has a different background and different experiences than me. Uppermost in my mind at all times is the question 'How does this dream relate to the dreamer's present-day life? What is it trying to tell us that may be new or that involves our looking at experience in a different way?' There is no way to reproduce the dialogue between me and the dreamers for all the dreams here, but I have selected comments that the dreamers made that seem to have a direct bearing on the meaning. In a very few instances, which I have noted in each case, it was not possible to discuss the dream with the dreamer, and I have had to interpret them on the basis of my knowledge of the dreamers and their situations, and of other dreams of theirs that I have been able to discuss with them.

At the close of each interpretation, I refer back to material in this book that may be helpful in understanding the points discussed. In very many cases, perhaps all, there is no single 'right' interpretation; the dream may be seen from a number of perspectives, and what at first look like contradictory interpretations may be seen as supplementing one another. When you find a major divergency between your interpretation and mine, consider whether they may complement one another, rather than exclude one another. But if you strongly disagree with my interpretation, or if you feel you might shed some light on points that I have missed, then you might like to send me your thoughts (write me care of the publisher) you may have some insights that will prove valuable for future editions of this book! I will try to reply to all such correspondence.

The aim of this exercise is to gain practice in interpreting dreams; but I hope that you will enjoy exercising your ingenuity. Because some readers may come to this book with no background at all in dream interpretation, while others may be quite skilled at it, I have tried to include a range of dreams, from easy to difficult, in this collection.

SAMPLE DREAMS

DREAM 1

The dreamer is a professional woman in her early twenties. She is a university graduate and holds a responsible job. She is unmarried and lives with her friend, Renée, whom she has known for many years and is almost a sister to her. Renée is, perhaps, the one person who knows her best and to whom she might confide that she is consulting me. The dreamer visits her parents on occasion, but does not feel very close to them. She came to me worried about her relationship with her boy-friend. For four sessions, we discussed this and her general life history, then she brought me her first dream, as follows:

> *In the new place, I've got exams on. I'm unclear about whether I have to take the exam or go see Don Broadribb for this unit, then I decide it's to see him. I'm running a bit late so I telephone. I have trouble dialling—the numbers slip and the radio seems to be going. I have to ask Renée if it's switched through to phone okay. I know the number 865173. Then Mommy and Daddy arrive—Mommy's dressed for squash. Unfortunately, I can't play, I've got to go and see Don Broadribb. They hand me a newspaper article about squash not doing any good over a long period. I'm busy with exams and haven't time to read, yet they suggest I do. Then I'm going to have a bath—rice is being cooked in it.*

The dreamer had not, in fact, moved house, nor was she a student taking exams. The 'unit' refers to an imaginary course in which she is enrolled. The telephone number given in the dream is accurate. The dreamer was very active in sports. The point about the rice, at the end, is very obscure. The dreamer was unable to shed any light on it.

Go through this dream carefully, in the light of what you have been told about the dreamer and specific references in the dream. Keep in mind that this is her first dream 'dreamed for Don Broadribb', and likely sums up her feelings about me and her sessions with me. What sort of image is implied about me? Let your imagination run wild for a moment as you consider all the possibilities that occur to you about the dream. Then hone your imagination by picking out those items you feel most in tune with after reading the dream and comments. Do not despair if you find it hard going. It is, after all, your first challenge in dream interpretation. Only after you have thought about the dream closely should you read my comments and interpretations. Be sure to study the dream and my suggested interpretations before proceeding to dream #2.

(For suggested interpretation, see p. 212.)

DREAM 2

This dream is from a woman in her late twenties, the youngest of three sisters, her two sisters being about twenty years older than her. Her conception had not been planned, and her birth was not welcomed. Her mother, a perfectionist, was prepared for a long drawn-out quarrel whenever there was any disagreement, no matter how minor. As a result, the dreamer had expectations of herself that could never be met. Though not a high school graduate, she managed to get into university at about the time of this dream, and there she performed brilliantly. But nothing she did was good enough in her eyes. When she got 92%, she cried because it was not 100%. However, she constantly trumpeted her abilities, claiming that, if given the chance, she could be successful at anything to which she turned her interest. Yet she gradually withdrew from her university courses, on the grounds that she was not cut out for these subjects.

The dreamer was married to a very affectionate man who, like her father, was given to outbreaks of violent temper. Discord in the marriage had led to a separation several months before this dream.

She thinks of herself as ugly, and enforces this opinion of herself by covering herself up completely, even in hot weather. She wears her hair wound up in a turban, for reasons she cannot explain. On a very few rare occasions when I see her hair falling down naturally, I discover that she has a beautiful face and hair that any movie star would envy.

She is seriously overweight, and never manages to lose weight, despite constant attempts to do so. She feels starved, not only for food but also for affection, and this goes back as far as she can remember, for her parents had no love to give, neither to each other nor to her. Shortly before this dream, she tried staying with her parents, but found it necessary to move out because of the tension in the house. She came to me for analysis for a couple of years. She found it hard to cope with the separation from me between sessions. She would telephone me frequently each week, and use any excuse to talk for, literally, hours. While I was on vacation, after the first two years, she had this dream:

> We are at my parents' house, in their living-room. There in the centre of the room is a humidicrib with a baby inside. The baby is several months old. It is badly disfigured, with large gashes on its face, pieces of flesh falling from its cheeks. It is so ugly and horrible-looking, I wonder if it is mentally retarded. My mother is cold and uninvolved, completely ignoring the baby, while she sews on a tapestry. My father is also removed and unconcerned about the baby. I think about the baby— 'How terrible. What can be done for it?' I am in a panic. Then I am at my sister's house (younger sister), and I am telling her about the baby. We hug each other. Then her husband hugs me.

The 'younger sister' refers to the younger of her two sisters, both of whom were about twenty years older than the dreamer. The 'several months' age of the baby could relate to the fact that the dreamer had both separated from her husband and begun university studies several months before this dream. A hint for interpreting this dream: there seems to be a close connection between her concept of what she herself looks like and the appearance of the baby in the dream.

(For suggested interpretation, see p. 215.)

(For suggested interpretation, see p. 215.)

DREAM 3

This dreamer is a married teacher in her late forties. Her husband has a responsible job that takes him away from home frequently. He is very tired, unaffectionate, and spends most of his free time working on his hobby, one that the dreamer neither shares nor finds interesting. They have been married for about thirty years and have grown children. Hungry for affection and attention, the dreamer has turned to a friend and has been carrying on an affair with him, unknown to his wife and to her own husband. The dreamer is well paid and kept very busy, but does not get on well with her superiors. She has done post-graduate university study and rightly feels that most of her talent is being wasted. For some years now, she has been having nightmares of a most gruesome kind several times a week. She feels quite close to a breakdown, and her nightmares seem to her to indicate that something is drastically wrong.

There appears to be nothing happening in her life to account for the spate of nightmares, which are of many years' duration. In them, she regularly dies a horrible death, is tortured excruciatingly, is involved in natural disasters, etc. There is no indication of any mental illness, nor has there ever been. Physically, she is very healthy. A friend loaned her a book on

Jung, and from this book, she came to feel that perhaps there could be some relief from her nightmares. She consulted a psychologist, who referred her to me for analysis.

Vivid in the dreamer's memory is an incident that happened when she was about ten. She and her family were on a train, and she was sitting by the window alongside a man who had covered his lap and hers with a blanket for warmth. Unexpectedly, he moved his hand up under her dress and began to fondle her genitals. She was very frightened, but did not dare cry out. Later, when they left the train, she told her mother, but her mother scoffed and said that she had been imagining things, and refused to believe her. She never dared mention the incident again. But the fear remained with her and haunted her frequently.

She brought me a number of nightmares at her first consultation, and one of them was the following:

> *I am walking along a railway line out in the country accompanied by a young girl. A big burly man comes up to me from the opposite direction and engages me in conversation. I know within myself that he is trying to allay my suspicions by being nice but that he intends to rape the child. I know that on no account will I allow him to do this. Then I look down and I see that, in my hand, there is a pair of scissors.*

Before turning to the interpretation of this dream, it is valuable to think about the dream in two respects: the relation of the dream to the traumatic event of her childhood, and its possible relation to present-day events.

(For suggested interpretation, see p. 217.)

DREAM 4

Our dreamer is a woman in her early twenties. She married a man named Erik five years ago, but separated from him one year ago. Their son, Robin, is in her husband's custody. Soon after leaving her husband, she began to live with Jim, whom she loves dearly but about whom she feels very insecure. One of Jim's close friends is Mark. Not long ago, when the dreamer was sick in bed, Mark got in bed with her and raped her. She is afraid to tell Jim about this. Her mother and brother live in a distant city, and have not ever visited her. There were no known possibilities of legal problems at the time of her dream. It may be of interest that the dreamer has been employed as a semi-skilled labourer with a very low income, but, quite recently, has found a job with a much larger salary, which makes her financially independent for the first time. Paradoxically, her husband Erik wants a reconciliation, just at the time when she finally feels free to choose her own life.

To help follow her dream, the following table of the cast of characters may be helpful:

Erik = her now separated husband.

Mark = the close friend of her lover, who raped her when she was sick.

Robin = the son of the dreamer and Erik.

Jim = the dreamer's lover.

Mother and brother: live in a far distant city.

This is her dream:

> *Erik had been put into prison for running someone over. Also Mark was in prison for murder. I found myself at Erik's house with Mum and Robin. I said to mum that Erik running that person over was an accident and not deliberate. We were going to the prison to see how Erik's trial would go. I was afraid because, if he was found guilty, he would be put away for five years. And Robin would have no home, apart from me, and Jim would leave. I was thinking so selfishly. Of course I didn't want Erik to go to prison. Mum and I made our way to X Street and went inside the prison. We walked through the corridors, and then down to the end where Erik was. His trial was just about to begin. Mum and I gave Erik our assurance that everything would be alright. Then Erik was asked some questions. Then a question came up about if he could manage with a son. Erik said he was struggling and could not always find enough food. I thought, 'You liar'. No more was said. We went out to look for Mark. He was in the next room. I felt happy to see him in jail. An hour later, we went back to Erik. Instead of Erik being there, it was my brother. He said that he was free to go, so I cuddled him. I said, 'I knew you would be okay, I knew it'. We all walked out of the prison, got in the car, and made our way home.*

The reference to losing Jim becomes clear when we realise that Jim disliked the dreamer's son Robin, and refused to have him in the house with him.

(For suggested interpretation, see p. 218.)

DREAM 5

This dreamer is a university-educated woman holding a responsible job. She is in her early thirties, single, and lives alone. She came to consult me primarily because of dissatisfaction with her life, a fairly deep depression and plenty of anxiety. There was good reason for some of this anxiety, she had undergone a number of self-caused 'accidents' that, to an outsider, look very much like unplanned suicide attempts. The dream presented here is an 'initial' dream; that is, it was dreamed the night before meeting me for her first consultation. As generally is the case, she had never seen me and knew little or nothing about me before this first consultation.

> *A large open air place with lots of people crowded together eating. I managed to squeeze up next to my father who is sitting next to a most attractive man. They give me a gin and tonic. I noticed that my mother is serving tables behind us, without difficulty, which surprised me.*

The dreamer and I discussed this dream quite extensively, and she devoted a great deal of thought to its possible meanings. Some of the salient points that came out of this cogitation are:

Gin and tonic: a pleasant drink with romantic feelings attached. But there is also an unpleasant memory: as a teenager on a date, she went with a boy who gave her gin to loosen her up sexually. She feels some similarity between this boy and her father, in build and perhaps personality.

Father: she calls him selfish, self-centred, thoughtless, unloving, ungrateful, hypocritical, and (like her mother) uses alcohol as a crutch.

Lots of people: she finds the setting pleasant, but would hate such a crowd, though her parents enjoy such gatherings.

(For suggested interpretation, see p. 221.)

DREAM 6

Our dreamer is a woman in her early thirties. She is divorced and works as a professional woman, but her duties are allotted to her by her boss, whom she heartily dislikes. She has a university diploma, but recently, the university upgraded her course to degree status, and diploma holders could convert their diploma into a degree by doing one semester of full-time study in the final year of the revised degree programme. This would open new horizons for the dreamer, who would now be eligible for positions for which she is now unqualified, and she could also consider the possibility of post-graduate study. But she wants to keep her present job open; partly in case she does not get the degree, and partly with the hope of doing part-time work to help finance herself if she should be able to continue on into post-graduate study. The simplest solution would be a leave of absence from her work for one semester, but because she and her boss do not get on at all well, she doubts that this would be granted. Whatever is to be done needs to be done by January 5, since enrolment for the semester closes soon after that date. She does not like her present job, since she has no say in what she is assigned to do, and would like to resign, but she realises that this would mean depending on the conviction that she will succeed in the university work, because she feels sure that, if she resigns her job, her boss will in no way take her back. Her dream:

> *I am talking with my boss. I tell her that I want a semester off to finish my degree. She eagerly agrees, tells me I can have the semester off with pay, also tells me I can have a two-week vacation starting January 5, and gives me a passport and ticket for the vacation. She shows me my desk. I notice a big B embroidered on the carpet under the desk. I ask if this is the desk the previous director used. She tells me no, all the desks have this monogram under them.*

There are, the dreamer feels, two references to me in the dream. One is the date January 5, which is the date when I am scheduled to resume work after the Christmas holidays. The other is the monogram B under the desk(s), which she thinks relates to my surname. About the ticket and passport, she has no idea; she is not planning any trip, and she would do her university studies in the same city where she works.

(For suggested interpretation, see p. 221.)

DREAM 7

This dreamer is in his late forties. He has three children. When his marriage split up, the two older children stayed with their father, but the youngest, Linda, aged 2½, had to be placed in a foster home, with the Jones family. Later, she was adopted. Following the adoption law, neither parent was informed of the name or whereabouts of the adopting parents. The dreamer and his two older children feel the loss of Linda very deeply, and now, several years later, on the anniversary of Linda's entering the Jones' foster home, he has fallen into a mixture of deep depression and anxiety. This at first puzzled him, but his dream seems quite straight-forward and he came to me to discuss what to do about it. Here is the dream:

> *I become a university student again. It is night and I think that I am asleep and dreaming. I wish I could be sure Linda is all right. Why not send a letter to the adoptive parents via the foster family to ask. What is their name, Jones isn't it? I must look it up in the phone directory, to find the address—they would have moved since I last saw them. I am wandering about the house in the dark now. I am not sure that I am dreaming it all. I pinch myself and it hurts. I feel the floor, it is carpet. So I must be awake. I try to turn the living-room light on, it won't go on. I try another switch, it too won't work. So I must be*

dreaming after all, that sort of thing is obviously a dream motif. Can I wake myself up? I try, and feel the bedding around me. (In the dream, I look in the kitchen cupboard and think how Linda would like the things there. The children can raid the cupboard at will.)

There are some relevant comments gleaned from the dreamer:

University student: the dreamer is a university graduate, and one of his friends, who has just had his first baby born, is doing post-graduate research. The friend shares the universal fear among new parents, that something might happen to his new baby daughter.

It is night: the dreamer had severe insomnia this night, and only fell asleep in the wee hours of the morning.

I wish I could be sure etc.: the dreamer often expresses the wish that he could know whether his now school-age child Linda is alive and well.

Letter via the foster family: because of the age of the child when adopted, a gradual transition from the foster home to the adoptive home had been made, so that the foster family knows the adoptive parents fairly well.

Wandering . . . in the dark now: One of the most common dream images for anxiety is the theme of going about the house in the dark, while the lights refuse to turn on. Having attended many of my seminars, the dreamer was well familiar with that motif.

I feel the bedding around me: He had not, in fact, actually got out of bed at all, so that the feeling of the bed covers reassured him that his tests for being awake, in the dream, were imaginary.

(For suggested interpretation, see p. 222.)

DREAM 8

This dreamer is a woman in her thirties. She is married to Barry, and has two children, one of them a pre-schooler named Margaret. She has been having problems with her marriage, and had a brief separation while she visited relatives in England. She feels lonely, and that she has made a mistake in marrying Barry. She feels that, as a woman, she has been taken advantage of, both sexually and socially. She is close to her brother Bob, though he tends to be felt as a nuisance. Her young daughter Margaret is a very troublesome child in the dreamer's view. The dream goes as follows:

I flew home from England. Barry unpacked my suitcases upstairs. On coming down, we were eating or drinking when he asked me if I'd remembered to bring Margaret home. I said he should know as he'd unpacked the suitcase. Realisation that I'd left Margaret in England at her grandparents' house. They were not there though, having gone to stay with Barry's aunt and Bob after dropping me at the airport. The horror of our little girl all on her own in grandparents' house. She would already have spent a whole night on her own—vision of her crying, hungry, unable to reach light switches, etc. In absolute panic, drafting telegram to grandparents—took for ever to do it in the way of dreams. Was frantic. Having drafted telegram, then decided it would be a better idea to ring. Woke here, quite exhausted.

(For suggested interpretation, see p. 223.)

DREAM 9

Bill, our dreamer, is a single man in his twenties, a labourer. Knowing that I was looking for dreams to use in this book, he left a large sheaf of typed dreams with me, and from them, I picked this one. Since it was not possible to discuss the dozens of dreams he had typed up with him, the interpretation will have to rely largely on impressions.

Bill is a large, muscular Irishman, used to heavy work. He strikes me as highly intelligent, but true to his working-class background, he left school at the minimum age. His discontent with life oozes forth, and he seems to be heading in no particular direction. I get the impression that he does not look farther ahead than the next month or two. He is attractive, and it is surprising that he has not yet been snapped up by some young woman.

War themes run through Bill's dreams. The warring parties vary, but inevitably, Bill is in jeopardy. However, war is by no means the central feature of his dreams as a whole. Most of them have to do with family and friends. Often, he is portrayed as getting things right when others have failed. Competition is a very frequent theme; the impression is that he is very unconfident about his abilities and has to continually prove himself. Mixtures of past and present are common, scenes of childhood being about as frequent as scenes of today. But is is striking how people from childhood are mixed together with friends of today to an extent unusual in dreams.

I get the impression from the set of dreams that inner concerns are much more important than outer ones. There are very few that deal with work or events of the day. The dreams seem to portray largely his attempts to come to grips with his family and friends. There are no grandiose fantasies, and nightmares of the type presented as follows are rare.

I am in bed with a very masculine type of guy and he is performing oral sex on me. I go along with it just for the physical pleasure, but I am not attracted to him in any way. Then he wants me to do the same to him, but I refuse.

Then I am in Vietnam, next to a round concrete water trough on

*the outskirts of a village. The village is being shot up and plundered
by the Vietcong, I think. I am lying low in the grass and am safely out
of sight of the enemy. The only danger is if somebody happens to let
off a burst of fire into the grass that I am hiding in. Sporadic gun-fire
kept up for some time, but then everything went quiet. I got up and
went over towards the village. There were three girls there and they
were actually either sisters or they were not related at all. But to protect them from the Vietcong, they were playing the part of mother
and two daughters. Anyhow, they promised to hide me if the soldiers
came back. Well, I think the soldiers must have come back, because
the next thing I know is that I am being taken prisoner of war, but I
am going to be imprisoned in a camp which houses Vietcong prisoners
of war. I am being marched down a dirt road towards a group of
prisoners standing on the edge of a rice paddy. The guard in charge of
me says that, in these camps, each year, thirty-three thousand
prisoners are killed by their own inmates, and I think that these Communists are a pretty mean mob.*

We should take note that the dreamer, Bill, is far too young to have been
involved in the Vietnam war. Also that the confusion in the dream (is he a
Vietcong or an enemy of the Vietcong?) is very atypical of his dreams.

(For suggested interpretation, see p. 225.)

DREAM 10

This very brief dream is from an adult man who works as a labourer. He
grew up on a farm, living with his parents until his mother died when he
was in his early teens. Thereafter, he lived on the farm with his father. He
did very well in school, and was sent to a prestigious private high school,
where he was considered quite brilliant, and a very demanding career was
planned for him. His working-class wider family had gone to great pains to
rise in the social scale, and members of it became very prominent figures.
The boy felt very great pressures on him to achieve. At fourteen, he began
to have delusions, and eventually, he lost all contact with reality. He was
found wandering in a confused state, and was brought home by the police.
A doctor sent him to a mental hospital, where severe schizophrenia was
diagnosed. He was given an anti-psychotic drug, and advised that too
much study had driven him mad. He stopped school and eventually got a
secure job as an outdoors labourer. He continues to be maintained by the
drug, under the influence of which he appears quite normal to other persons, though he is obviously emotionally retarded.

Now in his thirties, he has never had a date with a woman. Some of this
emotional retardation may trace back to the loss of his mother and the fact
that he was sent to an all-male private high school. The lack of sexuality in

his life disturbs him greatly. He would also like to study to improve his work prospects, but is held back by the fear that to return to study would again drive him insane. In this regard, it may be noted that periodic attempts have been made to wean him off the anti-psychotic drug on which he is maintained, but each attempt has resulted in the reappearance of incapacitating schizophrenia.

His dream:

> *Dreamt I was back on the farm and about fourteen years old. We had to shift a newly shod giraffe to another paddock. We had a lot of trouble and I woke up when the giraffe ran towards me.*

(For suggested interpretation, see p. 227.)

DREAM 11

Our final dream comes again from a man in his twenties. He left school at the minimum age of fifteen, and eventually joined a profitable and successful business owned by his father. His marriage being on the rocks, he consulted me at the insistence of his wife. It has been possible to obtain a verbatim account of her presentation of his problem, and this will serve as an introduction to his dream:

> John's unpredictability is probably the thing that bothers me most. Given the same set of circumstances, but at different times, he will react in completely different ways. I often feel I am living with a Dr Jekyll and Mr Hyde character . . . I find myself for ever planning my conversation with him, no matter how trivial, and as tactful as I try to be, it depends on his mood as to the way he will react . . . John feels I am wasting money, and does not understand that, as I do not usually drink through the week as he does, I should be able to buy something little for people. On the other hand, he will lose a lot of money when betting heavily on the occasional card game or horse . . . He does not have much patience with people who disagree with him, and without realising it, he will raise his voice in a discussion . . . his father does exactly the same thing (even over the slightest matter), and I feel sure this is how most of their huge arguments begin . . . Another thing is John's negative and pessimistic attitude sometimes. He will often become depressed and not be bothered with anything. This can happen in relation to work, talking to people or myself . . . John's bad temper can terrify me. He can sometimes fly into a fit of rage over the slightest thing. If he does not break anything in the house, he will go to the yacht club and get drunk . . . I'm afraid of my not being able to control him at these times. As much as I try to calm him down, I cannot . . . All these characteristics of John's are not always present. Most

of the time, John can be a warm, loving, sympathetic, sincere and gentle man.

Independently of his wife's account, John told me that what worried him most was his very heavy drinking, and his tendency to explode in an uncontrollable rage. He said that he and his father disagreed on the details of how the business should be run, and this led to many violent quarrels between them. In the light of all this, we may now look at his dream:

> *Made a trip to capture a crim. However, he didn't fall for it. He had about three of us bailed up in a house. We had guns. One of the guys had a shot at him and missed then he turned and got his gun. We were in the bedrooms and one of the other guys still had a gun hidden. I tried to get the gun but he stopped me. He cut my knee with a knife to stop me doing it again. Then he went on a rampage of killing, etc. He also took the form of a snake.*

(For suggested interpretation, see p. 229.)

INTERPRETATIONS

In the following pages, I present my understanding of the sample dreams and their probable interpretation. In the comments that accompany each dream text, I have summarised the main points relating to the dreamer and the dreamer's thoughts about the dream. The interpretations I present here are the result of discussion of the dreams with their dreamers, for the most part. Naturally, I have also benefited from hindsight in many instances, but I have tried to keep this 'benefit' to a minimum, since it gives me an unfair advantage over you, the reader. When hindsight has been of special value, I try to point this out in my discussion.

INTERPRETATION OF DREAM 1

This is a transference dream; that is, it deals with the way the dreamer sees and feels about me. Transference is not limited to analytical experience, of course. One particular value of dreams is that they often reveal just how you see and feel about someone else, and that 'revelation' may come as a bit of a surprise to you, as well as to the someone else! Such a dream is a very helpful aid in keeping check of how you actually perceive and feel about another person. In the case of analysis, it is valuable for the analyst, as well as for the dreamer, to discover what feelings have been stirred up in the dreamer by the encounter with the analyst. In everyday life, there is not much opportunity to discuss such matters with an acquaintance, a boss, a relative or partner. But it does help *you* to understand just what is going on emotionally inside you. During an analysis session, this opportunity does exist, and it plays a very important role in sorting out just what is going on. It may not always be possible to discuss the dream fully, but, for the analyst, it serves as an important indicator of the state and nature of the relationship between herself/himself and the patient/dreamer. Nevertheless, the interpreter must always keep in mind that the interpretation of a dream is merely a useful tool for discussing the concerns and problems of the patient/dreamer. It must never be an end in itself. In working over a dream such as this one, our ultimate question must be: 'What is the dreamer trying to say to me via this dream?' And in all instances: 'What is it that this dream is saying to me that I or we were not fully aware of before?'

To sum the first dream up, its most outstanding feature is the dreamer's uncertainty, we might say ambivalence, towards coming to her session with me. This is portrayed by a theme that dream interpreters get to know very well — an effort to get in touch with the analyst that is blocked by various means. The failure to contact the analyst on the phone is a particularly common dream motif. It is important to examine what the difficulties are in the dreamer's attempt to 'get through to' the analyst. It is helpful to look at the difficulties in the dream, and to consider what each one implies.

The dreamer is unclear whether she is to take an exam, or to go and see me about her course. The dreamer was not, in fact, enrolled in any course of study, and had no examinations coming up. But since she refers to me as the person in charge of the course, it implies that the analytical sessions are a sort of course, with, undoubtedly, examinations going on all the time. Many people conceive of analysis as a learning situation, where they tell their problems and the analyst tells them the solution. There is also the universal preconception that an analyst is busily secretly examining and diagnosing. Our dreamer had had no previous contact with an analyst, and seems to have shared these misconceptions.

She attempts to telephone me that she will be a bit late. Usually, when a person is in such distress or need that they make a commitment for the long-term process that constitutes an analysis, she/he gets cold feet to some degree. When they discover that the analysis requires that they bare their soul completely, they become hesitant. A typical manifestation of this is arriving late for a session, because of an inner conflict over 'shall I go, or not?' (This is quite different from a situation in which a person is forced to be late by circumstances outside her/his control, such as a car breakdown, etc.) But in this dream, the situation is a bit different. She wants to notify me that she will be a bit late, but circumstances prevent this.

She has trouble dialling; the numbers slip. In other words, she finds it difficult to get through me, the lines of communication are apparently not free. The failure of a patient to get through to the analyst may be a fault on the analyst's part or on the patient's. But in this instance, the problem is at her end. She knows my number, how to get in touch with me, but has difficulty in making the apparatus of communication work. This is a way of saying that she does not yet have enough control of her means of expressing herself to get through to me; her attempt to make contact with me is hindered. Thus far, we have not learned what the difficulties are, only that they exist.

The radio seems to be going. Radio, in dreams, represents the perception of other voices and feelings than the dreamer's awareness of what is going on. These 'interfering sounds' may be external ones, such as worries and preoccupations not seen as relevant for discussion; or the attitudes and opinions of friends and family members; they may also be inner voices, i.e. conflicting thoughts and feelings that block off her ability to come across clearly to me.

There is a conflict of interest, between playing squash or seeing me, decided in favour of me. There is a strong hint that she feels a need to choose between her mother and me, that we represent opposite forces tugging at her for allegiance. This hints that she may be involved in a conflict of loyalties; me versus her parents. The dream puts it quite plainly: does she prefer to spend her time going to play squash with her mother, or come to consult me? Her father is mentioned as also coming, but he seems to play no role in the dream.

Now, some other aspects of the dream: 'In the new place, I've got exams on'. The new place presumably refers to where she's at emotionally. Exams imply a judgment being made. There are two areas of judgment that she might fear: one is her own self-judgment, what she feels about herself; the other is the assumption that I am going to judge her on the basis of what she brings to me. There is, actually, a third area of judgment that requires attention: her judgment of me and my adequacy for her.

Analysis is a unique situation in a very vital respect: it requires full, uninhibited openness, of a sort rarely or never known before. The closest parallel would be the small child's almost unlimited trust in her mother, but even the smallest child has secrets, and knows that some topics are not tolerated. The analyst is asking for an emotional intimacy unprecedented in her life. And this analyst is almost a complete stranger to her. He is, apparently, asking for unlimited trust and demanding confidences never shared with anyone before. No small demand! No wonder she feels uncertain about it. So the exams are on in this sense, too; not only in the feeling that the analyst is examining her, but in her need to examine the analyst and decide how much confidence she is prepared to give him. She decides to meet the challenge. But then the uncertainties take over.

She asks her friend Renée whether the phone is in working order, which I take to mean that she asks Renée whether it is appropriate to call me. Renée is asked to give an opinion as to whether the lines of communication with me are open. I have no reason to think that she really spoke with

Renée about the advisability of opening herself to me, but if we take it that Renée here stands for an outside opinion that she values, the dream reference makes sense.

When the parents arrive, there is a paradox. Though the dreamer's mother is dressed for squash and invites her to play squash, she also gives her an article to read about the ill effects of long-term squash-playing. Might the dream be hinting that her mother has used athletics as a substitute for delving into her own emotional depths and sorting out her problems, and the dreamer feels a tug to do the same?

The final sentence of the dream contains some bizarre imagery. To have a bath is to clean oneself, and that is what she wants to do, to cleanse herself of the muck that has come to cover her soul during her life (the 'muck' being a very serious problem in her sexual relationship with her boyfriend). Rice might represent fertility and the basic foodstuff of much of the world. The rice bath follows directly upon the point that she must hurry to see me. Discussing emotional experiences and problems involves a great deal of self-exposure. Long before this, a bath has been familiar as an image for the process of being cleaned of the muck of one's life through discussion in analysis. Rice is also traditionally thrown at weddings, and the idea of a marriage may not be too far-fetched for this part of the dream, a marriage not so much with me as of her rational and emotional selves, perhaps.

In working over this dream, you might find it helpful to consult Chapter 2, 'The People in our Dreams', and Chapter 6, 'Sex in Dreams'. The discussion of Roger H.'s dream #1 in Chapter 2 may be particularly relevant here.

A question for you, the reader: were there any conflicts between your understanding of the dream and mine? Would you add anything to what I said? If you are already well used to working with dreams, much of what I have said may come easily to you. If you work from a different viewpoint, you may see something quite different in the dream than I did. (If so, I'd like to hear the details from you.) If, on the other hand, you are only just beginning to work with dreams, much of the interpretation may not seem as easy as it looks on paper, and it may be difficult to see how some conclusions were reached. In a live situation, most of the interpretation would not be clear from the start, but would emerge slowly as you discuss the dream with its dreamer, each contributing her/his quantum of bewilderment, pondering and bright ideas. For those of you who found the going rough, I say 'Take heart. Your feeling should be "see what can be gained if enough time and effort and discussion are taken", *not* "oh my God, I could never think of all that!"'

INTERPRETATION OF DREAM 2

The dream takes place in her parents' house, at which she recently stayed after separating from her husband and starting her university studies. It was in this house that a strong quarrel took place, when she and her mother disagreed about the pronunciation of a word. She sees herself as a baby again; but she sees herself through the eyes of her mother, an image drilled into her from infancy and apparently not much affected by later experiences. The dream baby seems premature, for it is in a humidicrib. Perhaps this has to do with her feelings about university study, for she thinks, in the dream, that perhaps the baby is mentally retarded. The prematurity could also be linked to my vacation: she feels herself thrown out into the world, with no substitute-father to care for her and whom she can contact in time of crisis.

The baby has gashes on its face, pieces of flesh falling from its cheeks, it is ugly and horrible-looking. This seems to fit in with her own self-perception of her body, which she usually takes such care to hide. Why the face? Possibly because it is about her head, rather than her heart, that she feels so deformed. It is her head-work, intellect, that she feels can never be good enough; what, to others, would seem an achievement, to her, seems like a hideous failure.

But the dream emphasises the emotional aspect of it all. Neither parent is interested in this baby, they quite ignore it. Only she is concerned, and the concern turns into panic. What indeed could she do? Interest and affection are obviously not to be found in her parents' house. Where then? She can turn to her sister, who can give her some warmth, and (daringly) to her sister's husband, who can also give warmth. (Could this be a fantasy about me?) But where is her own home and the warmth she needs to find in it. Her husband, an affectionate man, has been left behind. She has hope, but can it be fulfilled?

If we are right in seeing the ugly, maltreated baby as the way she sees herself, an image taken over from her parents, may we not be justified also in seeing the cold, insensitive, ignoring, uninvolved mother and father in the dream as representing the self-critical element in herself that demands perfection and can never accept anything she does as good enough? (the subjective level of interpretation). Does the dream not say to her: 'Look! You must rescue this deformed baby which is your emotional soul, get it away from the cold-hearted judgmental side in yourself that sees your beauty as ugliness and your intelligence as mental retardation. You must escape to the position your sister is in: daring to show and rejoice in her physical beauty and her mental abilities. She is your real, adult soul, which is waiting to embrace you if you only give it a chance. And the achievements you envy so much in your husband [in her view, her husband, a very successful executive, lacks the initiative to increase his status and prestige] are available to you, they are the husband to your soul, from whom you need never be parted'?

Chapter 4, 'A Dream Has a Purpose', is specially relevant to this dream, and I suggest particular attention be paid to Margaret J.'s dreams #2 and 3 and the comments on them.

INTERPRETATION OF DREAM 3

Essentially, the dream represents the continuing fear that has been with the woman for so many years. But it is not a simple re-enactment of the actual event. There are several major differences. First of all, in the dream, she is walking along a railway track, rather than riding in a train. Secondly, she is her present age, accompanying a young girl who might be about her age at the time of the actual molestation. Thirdly, the man tries to con her into forgetting her suspicions by talking, whereas in the real event, there had been no conversation. Fourthly, there was no suggestion of rape in the actual event, as there is in the dream. And finally, she is armed, even if with a strange weapon, a pair of scissors. These differences lead us to think that the dream is commenting on her present-day state, and not merely repeating the trauma of her childhood. It would be a serious error to ignore or overlook the childhood event in favour of focusing only at the present, because the fear that was aroused in childhood is obviously still alive and active in her. To ignore it would be to imitate her mother, and pretend the very real hurt does not exist. But it would equally be wrong to concentrate only on the past, because, as the dream points out, she is now an adult and able to confront head on the threat she felt as a child. She is both a wounded child and a capable adult, the dream is concerned with both aspects.

The differences between the actual event and the dream's portrayal require examination, because they provide the link between the still powerful child's fear within her and events of the present day. In the dream, she is following a railway track, as if life were a pre-ordained path. She knows where it leads to, but there is not much interest in it. She is in a soul-destroying rut, as the continuous series of nightmares indicates: somehow she is dying each day, or very nearly so. She has taken one step of great importance, she has found a lover who can give her the emotional warmth she needs so badly, but it has to remain undercover, covert, it cannot really satisfy. What can she do about her job? Is that also killing her day by day? What can she do about that?

She is both an adult and a child, side by side, going along that track. How can she allow the child to grow and to merge into her adult personality? Perhaps by confiding her fear in someone, preferably a woman (because it was her mother who refused to hear her), who will accept the reality and appropriateness of the fear and not try to argue her out of it.

A male voice tries to lull her into not recognising what is happening. As a child, she may not have consciously known what the man on the train was up to, but her body knew. In his heart, it was rape he was intent on, even if he knew that he would not be able to carry it through outside of his fantasies. It is very likely that she has told herself innumerable times that, after all, he did nothing really harmful. But her heart knows better: what, to an adult, may be passed off as a sexual aberration, to the child, felt like an attack on her very being, as indeed it was (otherwise it would not continue to haunt her). Question: is she under threat now, at the present time; is her soul being raped while a smooth voice tells her everything is all right? The hindsight answer proved to be yes, although it took her several years to find it out.

The dream warns her of the presence of danger, and tells her that she has a weapon to protect herself, strange though that weapon may appear. Scissors are for cutting. What fabric of her life needs to be cut off in order that she can survive? Again, the dream poses questions that must be asked before they can be answered. Wisdom is to know what questions to ask. Folly is to assume that the answers are already known.

Chapter 4, on 'Nightmares', is most relevant to this dream; in particular, Carl N.'s dream #5.

INTERPRETATION OF DREAM 4

This dream is, in many respects, a fairly clear representation of the dreamer's feelings in the complicated situation in which she finds herself. We may see the feelings more easily if we take the persons one at a time.

First, there is her husband Erik, whom she left a year ago and who has custody over her son. She feels that he has committed no crime: what he did was accidental. The 'crime' was that he ran over someone, namely her. He 'ran her down' (criticised? in any event, paid no attention to her feelings). But she feels that he did not mean to do so. He is in prison, about to be tried for his 'crime'. Interestingly, the penalty if he is found guilty is a prison sentence equal to the length of their marriage. She would like to let him go free, both in a legal sense (= divorce), and in an emotional sense (= no longer kept cooped up in her mind, but allowed to go his own way, she and he totally free of one another).

She is at Erik's house, which I think we can take as her imagining herself in his shoes, together with her mother and her young son. She imagines telling her mother how she sees what had happened in the marriage, now. She reassures Erik that there is no guilt, everything will be alright (i.e. she forgives him). But she realises she has a hidden motive in this, namely that as long as he is free to care for their son, she can be free in her new relationship. Unless she considers him blameless, how can she justify leaving her child with him? Unfortunately, at the trial, Erik claims that he cannot always fill his son's needs. That would mean that she would have to care for the child, and she fears Jim would leave her if she did so.

Mark, she feels, is really the person who deserves prison. What Erik did to her was uncalculated, unintentional. But Mark's rape of her while she was helpless and trusted him is tantamount to soul murder; she would rejoice to see him in jail (I think in waking life too, not just in her dream.)

Robin, unfortunately, is the victim of the emotional struggle between her, her husband and her lover. She realises she is being selfish by putting her love for Jim above that for her son. But what to do?

The dream finds a solution for her: what if she loved Erik like a brother instead of as a husband? Could she not have him and Jim too? Erik really is a kindred spirit. He was trapped in the marriage just as she was. Can she not hold him in her feelings as a brother, absolve him of guilt, and they can all co-exist? — because in reality, he lies when he says he is unable to care adequately for their son.

Essentially, the dream is not talking about actions, but about feelings. She is trying to work out the most satisfactory way of feeling toward the present situation. This involves re-evaluating what has happened, and what her motives are. It involves ceasing to hate Erik, without having to feel it necessary to return to him as a wife.

Chapter 8, with the dream of the 'Reporter in Russia', is relevant for study in working over this dream.

INTERPRETATION OF DREAM 5

There are many possible approaches to this dream. One point needs to be kept in mind: the young woman who dreamed it had never seen me before consulting me the day after this dream. Since she was in a severe emotional crisis, it is possible that the dream relates to her hopes and fears about what I would be like. It is possible that the 'most attractive man' was her dream fantasy or hope of what I would be like, since she knew nothing at all about me. The young man is seated next to her father, and it may be that, at the same time as this hope, she held a fear that I would be a younger version of her father, of whom her opinion was very low, as can be seen from her description of him. The dream came as quite a surprise to her; she could make nothing of it, except to notice that virtually everything in it is contrary to what she would expect in real life. But she worked industriously over the dream, trying to understand it.

A large open-air place: If we assume that this dream, brought to me on the first day, is a communication about 'where she's at', the setting is significant. Everything is out in the open, a feeling she would normally enjoy. There are no secrets to be kept hidden. It should be noted, at this point, that she was deadly serious about her analysis, and was intent on holding nothing back, no matter how painful.

But there are *lots of people crowded together eating.* This is a situation she firmly dislikes. But if taken on the 'subjective level', as a statement about her own condition, it indicates that, when she opens up her soul, it is found to be absolutely crowded. She is not, if you like, one but a vast number of people crowded into one personality — a way of saying that there are so many facets to her life and emotional history, that there is hardly any place left for the real her to squeeze in. She feels that she is not really herself, a feeling that manifests outwardly in deep depression and severe anxiety.

I managed to squeeze up next to my father: That her problems trace back to family relations to a considerable extent comes as no surprise. Father and Mother figure prominently in the dreams of many adults who had never fully shaken off their childhood view of the parents as superior beings with moral and physical authority. Emotionally, most of us remain our parents' children, still taking them as having authority that they do not, in fact, possess. It is most difficult, of course, for those of us whose parents are within reaching distance and who actively attempt to meddle in our lives. But those of us who have shaken off the live parents, or whose parents are dead, remain dominated by the attitudes and judgments derived from our parents.

The dreamer's comments about her father are not so much a description of him as an emotional evaluation of him. Does this all dark picture of him cover up a deep love for him, and is she trying to find a way to shove herself in alongside him, to have a part in his life? This is a question that requires investigation.

The description of her father, which I have quoted verbatim, is a long series of negatives. We are led to wonder: are these really qualities of her father or is the string of negatives a sort of agenda for examination of her own bad side? They are a way in which she sees her father. But are they also his legacy to her? Probably all of us share those same qualities, but not all of us are prepared to do something about them. This young woman was.

Who is sitting next to a most attractive man. They give me gin and tonic. I have already made the suggestion that this young man might be a fantasy of me, whom she had never seen. He could also be the other side of her father, especially as seen when she was a child and he was much younger and more attractive. Being next to her father, perhaps the man shares some of her father's qualities, especially the not-so-unsexual feelings a little girl has towards her father. There may be both a taste of fear and a taste of hope present in the gin and tonic. She considers gin and tonic to be a romantic drink, but it also conjures up for her memories of an unpleasant sexual experience.

Ultimately, the attractive young man will turn out to be a romantic potential in herself, waiting to be transferred to some suitable partner. Just as she has internalised the negative qualities of her father (she is only too aware of this and it drives her to despair), there are genuinely attractive and romantic qualities, too. She is surprised by this suggestion, and cannot yet imagine what they might be.

The attractive man is an example of an *animus* figure. In other words, he represents the as-yet-undiscovered potentialities within herself. Maybe, who knows?, he may even represent the possibility of finding her very own 'attractive young man' in life, who will rescue her from the dreary spinsterhood she anticipates. At first, she will probably imagine him to be me, her analyst, who she will fondly imagine to incarnate all the good qualities of a loving male companion, though with a price — for, being seated so close to her father, she may also come to feel that he personifies all that she feels bad. Eventually, however, she will find herself a mate who will personify for her those qualities on which she has missed out, and be able to inspire her own hidden potential to come to the surface. That is what an *animus* is, an inner image of a man who personifies the woman's true hidden qualities and brings them into the open. An ideal seldom achieved, but an ideal nonetheless.

I noticed that my mother is serving tables behind us, without difficulty, which surprised me. The dreamer thought she had already come to grips with the problems and influence posed by her mother in her life. But evidently, her mother is still an active force, not only as a living woman but also internally as the spirit of the dreamer's own attitudes towards life.

The interpretation of this dream relies heavily on the discussion of 'The People in Our Dreams', with special emphasis on the six principles listed at the end of that chapter.

INTERPRETATION OF DREAM 6

At first sight, this looks like a simple wish-fulfilling fantasy. It looks as though the dream is trying to reassure her that her hopes will be fulfilled, she will get her leave of absence, with pay (!), and her two weeks' holiday pay to boot. Alas, this was not to be the case. The leave of absence was not granted, and she had to decide on quitting or giving up the hope for the university degree. When it came to the crunch, she resigned from the job.

The day-dream quality of the dream ends at about the middle of the text. From there on, it becomes hard to explain. Why should she be given a passport and ticket? Perhaps an expression of goodwill. Why does her 'vacation' begin on the date when I resume work? Perhaps a feeling that what will be a working period for me will be a vacation period for her, i.e. a vacation from analysis. (In the event, she did not resume analysis when my Christmas vacation ended, so the 'vacation' from analysis did take place.) Why is my initial embroidered on the carpet underneath all the desks? Am I identified somehow with the director, seen as the male who controls her life as the female director controls her work?

One thing seems clear, that farewelling the boss and work also means farewelling me, in that it is the desks at work that all have my monogram under them. Perhaps she hopes that I will give her as good a send-off as her boss does in the dream.

INTERPRETATION OF DREAM 7

> Is there not balm in Gilead any more?
> Is there no doctor there?
> Then why does it make no progress,
> this cure of the daughter of my people?
> Who will turn my head into a fountain,
> and my eyes into a spring for tears,
> so that I may weep all day, all night . . .
>
> JEREMIAH 8: 22–3,
> *Jerusalem Bible*

On the anniversary of the departure of his child from his home, the father felt an overwhelming sadness, and the wish/hope that it had all been a bad dream. I suggested that he do precisely what he planned in the dream, to contact the one-time foster parents and ask them to forward a letter to Linda's adoptive parents. Generally speaking, it is important to take dreams as literally as possible, particularly when a real-life situation is involved. In the face of enormous worry and depression, the dream is suggesting an eminently practical action that could alleviate the worst of the man's misery over the loss of his child. He is pictured as wandering about, groping in the dark, unable to find any light at all — a very familiar dream image for the feeling of total despair.

The realisation that it is a dream takes place in the dream itself, not an unusual event. But this time, there is an unusual twist to it. In the dream, he seeks to prove to himself that he is awake, and at first succeeds in doing so. He uses the time-honoured cliché of pinching himself to see if he feels pain and therefore must be awake. The result is yes, he is awake. He then feels the texture of the floor, to see whether it has its normal feel. Again, the answer is affirmative. He must be awake. All this is real, not a bad dream.

But the third 'test' shows otherwise: he is still in the dark, the lights will not go on. At this point, the anxiety becomes too great for him and he awakens, despite the massive dose of sleeping pills he had taken in the early hours of the morning. He had dreamed tht he was dreaming, a pretty common occurrence. It signifies that an important insight has come through in the dreaming process. His anxiety and depression were ready to wake him up and resume their current task of censuring him for having allowed his daughter to be adopted.

He feels like a university student again, like his friend whose new-born baby daughter reminded him so of Linda's birth. He feels that he is dreaming, and that is quite correct. But what does the feeling of being asleep and dreaming signify? In dreams, raw, pure emotions come through, uncensored, lacking the inhibitions that we have taught ourselves to use during waking life in order to prevent our emotions from disrupting our life. One of the greatest values of dreams is that they supply the weakened or missing emotions that present events evoke in us (in this case, the present events being the birth of his friend's daughter, and the anniversary of Linda's departure from his life). That is why so many people fear or refuse to look at their dreams, because they are unwilling to accept that the emotions portrayed in the dreams are really there inside themselves. In this case, the father had been talked (brainwashed) into believing that what had happened to his daughter was all for the best. His brain could believe this, but his heart, which controls his dreams, could not.

The father's heart, which had never been and never could be convinced that all was for the best, was beaten into submission during waking periods by logical arguments; whether his head would have ever come to such logical arguments without the aid of outside authorities and friends is questionable. His heart, forcibly prevented from expressing itself, had to retreat into emptiness and worry, manifested clinically as depression and anxiety.

The dream suggests a compromise: his heart must accept the *fait accompli*, that Linda, his daughter, is gone from his life; but his head must give way to his heart's demands, and make enquiries to discover Linda's welfare. (I suggest also: photos and some description of her activities and likes and dislikes. The dreamer's sister had sent Linda a very big, cuddly teddy bear for her to grow up with. Did this, a lasting expression of the emotional link between the dreamer, his sister, and his child, go with her to the adoptive home to be her steady companion?)

Raiding the cupboard: a peculiar image, until we remember that the cupboard is the container of sweet, delicious experiences within himself, ready to be 'raided' by his children at any time, day or night. His love for Linda continues undiminished, though she has disappeared from his life, and he wishes he could make available to her the 'cupboard' within himself that his other two children enjoy. The paternal and maternal instincts in a person do not cease when the child has been adopted, as countless parents know. To some extent, at least, the gap in his heart can be filled by the compromise suggested in the dream. The anxiety and depression can, at least, be converted into grief and sadness, leaving room for a subsequent ray of joy and gladness to enter in.

For this dream, June T.'s dream #3 and the brief description of it in Chapter 4, 'A Dream Has a Purpose', are helpful reading.

INTERPRETATION OF DREAM 8

This dream obviously relates to the dreamer's feelings about returning to her husband, the trip to England, her children (Margaret in particular), the marriage, her family and the emotional chaos she is undergoing. There is a striking ambivalence about her daughter Margaret. On the one hand, so the dream goes, she flew all the way back home without noticing that her daughter was not with her, and even when Barry asks about Margaret, the dreamer seems at first unconcerned. Then her empathy with the child surfaces; she realises that she left Margaret behind in an empty house, feels the child's panic and tries to work out a way to get in touch with Margaret's grandparents. It is intriguing that the dream does not say whether she means her own parents or Barry's parents, as if it did not really matter. It is also intriguing that the dream puts Barry's family (his aunt) and hers (her brother) together as if they were one. The feeling that comes out of this is that both families have been left behind in her emotions.

There is clearly a feeling of guilt on the dreamer's part. Although, in reality, she did no such thing with Margaret, in her dream, she leaves her behind, and only belatedly realises what it must feel like for the child. On one level, the dream is saying 'Look, you would rather leave Margaret behind, just like the grandparents and relations. Admit it. But imagine how Margaret is feeling without her mother. You may be present with her physically, but emotionally, you have lost sight of her. How would you feel, treated like that? How about showing some concern for the child?' This is quite true, as far as it goes. But there is more to it than that.

The dream is not only a statement about her feelings towards the child; it is also a statement about her feeling towards herself. The dreamer can identify with her child's plight, because she herself feels the same way right now. With the breaking up of her marriage, she feels as if she has been abandoned and left to cope with life when she does not feel able to exist on her own. Internally, she feels starved for affection and care, life feels like groping in the dark, her soul is crying, but there is no one to hear. We need to ask ourselves why it is Margaret who is left behind unnoticed. Margaret is the rebellious one, the independent one who knows her own mind. She is also a young child, and that is how the dreamer feels, like a little child left to cope with no one to care for her. She is an adult, a mother, a person trying to find her own way; but she is also a small child, lonely and frightened, crying out in desperation to a world that does not even know she is there.

The dreamer wants to communicate this feeling, but does not quite know how. Who does she want to tell? The grandparents. Who are they? If they are Barry's parents, is it too much to suggest that they represent, in the dream, the paternal and maternal instincts in Barry? That she is trying to call out to him to be a father and mother to the abandoned little child she feels like inside? In many marriages, this is the case: the wife is looking for a parent in her husband, and, equally often, the husband is looking for a parent in his wife. Many marriages fall apart because of this; each is unaware of the other's emotional needs, each assumes the other is exclusively an adult, and becomes disappointed, even desperate, on discovering that this is not the case.

In dreams where a son or daughter appears, it is often difficult to know whether the plight of the child is meant, or the plight of finding that child's situation in yourself. Very often, both seem to be meant. Children do, in reality, quite often absorb their parents' emotions and act them out as if a mirror image of what is happening inside the most important people in their lives, their parents.

Barry's parents in England would have reminded the dreamer very strongly of Barry's personality. But, being of an older generation, they would have seen the dreamer more as a daughter than an independent adult. This would be equally true if her own parents were meant. Here comes the paradox, of wanting to be on her own, yet also wanting to be cared for as a little child. She wants to cry out to them, 'I brought you a needy, starving child, take care of me!' She wants to be loved and cared for, both as an adult and as a little child, needing independence within the framework of a parental type of love. Very probably, if we could look into her husband's dreams, we would find the same need on his side. The goal is not to abandon this child-like need, which is in all of us, but to bring it into the open and have it cared for. The first step in that direction is to recognise that the little abandoned child still lives. Once the dreamer has discovered that, she can find a way to express her need in a fashion that it can be met.

Alfred M.'s dream #3, in Chapter 2, 'The People in Our Dreams', is a relevant parallel for comparison with this dream and its interpretation.

INTERPRETATION OF DREAM 9

The feelings of being under threat and of sexual uncertainty stand out strongly in this dream. The dreamer entertains the feeling of enjoyment of homosexual sex, but has no interest in performing it; it is one-directional only. In the major section of the dream, three women promise to hide him in the event of the soldiers' return; but there is no further mention of this, and evidently, they do not attempt to hide him. If the central theme of the dream is the desire for homosexual oral sex, then he feels under threat for having such feelings, and being with women does not protect him from the guilt (if such it is).

It appears that he is on the losing side of the Vietnam War. His enemy is the local rebellious people (the Vietcong) who are seeking to destroy the government, to stage a revolution. But there is an incongruity in the last sentence of the dream: the statement is made that, each year, 33,000 prisoners are killed by their own inmates, who are apparently the Communists. This causes us to look back and wonder which side he is really on. Is it the soldiers who are the Vietcong, or is it the prisoners they are taking? Is it because the soldiers who capture him are not Vietcong but government troups that the women do not, in fact, hide and protect him?

Bill's dreams are not inarticulate, and there is no such confusion in any of the other dreams. It is not that he is unable to express himself clearly. I think the confusion is a part of the dream itself; that he does not himself know which side he is on, the rebellious Communist side or the Saigon Government. A couple of other thoughts arise here: politics does not turn up in the other dreams, there is no suggestion that Bill has any active political interests. And a curious twist; the dream occurred many years after the end of the Vietnam War, so that Bill, in waking life, knew quite well who won. If, as the last sentence of the dream implies, he identifies with the ultimate victors, then the victors are, simultaneously, losers. The inmates of the camp kill each other off, and these inmates are the Communists. Whose side is he on? The attitudes of his parents and family (the traditional government), or of the rebellious son trying to find his sexual identity and to overthrow the established order in which he was reared (the rebellious Vietcong)? Is the feminine group who fail to keep their promise to hide him in actuality his mother and two sisters as they make themselves out to be to the rebellious element in him? Or are they three sisters? Or are they related to each other at all? This last question may be quite important. Does he view women as a homogeneous grouping (three of a kind) or as individuals? Does he have social problems because of an inability to relate with women as individuals?

The problem is more complicated than this, I think. His opening sentence is *I am in bed with a very masculine type of guy and he is performing oral sex on me.* Why the stress on 'a very masculine type of guy'? I am reminded that he, himself, is very muscular, a heavy labourer, and appears to me not to have developed his very strong intellectual ability. There is nothing about him that seems effeminate. He seems to have gone to lengths to present a 'very masculine type of guy' image to the world. Does he do this to compensate for a fear of feeling effeminate inside himself? Has he emphasised bodily appearance to the detriment of developing what I suspect to be a high intellectual ability, in a deliberate attempt to seem more 'masculine', according to his own understanding of masculinity?

Some of the details are of special interest. *I go along with it just for the physical pleasure*, etc.: is he telling us, via his dream, that he is not really as attracted by the 'very masculine type of guy' image as he presents himself to be? His other dreams suggest that he has never felt accepted by his family and by his childhood chums. The motif of competition and the need to continually prove himself run through all the dreams. For the social class from which he comes, physical appearance and strength are considered the hallmarks of manliness. And the strongly male-centred cultural tradition considers an 'unmanly' man to be very inferior.

The appearance of the *round concrete water trough* is intriguing, for it plays no role in the dream story. It may suggest a farm setting, which would be appropriate for the events that follow. Symbolism is interesting here. Mandala motifs, i.e. emphasis on a circular formation, turn up when people feel their very being under threat, which is very much the theme of the story. The 'magic circle' is a well-known mandala image. The water trough is presumably for animals on the farm. Would it be too much to imagine that Bill's instinctual drive to be himself is being thwarted in his waking life, and the dream is trying to compensate by bringing up the traditional symbol for wholeness?

Thirty-three thousand prisoners are killed by their own inmates. The 33,000 gives a hint as to what is meant here. Being very strongly Irish in accent, Bill's way of pronouncing the number 33 is strongly ridiculed by workmates and casual acquaintances. (The Irish accent pronounces the number as 'tirty-tree'.) These Irish-toned inmates are at work killing each other off, according to the dream. Bill has great difficulty in coming to grips with his peasant Irish background. There is a self-destructive force at work, noted in this dream. Whichever side he is on, Bill's chances of survival, in the dream, are slim. This should not be taken as an indication of his prognosis in solving real-life problems. As said before, this nightmare is not typical of Bill's series as a whole, but it does pick up and expand upon feelings that turn up in various of his other dreams. We do not know what specific events set off this nightmare, but that it involves an active identity crisis seems certain. In the dream, the war that took place many years ago is still going on. In real life, we know which side won. But for him, at the moment, the rebellious side appears to be losing. Yet we know that if he perseveres, the revolution will succeed.

For further study of these themes, Chapter 1, 'A Dream Tells a Story', and, in particular, John W.'s dream #1, are helpful.

INTERPRETATION OF DREAM 10

This dream takes the dreamer back to the period when he had his break-down, and the farm where he lived as a child. The presence of a giraffe on the farm, of course, is a dream invention, the symbolism of which we need to consider.

A giraffe has one outstanding feature for which it is renowned, namely that it has its head so far off the ground, up in the clouds, we might say. It is not usual to shoe a giraffe like a horse, nor, for that matter, to have it grazing on farmland. The giraffe seems to be treated as a horse. It certainly would be a frightening thing to have a giraffe run towards you.

The idea that he had his head in the clouds while at school fits in with his own belief, shared by his father, that too much study had driven him crazy. Although this used to be a popular medical opinion, and is still current in popular folk belief, psychiatry no longer accepts it as valid. The prevalent view at present is that schizophrenia is a potential that may be triggered off by external forces that have been internalised. We can make a pretty good list of some of these for our dreamer: living isolated on a farm, still grieving over his mother's death, pressed on by the family's pre-occupation that they must rise to social heights, the boy is sent to a rich man's private school where, in an exclusively male environment, he is expected to excel in very difficult subjects. The fact that he apparently has a very high level of intelligence seems to justify this expectation.

In this context, the giraffe seems to signify the high expectations that were placed on the fourteen-year-old boy. These expectations are treated as if they were a normal part of farm life: the giraffe is treated like a horse. Horses were work animals on the farm, the family did not go in for horse-racing, but the giraffe's tall legs may imply the feeling that he must treat life as a race to be won, and prizes take precedence over other interests. The moving of the giraffe from one pasture to another points to the fact that nourishment must now come from another field; with the death of his mother, he had to get his emotional nourishments from books. It is curious that there seems to have been no upheaval in the boy's life when his mother died. The father did not remarry or apparently show any further interest in female relationships. It was as if the family dynamics changed when the boy's mother died, but his life was expected to proceed as planned.

There are probably a number of other images that could have been used by the dream to represent the theme of lofty expectations. The choice of a giraffe may have been conditioned by quite another connotation as well. By the age of fourteen, the boy would have become aware of his sexuality, in particular, his erect penis. Though erection of the penis is usual from birth onwards, the child usually only becomes concerned about it at puberty. A giraffe's neck is a good image for an adult's erect penis as per-ceived by a young boy. Two shifts had taken place in the sexual realm just before the boy's puberty: his mother, the only female influence in the family, died; and he was sent to an all-male school where there was no opportunity for the usual heterosexual relationships to develop.

There is no reason to suppose that the schizophrenia prevented his sexu-ality from developing. The reverse may hold, however, that the lack of normal sexual development contributed to the schizophrenic breakdown, which then perpetuated the abnormal socialisation of the boy. Sexuality was very much on his mind at the time of the dream, and the imagery in the dream may be intended to point my own attention and his to the state of the sexual atmosphere at the time of his breakdown. Given the man's great pride in his family's social achievements and disappointment at his own situation in life, both the social and the sexual aspects of the dream are probably to be equally emphasised.

In thinking about this dream, you might refer back to Chapter 3, 'Dreams and Symbolism', giving perhaps special emphasis to Marilyn Q.'s dream #1, which employs a different sort of sexual symbolism.

INTERPRETATION OF DREAM 11

John's dream portrays very vividly the basic problem that faced him, particularly in view of his wife's description of his problems. The most likely
reason for the dream was his inability to comprehend the serious nature of
the violence that was in him, and the profound split within his personality
which, as his wife said, was so strong that he seemed almost like two different people, as did Dr Jekyll and Mr Hyde. As she said, it was quite unpredictable which 'person' would be uppermost in his body, the 'warm, loving,
sympathetic, sincere, gentle man' or the aggressive, violent, raging
drunkard. This 'double personality' was a serious matter. He got into his
violent side several times a week. It threatened to destroy his job, because
his father, who owned the business, was becoming unwilling to entrust
work to him. And it threatened to destroy his marriage, for after six
months of this experience, his wife was giving serious thought to leaving.
The dream was, therefore, trying to bring John's attention to the fact that
his double nature was a real threat which he was not taking seriously
enough. It used very dramatic imagery indeed, powerful and intense.

Made a trip to capture a crim. The criminal seems very clearly to be
himself, and his 'trip' to capture this criminal is his self-examination as
aided by consultations with me. The gun battle that ensued is the attempt
to subdue one part of his character by the other. There is a paradox: in
hunting down the criminal, he allies himself with two other men, one of
whom gets totally out of control and goes on a rampage of killing; like a
snake, he is poised, hidden, ready to strike out and destroy without warning. This indicates how much the theme of violence had come to grip him.
He tries to fight the criminal with violence, to ally himself with a character
that may get out of control. We are justified, I think, in seeing all the
characters in this dream as aspects of John's personality: not just two but
four splits. Violence by one part of yourself against another part is a
dream's way of portraying the theme of fighting your disapproved nature
violently. This is almost always the automatic reaction of a person when
first brought face to face with a very disagreeable and dangerous aspect of
their personality. The first reaction is usually to deny its existence; the
second, to determine to destroy it, through the use of will power and determination. If that were possible, all would be well. But usually, it is not
possible, and it is necessary to work long and hard to discover the roots of
this 'criminal nature' and to recognise when it is being triggered off, and to
find some way of coping with it.

He cut my knee with a knife to stop my doing it again. In this battle with
himself, all John gets is being crippled. The gun-fire of the supposed
'goodies' bears no fruit. The attempt to destroy the 'criminal' side of himself merely culminates in crippling John and letting loose a killing spree,
the exact opposite of what was intended.

In the bedrooms, and *he also took the form of a snake.* Snakes usually refer to a basic instinctual problem, pretty nearly always a sexual disturbance. This seems to be confirmed by the point that, in the dream, John is confined to the house and, specifically, the bedrooms. His life history did, in fact, show some serious sexual problems and an inability to relate smoothly with a woman. John needs, then, to examine not only his method of dealing with violence by violence, but also the whole area of his sex life, past and present.

For working on this dream, several of the discussions in Chapter 5, 'Nightmares', would be helpful. In particular, the contents and commentary on John W.'s dream #8 seem relevant.

Index

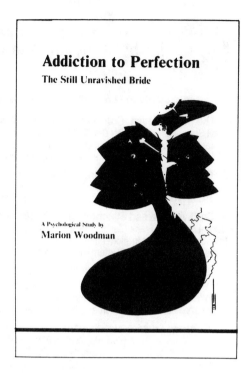

Addiction to Perfection
The Still Unravished Bride

A Psychological Study by
Marion Woodman

12. Addiction to Perfection: The Still Unravished Bride.
Marion Woodman (Toronto). ISBN 0-919123-11-2. 208 pp. $15

"This book is about taking the head off an evil witch." With these words Marion Woodman begins her spiral journey, a powerful and authoritative look at the psychology and attitudes of modern woman.

The witch is a Medusa or a Lady Macbeth, an archetypal pattern functioning autonomously in women, petrifying their spirit and inhibiting their development as free and creatively receptive individuals. Much of this, according to the author, is due to a cultural one-sidedness that favors patriarchal values—productivity, goal orientation, intellectual excellence, spiritual perfection, etc.—at the expense of more earthy, interpersonal values that have traditionally been recognized as the heart of the feminine.

Marion Woodman's first book, *The Owl Was a Baker's Daughter: Obesity, Anorexia Nervosa and the Repressed Feminine,* focused on the psychology of eating disorders and weight disturbances.

Here, with a broader perspective on the same general themes, she continues her remarkable exploration of women's mysteries through case material, dreams, literature and mythology, in food rituals, rape symbolism, Christianity, imagery in the body, sexuality, creativity and relationships.

"It is like finding the loose end in a knotted mass of thread. . . . What a relief! Somebody knows!"—**Elizabeth Strahan,** *Psychological Perspectives.*

Studies in Jungian Psychology
by Jungian Analysts

Limited Edition Paperbacks

Prices quoted are in U.S. dollars (except for Canadian orders)

1. The Secret Raven: Conflict and Transformation.
Daryl Sharp (Toronto). ISBN 0-919123-00-7. 128 pp. $13
A practical study of *puer* psychology, including dream interpretation and material on midlife crisis, the provisional life, the mother complex, anima and shadow. Illustrated.

2. The Psychological Meaning of Redemption Motifs in Fairytales.
Marie-Louise von Franz (Zurich). ISBN 0-919123-01-5. 128 pp. $13
Unique approach to understanding typical dream motifs (bathing, clothes, animals, etc.).

3. On Divination and Synchronicity: The Psychology of Meaningful Chance.
Marie-Louise von Franz (Zurich). ISBN 0-919123-02-3. 128 pp. $13
Penetrating study of irrational methods of divining fate (I Ching, astrology, palmistry, Tarot cards, etc.), contrasting Western ideas with those of so-called primitives. Illustrated.

4. The Owl Was a Baker's Daughter: Obesity, Anorexia and the Repressed Feminine. Marion Woodman (Toronto). ISBN 0-919123-03-1. 144 pp. $14
A modern classic, with particular attention to the body as mirror of the psyche in weight disturbances and eating disorders. Based on case studies, dreams and mythology. Illus.

5. Alchemy: An Introduction to the Symbolism and the Psychology.
Marie-Louise von Franz (Zurich). ISBN 0-919123-04-X. 288 pp. $18
Detailed guide to what the alchemists were really looking for: emotional wholeness. Invaluable for interpreting images and motifs in modern dreams and drawings. **84 illustrations.**

6. Descent to the Goddess: A Way of Initiation for Women.
Sylvia Brinton Perera (New York). ISBN 0-919123-05-8. 112 pp. $12
A timely and provocative study of the need for an inner, female authority in a masculine-oriented society. Rich in insights from mythology and the author's analytic practice.

7. The Psyche as Sacrament: C.G. Jung and Paul Tillich.
John P. Dourley (Ottawa). ISBN 0-919123-06-6. 128 pp. $13
Comparative study from a dual perspective (author is Catholic priest and Jungian analyst), exploring the psychological meaning of religion, God, Christ, the spirit, the Trinity, etc.

8. Border Crossings: Carlos Castaneda's Path of Knowledge.
Donald Lee Williams (Boulder). ISBN 0-919123-07-4. 160 pp. $14
The first thorough psychological examination of the Don Juan novels, bringing Castaneda's spiritual journey down to earth. Special attention to the psychology of the feminine.

9. Narcissism and Character Transformation. The Psychology of Narcissistic Character Disorders. ISBN 0-919123-08-2. 192 pp. $15
Nathan Schwartz-Salant (New York).
A comprehensive study of narcissistic character disorders, drawing upon a variety of analytic points of view (Jung, Freud, Kohut, Klein, etc.). Theory and clinical material. Illus.

10. Rape and Ritual: A Psychological Study.
Bradley A. Te Paske (Minneapolis). ISBN 0-919123-09-0. 160 pp. $14
Incisive combination of theory, clinical material and mythology. Illustrated.

11. Alcoholism and Women: The Background and the Psychology.
Jan Bauer (Montreal). ISBN 0-919123-10-4. 144 pp. $14
Sociology, case material, dream analysis and archetypal patterns from mythology.

12. Addiction to Perfection: The Still Unravished Bride.
Marion Woodman (Toronto). ISBN 0-919123-11-2. 208 pp. $15
A powerful and authoritative look at the psychology of modern women. Examines dreams, mythology, food rituals, body imagery, sexuality and creativity. A continuing best-seller since its original publication in 1982. Illustrated.

13. Jungian Dream Interpretation: A Handbook of Theory and Practice.
James A. Hall, M.D. (Dallas). ISBN 0-919123-12-0. 128 pp. $13
A practical guide, including common dream motifs and many clinical examples.

14. The Creation of Consciousness: Jung's Myth for Modern Man.
Edward F. Edinger, M.D. (Los Angeles). ISBN 0-919123-13-9. 128 pp. $13
Insightful study of the meaning and purpose of human life. Illustrated.

15. The Analytic Encounter: Transference and Human Relationship.
Mario Jacoby (Zurich). ISBN 0-919123-14-7. 128 pp. $13
Sensitive exploration of the difference between relationships based on projection and
I-Thou relationships characterized by mutual respect and psychological objectivity.

16. Change of Life: Psychological Study of Dreams and the Menopause.
Ann Mankowitz (Santa Fe). ISBN 0-919123-15-5. 128 pp. $13
A moving account of an older woman's Jungian analysis, dramatically revealing the later
years as a time of rebirth, a unique opportunity for psychological development.

17. The Illness That We Are: A Jungian Critique of Christianity.
John P. Dourley (Ottawa). ISBN 0-919123-16-3. 128 pp. $13
Radical study by Catholic priest and analyst, exploring Jung's qualified appreciation of
Christian symbols and ritual, while questioning the masculine ideals of Christianity.

18. Hags and Heroes: A Feminist Approach to Jungian Therapy with Couples.
Polly Young-Eisendrath (Philadelphia). ISBN 0-919123-17-1. 192 pp. $15
Highly original integration of feminist views with the concepts of Jung and Harry Stack
Sullivan. Detailed strategies and techniques, emphasis on feminine authority.

19. Cultural Attitudes in Psychological Perspective.
Joseph Henderson , M.D. (San Francisco). ISBN 0-919123-18-X. 128 pp. $13
Shows how a psychological attitude can give depth to one's world view. Illustrated.

20. The Vertical Labyrinth: Individuation in Jungian Psychology.
Aldo Carotenuto (Rome). ISBN 0-919123-19-8. 144 pp. $14
A guided journey through the world of dreams and psychic reality, illustrating the process
of individual psychological development.

21. The Pregnant Virgin: A Process of Psychological Transformation.
Marion Woodman (Toronto). ISBN 0-919123-20-1. 208 pp. $16
A celebration of the feminine, in both men and women. Explores the wisdom of the body,
eating disorders, relationships, dreams, addictions, etc. Illustrated.

22. Encounter with the Self: William Blake's *Illustrations of the Book of Job.*
Edward F. Edinger, M.D. (Los Angeles). ISBN 0-919123-21-X. 80 pp. $10
Penetrating commentary on the Biblical Job story as a numinous, archetypal event.
Complete with Blake's original 22 engravings.

23. The Scapegoat Complex: Toward a Mythology of Shadow and Guilt.
Sylvia Brinton Perera (New York). ISBN 0-919123-22-8. 128 pp. $13
A hard-hitting study of victim psychology in modern men and women, based on case
material, mythology and archetypal patterns.

24. The Bible and the Psyche: Individuation Symbolism in the Old Testament.
Edward F. Edinger (Los Angeles). ISBN 0-919123-23-6. 176 pp. $15
A major new work relating significant Biblical events to the psychological movement
toward wholeness that takes place in individuals.

25. The Spiral Way: A Woman's Healing Journey.
Aldo Carotenuto (Rome). ISBN 0-919123-24-4. 144 pp. $14
Detailed case history of a fifty-year-old woman's Jungian analysis, with particular attention
to her dreams and the rediscovery of her enthusiasm for life.

26. The Jungian Experience: Analysis and Individuation.
James A. Hall, M.D. (Dallas). ISBN 0-919123-25-2. 176 pp. $15
Comprehensive study of the theory and clinical application of Jungian thought, including
Jung's model, the structure of analysis, where to find an analyst, training centers, etc.

27. Phallos: Sacred Image of the Masculine.
Eugene Monick (Scranton/New York). ISBN 0-919123-26-0. 144 pp. $14
Uncovers the essence of masculinity (as opposed to the patriarchy) through close examination of the physical, mythological and psychological aspects of phallos. 30 illustrations.

28. The Christian Archetype: A Jungian Commentary on the Life of Christ.
Edward F. Edinger, M.D. (Los Angeles). ISBN 0-919123-27-9. 144 pp. $14
Psychological view of images and events central to the Christian myth, showing their symbolic meaning in terms of personal individuation. 31 illustrations.

29. Love, Celibacy and the Inner Marriage.
John P. Dourley (Ottawa). ISBN 0-919123-28-7. 128 pp. $13
Explores the challenge of Jung's work to traditional theological thought, particularly his belief in a religious dimension to the psyche and his expressed concern for the soul.

30. Touching: Body Therapy and Depth Psychology.
Deldon Anne McNeely (Lynchburg, VA). ISBN 0-919123-29-5. 128 pp. $13
Illustrates how these two disciplines, both concerned with restoring life to an ailing human psyche, may be integrated in theory and practice. Focus on the healing power of touch.

31. Personality Types: Jung's Model of Typology.
Daryl Sharp (Toronto). ISBN 0-919123-30-9. 128 pp. $13
Detailed explanation of Jung's model (basis for the widely-used Myers-Briggs Type Indicator), showing its implications for individual development and for relationships. Illus.

32. The Sacred Prostitute: Eternal Aspect of the Feminine.
Nancy Qualls-Corbett (Birmingham). ISBN 0-919123-31-7. 176 pp. $15
Shows how our vitality and capacity for joy depend on rediscovering the ancient connection between spirituality and passionate love. Illustrated. (Foreword by Marion Woodman.)

33. When the Spirits Come Back.
Janet O. Dallett (Seal Harbor, WA). ISBN 0-919123-32-5. 160 pp. $14
An analyst examines herself, her profession and the limitations of prevailing attitudes toward mental disturbance. Interweaving her own story with descriptions of those who come to her for help, she details her rediscovery of the integrity of the healing process.

34. The Mother: Archetypal Image in Fairy Tales.
Sibylle Birkhäuser-Oeri (Zurich). ISBN 0-919123-33-3. 176 pp. $15
Compares processes in the unconscious with common images and motifs in folk-lore. Illustrates how positive and negative mother complexes affect us all, with examples from many well-known fairy tales and daily life. (Edited by Marie-Louise von Franz.)

35. The Survival Papers: Anatomy of a Midlife Crisis.
Daryl Sharp (Toronto). ISBN 0-919123-34-1. 160 pp. $15
Jung's major concepts—persona, shadow, anima and animus, complexes, projection, typology, active imagination, individuation, etc.—are powerfully presented in the immediate context of an analysand's process. And the analyst's. We are there as they struggle with the conflict between the security of a hard-won, successful lifestyle and an inner imperative that demands a total reassessment of self—with no guarantees. Illustrated.

36. The Cassandra Complex: Living with Disbelief.
Laurie Layton Schapira (New York). ISBN 0-919123-35-X. 160 pp. $15
A close look at how hysteria manifests in the female psyche, and why it threatens patriarchal values. Includes clinical material and an examination of the role of powerfully intuitive, medial women through history. Shows how unconscious, prophetic sensibilities can be transformed from a burden into a valuable source of conscious understanding. Illustrated.

Prices and payment (check or money order) in U.S. dollars

Please add $1 per book (bookpost) or $3 per book (airmail)

INNER CITY BOOKS
Box 1271, Station Q, Toronto, Canada M4T 2P4